The Rev.

Robert P. Simonds

1846.

Xmas Day

1913

PRAYER-BOOK IDEALS

PRAYER-BOOK IDEALS

BY

HENRY PHIPPS DENISON, B.A.

PREBENDARY OF WELLS
VICAR OF ST. MICHAEL'S, NORTH KENSINGTON
AUTHOR OF "THE TRUE RELIGION"

LONDON: ELLIOT STOCK
7, PATERNOSTER ROW, E.C.
1913

CONTENTS

Contents

PRAYER-BOOK IDEALS

CHAPTER I

INTRODUCTORY

WHEN our Lord uttered, through St. John, His rebuke to the angel of the Church in Sardis, He prefaced it with these words of warning and of encouragement: " Be watchful and strengthen *the things which remain* that are ready to die." And as we read these wonderful words, we cannot but be conscious of their awful application to ourselves in England at the present day.

We have, thank God, " things which remain." We have in the Prayer-Book magnificent ideals of worship and of life; but when we begin to read and study the Prayer-Book, we find ourselves in an atmosphere that seems strange in the twentieth century. The Prayer-Book ideals do not square with everyday experience. This is abundantly manifest. One of two courses seems to lie before us :

1. We may try to alter the ideal to suit the facts.
2. We may try to find our way back to the old ideal.

A great deal is being said at the present day about Prayer-Book Revision. We may leave on one side for the moment the essentially dishonest motive that underlies a certain amount of the agitation for Revision—viz., that as it has now been found that Catholics are not " breaking the law," the law had better be altered so as to exclude the said Catholics. It needs no words to condemn the flagrant dishonesty of such intention. But leaving this on one side, and relegating it to the contempt that it deserves, there remains a considerable amount of honest desire to promote the welfare of the Church by revising the Prayer-Book. But when one comes to consider the discussions on Prayer-Book Revision, one is painfully conscious of the fact that the principle that underlies the various proposals is that the ideal should be trimmed so as to fit the actual. In other words, ardent Prayer-Book revisionists seem to have made up their minds that the former of the two courses above mentioned is the one that is best for them to follow.

But is this the method of God ? If we look at the history of the true religion in the Old Testament, we find God constantly sending His prophets in times when the children of the Church had corrupted their ways. And in no case does the prophet suggest a new departure. The message of the prophet is invariably to recall the people of God to the ideal that they had forgotten, and to show them that it was just the turning from the ideal that was the root and source of all their troubles. And the same Lord GOD Who spake to our fathers by the prophets spake in these last days by His SON; and as the message by the prophet was, " I am the Lord thy GOD Who brought thee out of the land of Egypt," so the message of our Lord to His children in Sardis was, " Strengthen the things which remain that are ready to die." GOD's method is to recall men to the ideal, and as with Him

2

there is neither variableness, neither shadow of turning, so we are quite sure that in twentieth-century England, He calls us back to the old ideal, and bids us be watchful and strengthen the things which remain. It is our life that wants revising at the present moment, not our Prayer-Book.

Now, assuming that we are to conform our life to our ideal, not our ideal to our life, it is clear that we have at the present time to get ourselves back to the ideal. But the first step towards such a return is to have a clear vision of the ideal itself. And the purpose of this book is to help its readers to an understanding of what is the Christian ideal that is authoritatively set before the English people.

And here let me say one word about myself: I do not write to suggest certain " views " or " lines of thought " that commend themselves to me. It would be an impertinence on my part to do so; for, of course, there is no reason in the nature of things why my " view " should be any better than your " view "; I write to set before you the faith and practice of undivided Christendom. If you can show that I misrepresent undivided Christendom in any particular, I will at once retract; for the faith and practice of undivided Christendom is, to the Catholic Christian, an infallible authority.

" Views " have no authority, and carry no weight. As a matter of fact, those who cling most pertinaciously to their " views," or to somebody else's " views," do recognize the principle of Catholic authority in many ways, without perceiving that they do so. I would ask those who are most wedded to their " views " why they believe in the Apostles' Creed ? Why they practise Infant Baptism ? And, perhaps most startling of all, why they all agree to discard the Sabbath and keep Sunday instead ? You do not do these things because you have elaborately thought them out and made a " view " about them. You take them for granted on the authority of undivided Christendom. And, as it is with these things, so it should be with everything else. If, in any particular, a man finds himself, or a body of men find themselves, at variance with the body of undivided Christendom, he is responsible, or they are responsible, before God and their fellow Christians for having thus isolated themselves from the main body. It is no use saying " that is my view," as if that made an end of the matter. It does not in the least matter what your " view " is, or what my " view " may be. God is the Judge; and " views," methinks, will fare badly in the judgment to come.

There are matters upon which undivided Christendom has not spoken. On these matters, a Christian may hold " views." For instance, you are welcome to a " view " as to whether the Incarnation was, or was not, in consequence of the Fall. But no Christian has a right to a " view " as to the Creeds, or the Sacraments, or the right way of worshipping God; for on all these matters undivided Christendom has spoken with no faltering voice.

In writing then, as I am now about to do, on the subject of " Prayer-Book Worship," I am merely going to put before my readers the faith and practice of undivided Christendom. Take it, or leave it ! But remember that, if you follow your " view," or anyone else's " view," instead of bowing to the authority of undivided Christendom, you will have to justify yourself before God for so doing.

Introductory

It is sometimes said: " These people do not recognize the authority of the Church; and, therefore, you should meet them on their own ground." But that is just what I *cannot* do; for I am bound by my Christian creed to believe in the Catholic Church quite as much as I am bound to believe in the Holy Trinity or in the Incarnation.

One word to my readers:

The purpose of this book is not to afford to its readers the intellectual pleasure of following an argument. The book fails altogether of its purpose if it merely is " interesting." The vision of the ideal at once implies a judgment. " The Word of God is quick, and powerful, and sharper than any two-edged sword." Englishmen are apt to think that their individual conscience is to be the supreme and sole referee: that if they individually think a thing right, it is right, and if they individually think a thing permissible, it is permissible. They ignore, for practical purposes, any standard outside of themselves. But this, I need hardly point out, is to ignore the ultimate judgment of God. Whatever Englishmen may think or say, it still remains that our Lord is the Judge, and that *all* judgment is committed to Him because He is the Son of Man. We English Christians, then, have to cease to " do that which is right in our eyes," and to look to it that we conform our lives to the standard of life authoritatively set before us by God in His Holy Church. And in this, as in everything else, we have to face the alternative. If we wilfully persist in following our own standard of life, instead of God's, we must be prepared to take the consequences of our disobedience in the judgment to come. The present Dean of Canterbury has said:

" It is not, in fact, simply a sense of duty which is aroused by the voice of the conscience. It is a sense, and a conviction, that there exists a sanction for that duty, and that a violation of it will be surely avenged. . . . It is a conviction that in ourselves and in others this claim *will be enforced.* . . . It is a conviction, in other words, *that we are responsible and that we shall be held to our responsibility.*"

Is there an authoritative standard of human life? At the present time men do not seem to be very clear on this head. " Individualism " is the watchword of the day. Men are impatient of any restraining power on their thoughts or on their actions. Men seem to think that if they do that which is right in their own eyes they are taking a rather high level; because, of course, it is possible for them to do that which is wrong in their own eyes. They acknowledge *a* standard: they will not let their lives run utterly wild; but the standard is a purely individual and personal one. Whether it be in the region of thought or in the region of action, whether it be in faith or in morals, they constitute their individual conscience, Judge, Jury, and Court of Appeal, all rolled into one. Their creed is that which they think they see to be true: their table of the law is that which they think to be right. It is of the extremest importance that we should fairly face the question whether every man is to be a standard for himself, or whether there is an absolute standard of right and wrong outside ourselves.

Put in this bald way, I suppose we should all shrink from saying that the beginning, middle, and end of right and wrong lies wholly within ourselves.

But we do not habitually put it in this bald way, but wrap it up in some slightly more decent covering.

Introductory

And the result is that men who would shrink from nakedly saying that they themselves are the complete measure of right and wrong, are really all the while making themselves the complete measure.

Let us take an instance of this: (1) In the region of Faith, and (2) in the region of Morals.

1. Let us suppose the case of two men whom we will call John and William. John believes that God is Three Persons and One God; William is a Unitarian. How does average English thought deal with these two men? Should we be wrong if we say that your average Englishman would say that, while it would be wrong for John to deny the Doctrine of the Blessed Trinity, because he would be going against his convictions, it would not be wrong for William to deny it because he is a Unitarian.

But what does this really mean? Stripped of its veil of spurious charity, it means that the Blessed Trinity has no real existence; that God does not really exist, but that He is merely the figment of men's brains. Given that God is a really existing entity, it follows that either He is Three Persons and One God, or He is not.

If He is Trinity in Unity, John the Christian is right, and William the Unitarian is distinctly wrong.

If He is not Trinity in Unity, William the Unitarian is right, and John the Christian is distinctly wrong. They cannot both be right if God exists at all.

Mere common sense will take us as far as this. But we are not left to mere common sense, for the Christian Religion is based upon the fact that it has pleased God to give us a Revelation of Himself. That Revelation is partial and progressive, but it is, and must be, always the same. It is of the very Essence of the

Being of God that He cannot lie. " He *cannot* deny Himself." He *cannot*, at one stage of human history, reveal Himself as Trinity in Unity, and at another stage of human history reveal Himself as a Monad. That which is behind the veil does not change as a veil is gradually lifted. It is not that God changes, but that those to whom He progressively reveals Himself see progressively more of that which is always there. " Now we see through a glass, darkly; but then face to face." But, if we see at all, it is the same thing which we now see partially and which we shall then see perfectly. And so we reach the certain conclusion that either all men must believe alike about God, or some men must be sinning against the Revelation of God and will certainly have to answer for that sin.

Go back once more to John and William. It is no use William saying, " I am a Unitarian," as if that settled the matter. That settles nothing at all. For the question is whether he has any right to be a Unitarian.

So much for our example in the region of faith. The doctrine of the Blessed Trinity is one of the revealed truths; and, as we deal with that, so we deal with every portion of revealed Truth. If John is right, William is wrong; if William is right, John is wrong; but they cannot both be right if anything outside of themselves exists at all.

2. Now let us see how the average Englishman acts in respect of Moral Truth.

Robert thinks that a man and his wife are bound to each other till death parts them, so that if either marry again in the lifetime of the other they commit adultery.

Richard, on the other hand, does not think so: he considers that the Divorce Act is all-sufficient, and that divorce sets people free to marry again.

Introductory

Here I shrewdly suspect the average Englishman will resort to his wiseacre formula, and say that it would be wrong for Robert to avail himself of the Divorce Act, while it would not be wrong for Richard to do so!

But this, like our example in the region of Faith, really means a denial of the existence of God.

" Every man has a right to his own opinion " is the parrot cry that we so often hear; to which I would answer: " Be it so—but Almighty God must have at least an equal right to His." And thus the matter resolves itself into a trial of strength between man and God!

The remarriage of divorced people is not wrong because Robert believes it to be wrong, nor is it right because Richard and the British Parliament think it right. The question is not what Robert or Richard or the British Parliament think, but what is God's mind about it. There is an absolute right and wrong in the matter. What this man or that, what you or I, think about the matter is of infinitesimally small importance. What is all-important for us is that our ideas about the matter should square with the absolute right and wrong that lies outside of, and is independent of, ourselves and our " views."

And in questions of right and wrong, as in the questions of truth and error, in the region of Morals, as in the region of Faith (if, for the moment, we may separate them in thought), we are not left to the mere commonsense aspect of the matter. That alone would tell us that there must be a positive right and wrong somewhere. But in morals, as in faith, we have God's Revelation of Himself. So that of the broad lines of morals, as of the broad lines of faith, we lay it down, that either all men will think alike, or that some men will be sinning against the Revelation of God.

9

But now, having put things in this bald and uncompromising way, let me anticipate the charge of " bigotry " and " uncharitableness " and " narrow-mindedness " which will certainly be brought.

If Richard thinks it right to have two wives at once or to marry his sister-in-law because the British Parliament says he may, I say emphatically that he is wrong, because I *know* that he is wrong; but I do not attempt to pronounce any judgment as to his individual guilt; I can know nothing of his opportunities; I cannot say how far his ignorance is " invincible," or his prejudice " inveterate." " Who art thou that judgest another man's servant ? to his own Master he standeth or falleth." We insist that there is an absolute right and an absolute wrong; we insist that it is the duty of every human being to conform his actions to that absolute standard. Less than this we could not do if we believe in the existence of God at all. But more than this we cannot and we will not do. The judgment of individuals is in the hands of the Only One Who has the right to judge; the One to Whom all judgment has been committed.

It is against the awful indifferentism in faith and morals alike, that is so rampant amongst us at the present time, that we need to be warned. Human thought never sank so low as it did when the Sophists taught their philosophy of despair. They taught men that there is nothing absolutely true, or absolutely false; they dared to say that that is true which appears to a man to be true, and that is false which appears to a man to be false. They were Individualists of the first water ! And inasmuch as truth of thought and truth of action are inseparably connected, the Sophists must bear the imputation of teaching that there is no absolute right or absolute wrong. They must be taken as teaching that that is right which appears to a man to be right, and that that is wrong which appears to a man to be wrong. And, as I have said, you have here the lowest degradation of human thought.

Men may be hideously mistaken as to the external standard of right and wrong; they may commit the most frightful crimes in their blindness, in the name of religion; but, as long as they believe that there *is* a standard outside of themselves, and are trying, however blindly, to conform themselves to that standard, they have not parted company with all nobleness of nature. But the Sophist is below the brutes that perish. He can see nothing beyond and outside of his own miserable self. He may be cultured and civilized, but he is the last, the most grovelling, and the most despicable of human beings.

Whatever you do, then, be quite certain that there is an absolute standard of right and wrong outside of, and independent of, whatever you or I may think about it. Lay fast hold on this great truth, and it *must* follow that you will see that your one aim and object must be to conform your life to that standard.

There is, then, an authoritative standard of right and wrong. If this were not so, we should have nothing before us but the blackness of despair.

To the man who is convinced that there is an authoritative standard of right and wrong, and that that authoritative standard is to be found in the consensus of the Whole Body of the baptized, life becomes at once the simple thing that God means it to be. To the faithful Christian there is no dividing line between things natural and things spiritual, between things secular and things religious, between the things of time and the things of Eternity. Creation to him is one solid whole, and God is the Ruler and Master of it all. He sees the whole creation reconciled to God in Jesus Christ, and the whole round world become one vast Temple of God and of the Lamb.

Thus we see that the phenomenon of the " Prayer-Book Man " takes us very deep indeed. If the " Prayer-Book Man " is the Englishman as God would have him to be, then, in the broad lines of his life, he is man as God would have him to be. For the Englishman is man first, and Englishman quite second! We Englishmen are very cock-a-hoop. It is the reverse side of that splendid courage and self-reliance that have made us, as a nation, what we are. But it has been laughingly said about us that it seems to be open to question whether the Anglo-Saxon race fell in Adam! When people nowadays speak of the Prayer-Book, they do it rather with a shrug of the shoulders. The Prayer-Book is looked upon as something very old-fashioned and early Victorian, that we need not attend to now that we have become so very *fin de siècle* and clever.

But think of it steadily, and you will see that the " Prayer-Book Man " is our authoritative standard of life. And if we, for any reason of our own, decline from that standard, we shall certainly one day have to answer for having so done.

PART I

IDEALS OF WORSHIP

CHAPTER II

PRAYER-BOOK WORSHIP

IN studying, as we are about to do, the ideal Christian life as set before us in the Prayer-Book, we begin, as the Prayer-Book begins, with the Christian ideal of worship. For Prayer-Book worship, of course, simply means Christian worship in the form in which it is authoritatively set forth for the English people. So that, in order to understand Prayer-Book worship, we must first of all have a clear idea of the principles that underlie all true worship—the principles that are carried out for the English people in the Prayer-Book.

Now, the attitude of the average Englishman towards the Prayer-Book is, *mutatis mutandis*, on the same plane as his attitude towards the Bible. The ideas of the average Englishman in respect of the Prayer-Book are hazy, shallow, and wrong, for the same reason that makes his ideas of the Bible to be hazy, shallow, and wrong—viz., that he does not begin by asking what is the subject matter of the book he is attempting to read. Now, the subject matter of the Prayer-Book is, primarily, worship. A man cannot possibly understand the Prayer-Book unless he has some idea of worship in its essence and in its history; and it is lamentable to see, as we so often do, teachers frittering away their time in minute commentaries on the English liturgy and offices, when neither they nor their hearers have any clear, definite idea of the scope and meaning of worship.

So we must boldly grapple with the great and tremendous subject of worship; and when we have mastered the principles of worship it will be easy to see how these unchanging principles are applied for practical everyday use in the Prayer-Book. But until we have mastered the principles of worship, it is mere waste of time to be fiddling round the details of the Prayer-Book.

Worship, whether true or false, whether Christian or heathen, is the touchstone of faith, and is the very heart and core and life of religion. Without worship, religion ceases to exist; it ceases, that is to say, to be a religion, and has become simply a speculative philosophy. Is not this just what is happening in India ? Some years ago great interest was aroused in this country in the Brahmo-Somaj movement; and unthinking people hailed it as a step towards the light, in that it discarded the idols of Hindu worship. But the Brahmo-Somaj is a philosophy rather than a religion, and it is at least open to question whether, in taking the backward step from religion to philosophy, it is not leading men farther from God, instead of nearer to Him. Lovers of the " truth as it is in Jesus " have no cause to rejoice over the Brahmo-Somaj movement, and it will be found a new hindrance in the way of the Kingdom of God in India. It is so silly of people to say that it must be a purer religion because it has cast off idols. If the Brahmo-Somaj draws Hindus out of the temples of Brahma, Vishnu, or Siva, it only means that it is drawing them away from religion into the chill regions of philosophy.

And when we come nearer home, we find (not to look farther afield than our own country) the same disintegrating force at work in Christian England as we see in heathen India. The altars are deserted, while clever men and women are eagerly chattering about religious questions. Christianity in England is rapidly ceasing to be a religion, while the intellectual few are trying to uphold it and cling to it as a philosophy.

History repeats itself, and we may well try and learn its lesson.

Dean Church, in his admirable lecture on Roman civilization, points out how high that civilization had been able to raise the world by the twofold idea of law and duty. Why did that civilization perish as it did ? He answers: " Because the Romans were untrue to their own principles." And how came it about that the Romans, in the mass, could be untrue to their principles ? He answers: " Because their religion had perished." The religion perished because of its falsity. On the wrecks of the religion arose the philosophy of the few; but (and this is the point I want to press) the philosophy of the few was powerless to hold together the splendid fabric of Roman civilization. " It fell, and great was the fall of it." To discard worship (whether Christian or heathen) is to discard religion. To be indifferent to worship is to be indifferent to religion. A keen interest in religious questions is *not* religion. If a man does not worship, he may chatter and discuss and write and philosophize about religion to the end of the chapter, but—he has parted company with religion.

In speaking, then, about Prayer-Book worship, we are speaking about English religion. Never for a moment let anyone suppose that he can retain *any* hold on religion when once he loses his hold on worship. Faith and worship are bound together, and nothing can part them. This is true of every false faith, and it is unquestionably true of the true faith; " The Catholic Faith is this, that we worship."

What exactly do we mean by worship ?

In order to arrive at an answer to this question, let us begin by ruling out certain things that clearly are not worship.

It is a curious thing that the expression " place of worship " is a Protestant rather than a Catholic expression.

Let us go into a so-called Protestant " place of worship," and look about us. We are in a large hall, furnished with seats, all facing a pulpit or rostrum at the end of the building. Occasionally, as I believe in the City Temple, the " auditorium " (properly so called) is curved as in a theatre. It is quite clear, from the very aspect of these buildings, that *hearing* is the first purpose for which they are built, and the main purpose for which they are required.

Now, to hear the Bible read or expounded no doubt is an excellent thing. There is ample need for instruction in the things of God. But a moment's thought will show that hearing is not worship. The very fundamental idea of worship is that of something that is given, or paid, to God. Strange, then, that the very places that especially come under the denomination of " places of worship " should be entirely arranged for something which, however excellent, can by no stretch of language be called worship.

We rule, then, out of our conception of worship all hearing of Scripture or sermons.

" But," someone will say, " you seem to forget that

prayer and hymn singing go on in these 'places of worship,' besides Bible reading and preaching." No, we do not forget it, but we do not think we should be wrong or uncharitable if we say that they are rather subsidiary to the preaching, which seems to be regarded as the most important exercise in the " place of worship." But even supposing that we are mistaken in this estimate, we must inquire a little into the nature of this " prayer and hymn singing."

Should we be very far wrong if we think that the " prayer " consists mainly of petitions and, perhaps, thanksgiving ? Petition for something that we need, and thanksgiving for something that we have received. Does this exhaust the idea of worship ? Have we nothing to do, when we come before God, but to ask for what we want, or to thank for what we have received ? Petition and thanksgiving, no doubt, have their place in worship, but it is a subsidiary place. If prayer and thanksgiving are all that are given to God, we must rule them out and say that, excellent and necessary as they are, they do not constitute worship.

But occasionally, among those advertisements which nowadays so largely adorn the doors of Protestant " places of worship," one sees a notice of Praise and Prayer Meeting. This sounds a little better; but, from its occasional appearance on the advertisement board, one would rather gather that it is a " meeting " of a more or less exceptional character. But, even if this were not so, we must say that even praise and prayer do not exhaust the idea of worship, and must, if they stand alone, be ruled out too. Praise and prayer will enter into worship, but if you say that worship is praise and prayer, you will feel instinctively that you have given a wholly inadequate definition of worship.

And the element of praise will include the hymn singing, not to mention the anthems and the " solos " that seem now to have become an almost indispensable feature of the Protestant " place of worship." But even here we must remember that there are hymns *and* hymns. The hymn, properly so called, is an act of adoration or praise addressed to Almighty God; but a vast number of hymns are what might be called " subjective hymns." How beautiful and touching these subjective hymns often are all devout Englishmen will know. Who, for instance, is not touched by that lovely hymn, " When I survey the wondrous Cross " ? But it touches one as an exquisite meditation. It is that rather than a hymn properly so called. And how large a proportion of English hymns will have to be put in the category of " subjective hymns " !

If, then, we rule out hearing, petition, thanksgiving, and even praise, and all " subjective " singing, what have we left in the Protestant " place of worship " ?

We shall feel that Dr. Littledale was not far wrong when he said that the Protestant idea of worship is " a few subjective hymns and an oblique sermon to Almighty God, followed by a direct one to the people." And akin to this is his definition of the Protestant idea of a minister—viz., that he is " a person who is paid to express once a week the thoughts of the congregation in better language than they could put them in for themselves."

But when we turn from the Protestant sects to the Church in our own land, we find again a failure to grasp the first principles of worship. Some fifty years ago the efforts of reformers in the English Church were directed towards the recovery of the idea of the Daily Office, which, preserved in our cathedrals and collegiate churches, had practically died out in the parish churches. In those days a well-known " Low Church " clergyman said: " Shall I leave my house-to-house visitation to *read prayers to a congregation of two or three ?*" But " prayers " are surely things that have to be offered to God, not "to a congregation." The good man had forgotten the first attribute of worship. We have, then, to rule out of our idea of worship all " reading " of " prayers to a congregation."

But, then, in these later days, we have a whole host of blatant vulgarities among us English Churchpeople that are equally subversive of the first idea of worship.

There is an assemblage of people on some particular occasion. It may be the Sunday School teachers of the district; it may be a temperance society, or the Girls' Friendly Society, or something of that sort. And on these occasions you hear the clergyman say: " I must *give them a service.*" " Give them a service "! What an expression ! And he forthwith cooks up some little hash of hymns and prayers, which he serves up to these people.

A good many years ago, in a country parish in the West of England, the village was *en fête ;* the vicar " gave them a service "; the Cathedral choir was hired to sing on this auspicious occasion. What was it all about ? Why, this: the squire's mother was that day one hundred years old !

Then we run through the gamut of vulgarity in such things as are called " bright and hearty services," " popular services," " elastic services "—the sort of functions that our dissenting brethren call " brief, bright, and brotherly." Then, in this connection, we have those new-fangled things that are called " memorial services," if only a man is sufficiently rich or sufficiently notorious to be treated to such luxuries. Poor Will Jones or Mary Smith must do without " memorial services." But as these aristocratic and wholly unauthorized functions seem to consist mainly of a few tags from the Burial Service, interspersed with the favourite hymns of the corpse, we may comfort ourselves that the common herd of the Christian family do not lose much by being deprived of the " memorial service."

So, if you please, we will rule out of the idea of worship all this congeries of vulgarities, with which, alas, we are so familiar: the " bright and hearty service," the " popular service," the " service " which is " given " to the temperance society or the G.F.S., and the " memorial service " so exclusively devoted to the rich and the great.

Having thus tried to clear away all this rubbish that cumbers the ground about the ideal of worship, we will now proceed to lay down the first solid piece of foundation as regards worship: and it will be found that this first fundamental idea is not exclusively Christian, but lies at the root of all worship, whether heathen or Christian.

The fundamental idea of all worship is simple adoration: the recognition by the intelligent creature that God is his Maker and his Lord, and that he is simply the creature and the slave of God, to Whom exclusively he belongs.

Directly a man really grasps the existence of God as a patent fact, directly he is really conscious of the Presence of God, adoration becomes the first necessity of his being. There is no room for thoughts of self in the awfulness of the Vision of God. " I have heard of Thee by the hearing of the ear "—speculative thought leaves the inner soul untouched—" but now mine eye seeth Thee: wherefore I abhor myself." So speaks holy Job. And when Isaiah, in the year that King Uzziah died, saw the Vision of Glory and the adoring seraphim, at once he cries: " Woe is me; for I am a man of unclean lips, and I dwell in the midst of a people of unclean lips." That hearing, or petition, or even thanksgiving, or detached praise, can usurp the place of simple adoration, indicates that the Vision of God is blurred and uncertain; while the blatant vulgarities that I have noticed are so obviously incongruous with any clear appreciation of the Reality and Presence of God, that they become doubly hideous by the contrast of their flippant impertinence with the proper and rightful attitude of the creature in the presence of its Creator.

Just think of " reading prayers to a congregation," of " giving them a service " ; just think of "bright and hearty services," " popular services," " elastic services," etc., and then, suddenly, think of Moses on Mount Sinai—" I fell down before God forty days and forty nights "; or think of St. John in Patmos, before the Vision of our Lord in glory—" I fell at His feet as dead "; and you will see how far away we have drifted, and how low we have sunk ! Even the heathen, hopelessly wrong as their conception of God is, and hopelessly wrong as their worship is, have, at any rate, retained the true instinct that the primary attitude of man to God must be that of profound adoration.

And this leads me to this last thought—viz., how it comes to pass that this obvious truth is forgotten and overlooked. Elijah tells us. It is because men are halting between two opinions. Men are not quite sure about their God; therefore, of course, they cannot worship Him. The clever fools and shallow philo-sophizers have so whittled away the conception of God that He has become a shadowy abstraction instead of being a living personality. You cannot worship a doubtful abstraction; you cannot fall down in adora-tion if you are not quite convinced that God is there. And so, all that seems left to poor man in the cold shades of philosophical speculation is to say: " O God, if there be a God, save my soul, if I have a soul."

The first element, then, of worship is adoration. And so we rule ruthlessly out of our conception of worship every sort of exercise in which adoration does not occupy the primary place. If men can content themselves with such things as we have been thinking about, it can only be because they have no adequate vision of God.

Hitherto we are only on common ground with the best of heathendom. In the next chapter we shall finally part company with heathendom.

Meanwhile, let us lay to our hearts the awful spectacle of the decay of worship in so-called Christian England, and let us be quite clear as to what it means. It means that Englishmen, to a large extent, are not sure about God; it means that Englishmen, to a large extent, have lost their faith, and are leaning upon " views " and " opinions "; that Christianity, to the majority of Englishmen, has ceased to be a religion.

What must we do in this appalling state of things ? May we not once more take to ourselves the words of our Lord to the Church of Sardis : " I know thy works, that thou hast a name that thou livest, and art dead " ? As we look at our empty churches and deserted altars, how should these words come home to us self-satisfied Englishmen ! Then let us take to ourselves the rest of the message: " Be watchful, and strengthen the *things which remain*, that are ready to die: for I have not found thy works perfect before God."

" The things which remain !" Still there remains the ordered worship of the English Prayer - Book ; though it seems " ready to die " in the scorn with which Englishmen leave it on one side ! Let us, at least, do what we can. Over our own spiritual life we have all power; and if we, any of us, are among those who affect to think that we can still have a religion while worship is indifferent, then let us get up out of this outer darkness, and go each one for ourselves, to strengthen, in Prayer-Book worship, " the things which remain, that are ready to die "; for, in spite of all our smug self-satisfaction, we may be very sure that our Lord has " not found our works perfect before God."

CHAPTER III

PRAYER-BOOK WORSHIP (*continued*)

IN the preceding chapter we cleared the ground by ruling out of our idea of worship any and every " religious exercise " in which simple adoration does not occupy the foremost place.

We have now to remember that adoration, which is the first necessity of man's being, is impossible if the worshipper is not in right relation with God Whom he worships. Sin makes worship impossible. Until, therefore, men are delivered from the bondage of sin (" saved from their sins "), adoration is an impossibility.

Now, this is what, from the days of Cain downwards, the fallen nature of man tends to make us forget.

By the fall it has come to pass that man's passions are no longer subject to reason, and that his reason is no longer subject to the will of God. Pride lies at the root of the dislocation of our fallen nature. And this pride brings it to pass that fallen man looks upon himself as the centre of things, and judges of all things, human and divine, from his own standpoint, and by a standard of his own making.

And so, from the days of Cain downwards, men have come to think that it is quite sufficient that they should have the wish to adore God. Man says to himself, " I wish to worship God," and he seems to think that forthwith he can go and do it. In our blindness and our pride, we have forgotten that it is quite one thing that we should want to worship God, and quite another that God should be willing to accept our worship. " The sacrifice of the wicked is abomination in the sight of God."

It is of the essence of our Christian faith that we believe that men can only be delivered from sin through the One Mediation of our Lord JESUS CHRIST. From the very beginning of human history, the people of God have always stood apart from the rest of the world. " Lo ! the people shall dwell alone, and shall not be reckoned among the nations." And what, all along the line of human history, differentiates the Church from the world is the stubborn and dogged belief of the children of the Church that the seed of the woman bruises the head of the serpent. While the children of the world in all ages are looking for salvation by the development and improvement of their nature from within, the children of God are always trusting to a Personal Saviour from without. So we lay down the great broad principle that finally separates Christendom and heathendom—viz., that Adoration is only possible through the Mediation of the Sacred Humanity of JESUS the Son of Mary.

Apart from the Sacred Humanity, there is nothing before man but everlasting damnation. By the very constitution of his nature, adoration is the first necessity of man's being, while, apart from the Sacred Humanity of Jesus the Son of Mary, it is impossible for man to fulfil or satisfy this first imperious need of his existence. Like Sisyphus in the old heathen myth, he is ever rolling the stone up the hill, only to find that, just as he seems on the point of reaching the top, the stone rolls back upon him. Put this heathen myth into Christian language, and you have exactly what is told us in the Athanasian Creed—" which Faith, except a man do keep whole and undefiled, without doubt he shall perish everlastingly." What is this despairing attempt to do what we wish to do, with the absolute impossibility of doing it, but " perishing everlastingly "? This is what theologians call the " pœna damni," the pain of *loss*, which is the essence of the existence of the lost, the life of hell.

The shallow impertinence that makes it possible for men to think, as they do, that God is bound to accept what they choose to offer, is the direct outcome of the fall, and the first of sins, cutting, as it does, clean across the first table of the law.

On all sides, Englishmen are saying: " It does not matter what you believe, or what denomination you belong to, provided you are a good man." To that, we Christians immediately answer: " How can you call a man a good man, if he is persistently breaking the first of all the Commandments ?" We Englishmen of to-day seem to have made up our minds that we may discard the first four Commandments, and confine our " religious " energies to the keeping of the last six !

Adoration, then, is the first necessity of man's being.

To be debarred from adoration is to perish everlastingly.

Adoration is only possible through the one Mediation of the Sacred Humanity.

Therefore, apart from the Sacred Humanity, we " perish everlastingly."

Let us try, then, to see something of what we mean when we say that we can only worship God through the Sacred Humanity of Jesus the Son of Mary.

In the first place, we mean that Jesus the Son of Mary is the one and only Revelation of God.

Our Lord said to the woman of Samaria: " Ye worship *ye know not what;* we know what we worship: for salvation is of the Jews." How hard and narrow these words must appear to twentieth-century Englishmen ! Yet they are not the heated words of a " bigoted denominationalist " on an education meeting platform, but the words of God Himself, the Eternal Wisdom, " the Word."

Why did our Lord say so emphatically that the Samaritans did not know what they worshipped ? Because they had separated themselves from the Jews, and had set up schismatical worship on Mount Gerizim. Separated themselves from the Jews ! What did this mean ? It meant, of course, that they were trusting to something else than to the Seed of the Woman that was to bruise the head of the serpent. They had separated themselves from Jesus Christ. And, of course, the immediate result of this was, ignorance of God. Remember the words of our Lord, " No man knoweth the Father save the Son, *and he to whom the Son will reveal Him.*" Remember the words of St. John: " Whosoever denieth the Son, the same hath not the Father." By their separation from the Jews, the Samaritans were " denying the Son "; consequently, they were worshipping they knew not what.

And this ignorance of the object of worship constitutes the sin of idolatry. Apart from Jesus Christ, men cannot know God; therefore they proceed to make a God of their own. This idolatry may take the form of making idols, " graven images," or it may (as it does in England) take the form of making idols with our own brains. It matters not; it is equally the sin of idolatry.

Now, remember what St. Paul tells us about idols. " An idol," he says, " is nothing at all in the world." It has no substantial reality that answers to it. So is every speculation about the Nature and Being of God, that is contrary to, or in disregard of, what God has revealed of Himself in Christ. It has no substantial existence. It is " nothing at all in the world." The god, for instance, of the Unitarians, is a god that never existed. It is " nothing at all in the world."

We cannot " worship we know not what." If we make to ourselves a conception of God and worship that, we are simple idolaters, paying homage to the work of our own brains. Jesus Christ is the one and only Revelation of God; we can, then, only worship God through the mediation of Jesus Christ, inasmuch as we can only know God through the Revelation of Jesus Christ.

Then we have to think of the position of our Blessed Lord as the great High Priest. Think of what is taught us about High Priesthood in the Epistle to the Hebrews. " Every High Priest taken from among men is ordained for men in things pertaining to God, that he may offer both gifts and sacrifices for sins. . . . And no man taketh this honour unto himself, but he that is called of God, as was Aaron. So also Christ glorified not Himself to be made an High Priest; but He that said unto Him, Thou art My Son, this day have I begotten Thee. As He saith also in another place, Thou art a Priest for ever after the order of Melchisedek."

We must remember that the whole purpose of the Tabernacle, the Sacrifices and the High Priesthood of Aaron, was to teach the people of God something more about Jesus Christ than they knew before. Now people are apt to say: " But all that has passed away now." Perfectly true ! But why has it passed away ? Simply because it is perfectly fulfilled in Christ. Do let us be on our guard against thinking that God has in any way changed. We can no more come to God now without the mediation of a High Priest than could the People of God under the old Covenant. We so easily slip into the way of thinking that the dispensation of the Old Testament was different in kind from that of the New. It is against this terrible, but not uncommon, error that the Article says: " The Old Testament is not contrary to the New." Men seem to think of the Old Testament dispensation as something that was entirely abolished in order that something entirely different might take its place. This, of course, is absolutely false. The Holy Ghost speaks of the Old Testament dispensation as *partial*, " that which is in part," whereas the New Testament dispensation is " that which is perfect." The difference between " that which is in part " and " that which is perfect " is a difference of *degree* not of *kind*. " That which is in part " is only " done away " because " that which is perfect " is come. The partial High Priesthood of Aaron has passed away not because God has changed His mind about High Priesthood, but because the perfect High Priesthood of Jesus the Son of Mary, the High Priesthood " for ever, after the order of Melchisedek," has taken its place.

And so, in the Epistle to the Hebrews, the Holy Ghost calls our attention to the great principles that underlay the High Priesthood of Aaron, in order that we may learn from them about the High Priesthood of Jesus Christ.

Now, think a moment what these great principles are.

First, the High Priest is taken from among men. If this were not so, he could not represent men. No angel could be a High Priest for men. So the High Priesthood of the Eternal Son is the direct consequence of His Perfect Manhood; of that Sacred Humanity that He took of the substance of His Mother. Jesus Christ is " taken from among men."

Secondly, the High Priest is ordained by God. " No man taketh this honour unto himself, but he that is called of God, as was Aaron." The High Priest, as a Mediator, must really represent both of those between whom he stands. He must be both " taken from among men," and " ordained of God." Aaron ful-filled, partially, both these requirements. Jesus Christ fulfils them perfectly. Aaron was " called of God " to be a High Priest. Jesus Christ was " glorified by " God to be High Priest when He said, " Thou art My Son, this day have I begotten Thee "; and when He " declared with an oath," " Thou art a Priest for ever after the order of Melchisedek."

Thirdly, the High Priest, taken from among men, and ordained by God, is ordained " for men." He is the one and only official representative of each man, and of all men, before God. Any worship that is not offered by him is an abomination to God; it is a blasphemy and a sin.

Adoration, then, is impossible, except through the One Mediation of Jesus the Son of Mary, because He is the One High Priest, taken from among men and ordained for men, and all human worship must be offered to God by Him.

Then, thirdly, we have to consider what it is that the One High Priest, the Priest for ever, is to offer for men to God. The Holy Ghost says: " It is *of necessity* that this man have somewhat also to offer." And we have now to think of the actual sacrifice offered by the High Priest.

The High Priestly sacrifice, in the Old Testament, was the great annual sacrifice of the Day of Atonement. It is then in the Day of Atonement that we are especially taught about the High Priesthood of Jesus the Son of Mary.

Now, when we think of the Day of Atonement, we remember that the great sacrifice consisted of two parts—(1) the killing of the victim; and (2) the offering of the blood in the Holy of Holies. These two acts, taken together, constitute the Sacrifice of the Atonement. The second part is as essential as the first. And this is the Divine " pattern," " showed in the Mount," of the perfect High Priesthood of Jesus Christ. The mediatorial office of the true High Priest, taken from among men, and ordained for men, is exercised in this twofold way, and when we speak of the Atonement we mean (1) the death of Christ on the Cross, and (2) the pleading of that death in " Heaven itself."

The Holy Ghost impresses upon our attention the difference between the partial and the perfect Atonement. In the partial Atonement, a victim had to be slain every year; in the perfect Atonement, Christ died but once: " Christ being raised from the dead dieth no more; death hath no more dominion over Him." But if, in the perfect Atonement, there is no pleading of the death in Heaven, then the pattern showed in the Mount was not a true pattern.

When Christ was about to die, He said: " It is finished." The One True Victim was slain, once for all and for ever. Then follows the second part of His mediatorial office. The great High Priest passes into the Heavens. Just what we should expect Him to do; even as the " partial " High Priest passed, after the death of the victim, into the Holy of Holies, to present the blood of the sacrifice there.

And so we are told of Jesus Christ as He is now in Heaven, that He " appears " before God " for us." That is His work to-day as the High Priest of humanity. From the day of the Ascension, when He entered upon this second division of His mediatorial office, right up to the Day of Judgment, the end of all time, our one plea before God is that our High Priest is " appearing " in Heaven itself—the true Holy of Holies—" for us." By His High Priestly office there in Heaven, and by that alone, the whole human race, and every individual member of it, is continually represented before God in the Highest Heaven.

Now, I think we are in a position to see what is the attitude of the people of God in reference to the High Priest.

Go back in thought to the Day of Atonement.

When the High Priest, on the Day of Atonement, had disappeared into the Holy of Holies, the people of God waited in the outer court. What did they wait there for ? They were waiting for the High Priest to come out again to bless them. That is to say, they were waiting for him to bring them the answer of God to the accepted sacrifice. In that moment of awful pause, their whole life was bound up in the life and work of their High Priest. For he was their official representative. He was " taken from among " them, and had been " ordained for " them. It was they, therefore, who were pleading with God in the Holy of Holies.

From the Ascension to the Day of Judgment seems to us a long time. But, with God, " one day is as a thousand years, and a thousand years as one day." And so, in the Creed, the Holy Ghost goes straight, and without a pause, from the Ascension to the Judgment. " He ascended into Heaven, and sitteth at the right hand of God. From thence He shall come."

The attitude, then, of the Church, from the Ascension of our Lord till the Day of Judgment, is just this, that her life is " hid with Christ in God." Her whole life and being hangs upon the High Priest in Heaven; and, by Him, the whole Church, and every member of it, is " appearing " in the Presence of God. He, there presenting His all-prevailing sacrifice (" He that liveth, and was dead ") is the One and only link between God and man.

And now we are in a position to understand what must be the nature of all true worship; what must be the nature, therefore, for English Christians, of " Prayer-Book worship."

The worship of the Church on earth must, of course, be identical with that of the High Priest in Heaven. The Church, in her worship on earth, must be continually doing the same thing as the High Priest is doing in Heaven. In Heaven and on earth it is the High Priest alone who offers acceptable worship to God.

In our next chapter we shall see how this great principle is actually carried out day by day in the ceaseless worship of the Church.

Meanwhile, let us put before ourselves, each one of us, this great vision of God and His creatures.

We have it set forth for us in the imagery of the fourth and fifth chapters of the Revelation of St. John the Divine.

In the fourth chapter we have the ideal. God and His creation: " He that sat on the throne," on the one hand; " the four beasts " (or " living creatures ") " and the four and twenty elders," on the other. In the fifth chapter we have that which hinders the carrying out of this ideal. There is a barrier in the way of the free and unrestricted intercourse between God and His creation—the sealed book. " No man in Heaven, nor in earth, neither under the earth, was able to open the book, neither to look thereon." What a terrible disaster has befallen the fair creation of God ! " I wept much because no man was found worthy to open and read the book, neither to look thereon." All apparently hopelessly gone wrong. Then the vision proceeds. The Apostle is weeping over the wreck of the beautiful ideal. What happens then ? " One of the elders saith unto me, Weep not : behold, the Lion of the tribe of Judah, the Root of David, hath prevailed to open the book, and to loose the seven seals thereof." At this message of comfort the weeping Apostle looks up, and the scene is changed. " I beheld, and lo, in the midst of the throne and of the four beasts, and in the midst of the elders, stood a Lamb as it had been slain."

" And He came and took the book out of the right hand of Him that sat upon the throne."

The Lamb stood " in the midst of the throne "; He represented God to His creation. He stood in the midst of the four beasts and in the midst of the elders;

He represented creation before God. The barrier is removed; the sealed book is taken out of the right hand of Him that sat upon the throne; creation returns, through the One mediation, to its right and normal conditions—viz., the true worship of God.

Such is the life and worship of the Church here on earth to the end of all time. Its life is " hid with Christ in God." It is bound up in the High Priestly mediation of Jesus the Son of Mary. Its worship is the perpetual exercise on earth of the High Priesthood of Jesus the Son of Mary.

Now let us just look back over the ground we have already traversed in our inquiry into " Prayer-Book Worship." The word " Prayer-Book " shuts out all those vulgar inanities that we glanced at in the last chapter. Thank God, there is nothing in the Prayer-Book about " popular services," " elastic services," " doll services," or " memorial services." The Prayer-Book delivers us from this sort of thing. But, when we have ruled out all this rubbish, there remains an idea of something prosaic and unromantic about the ideas that group themselves around the expression " going to Church." It is regarded as a somewhat wearisome performance that must be got through if it cannot be shirked; it forms the subject of many a witticism in our current literature; the badinage at its expense enlivens the luncheon table on Sunday. Yes ! " Prayer-Book worship " sounds to many a subject of what has been wittily called " a somewhat gritty texture."

A man one day said to a Priest: " Yes ! I go to Church, but I am one of those who think I am as well without it." And when we think of what " going to Church " too commonly means, shall we say he was very far wrong ?

But, as we begin to unravel this topic of " Prayer-Book worship," it grows in grandeur. We are driven by our faith to think of the knowledge of God, the adoration of God, and the High Priesthood of Jesus the Son of Mary. And, holding these great truths fast and firm, we shall see that " Prayer-Book worship," to us English people, is the reality, in everyday life, of the glorious vision of St. John. In the darkness and dulness and grey boredom of life, we shall hear the voice saying: " Weep not; behold, the Lion of the tribe of Judah, the Root of David, hath prevailed." And here, in dull, prosaic twentieth-century London, we shall look up and see that " in the midst of the throne and the four beasts, and in the midst of the elders, there stands a Lamb as it had been slain "; and we, in our Prayer-Book worship, shall take our stand, day by day, and moment by moment, with that happy, blessed throng, the new creation of God, who cry: " Blessing, and honour, and glory, and power, be unto Him that sitteth upon the throne, and unto the Lamb for ever and ever."

CHAPTER IV

CATHOLICITY

THE two fundamental principles of true worship are:

1. That the basis of all worship is simple adoration paid to GOD.

2. That such adoration can only be given to God through the Mediation of the Sacred Humanity of JESUS the Son of Mary.

We have now to see how the Church, in her worship, carries out and applies these great fundamental principles of worship.

But, first, we must arrive at a clear understanding of what we mean by the Church, whose worship we have to consider.

The present Dean of Canterbury, Dr. Wace, in his Bampton Lectures on the Foundations of Faith, impresses upon us the great truth that Faith is the faculty by which men lay hold of the things invisible; and that, both in heathendom and in Christianity, it is Faith that makes men realize, as they do, the things invisible. And by the exercise of faith it comes to pass that the things invisible are more real to men than the things that they can see; so that, in heathendom and in Christianity, we find multitudes of men and women regulating their everyday life, and governing their actions, by things unseen; yes, and willingly giving up, in suffering and in death, things seen for the sake of the things unseen.

And he shows that authority is the correlative of faith; how that men receive the subject-matter of their faith on some authority that they implicitly trust. The Moslem nations implicitly obey the authority of the Prophet; the Buddhists accept and follow the precepts of the Buddha; the Chinese accept as authoritative the philosophy of Confucius, etc. In any case, " faith cometh by hearing." It is taken on authority. Let go the authority, let it be undervalued or despised, or belittled in any way, and at once you have struck at what Dr. Wace so rightly calls " the foundations of faith."

And, as we have seen, faith and worship stand or fall together. Faith without worship is not faith at all. The faith that does not rest upon authority, and does not authoritatively express itself in worship, is merely speculative philosophy. And the very word " speculative " excludes all idea of authority. Speculations are the surmises of individual men or groups of men. They cannot come with any external authority. They are just " views " or " opinions."

Authority, then, is the correlative of faith; and therefore authority must be the correlative of worship. Our hold on the things invisible must come from authority.

Our worship, then, must bear the stamp of authority. In other words, it must be the worship " of the Church." It comes to us with the authority of the Church. It is the Church that will exhibit, in her worship, the carrying out of those great principles that, as we have seen, underlie all true idea of human worship.

Catholicity

The authority of the Church! What does that mean? Christians answer boldly: " The authority of Jesus Christ."

If there is one subject more than another that the Holy Ghost labours to teach us, it is the Unity of Christ and the Church. And of all Divine mysteries, there is none more mysterious and more out of the reach of the comprehension of the " natural man " than this.

The Holy Catholic Church, the Communion of Saints, is as much an article of the Christian faith as is the truth of the Holy Trinity or the Incarnation. And as being an essential article of the faith that all profess in their Baptism, it is as binding on the conscience of Christians as any other article of the Creed : and Christians, by the mere fact of their Baptismal profession are committed to belief in the Divine mystery of the Catholic Church.

It being a Divine mystery, we cannot expect to be able to do more, as regards the Catholic Church, than to see " through a glass darkly." If we could see it perfectly, and understand it thoroughly, it would not be an Article of Faith. Let anyone try seriously to meditate upon the simple words of our Lord, " I am the Vine, ye are the branches "; or upon the words of St. Paul, "As the body is one, and hath many members, and all the members of that one body, being many, are one body; so also is Christ "; let a man, I say, try seriously for a moment to meditate upon these words, and he will find at once that he can no more understand how this can be than he can understand how it is that " the Father is God, the Son is God, and the Holy Ghost is God; and yet they are not three Gods, but one God." He will find himself in the same intellectual difficulty as that which confronts him in the Athanasian Creed, when it says: " Like as we are compelled by the Christian verity to acknowledge every Person by Himself to be God and Lord, so are we forbidden by the Catholic religion to say there are three Gods or three Lords." The human mind fails altogether to form any adequate conception of the fact authoritatively revealed to us that Christ is as a body with many members, and that all the members of that Body, being many, are one Body.

Yet God, in His mercy, vouchsafes to throw certain lights upon this awful mystery—lights that are, at any rate, sufficient for our practical guidance.

" I am the Vine, ye are the branches."

One great truth strikes us here—viz., that the branches are an essential part of the vine. The branches may be more or fewer; they may be more fruitful or less fruitful; they may, to a certain extent, be taken away without injury to the vine; but a vine without branches would not be a vine. It is simply unthinkable. We see, then, that we can no more think of Christ without His Church than we can think of the Church without Christ; Christ without the Church would be a vine without branches. " I am the Vine, ye are the branches."

The same great truth is taught us by the Divine analogy of the body and the spirit. As we think of human soul and body, we see that, while it is possible for the human soul to exist apart from the body, yet a disembodied soul cannot express itself or make itself felt. It is only through the body that the soul can act; and the actions of the body, whether good or bad, are the actions of the indwelling soul. So here, too, we lay hold of the same great truth—viz., that you can no more think of Christ without His Church than you can think of the Church without Christ. "The body is for the Lord, *and the Lord for the body.*"

Then the mystery of the Oneness of Christ and His Church is taught us in all those places in the Holy Bible where the Church is spoken of as the "Bride" or "the Lamb's wife."

The Holy Ghost bids us remember the Divine mystery of Holy Marriage—a mystery that is beyond our powers of comprehension—viz., that a man and his wife are "one flesh." And this marvellous and mysterious oneness, the most complete of earthly unities, exists on account of the Oneness of Christ and His Church. "This is a great mystery; but I speak concerning Christ and His Church." And it is in connection with this great mystery that our Lord is spoken of as "the Second Man," or "the last Adam." Of the Second Adam, as of the first, the Mind of God is that "it is not good that the man should be alone." And as the mystery of the creation of Eve is that she was "taken out of man" when the "deep sleep" fell upon Adam, so have Saints delighted to meditate on the Church springing, as it were, out of the side of the Second Adam in His "deep sleep" upon the Cross. And (not to mention countless other illustrations of this great truth scattered up and down the Holy Bible) the devout meditations of saintly souls have seen a foreshadowing of the Resurrection of our Lord in the words spoken about Boaz: "It came to pass at midnight that the man was afraid and turned himself; and behold, a woman lay at his feet."

The first great fact, then, that we lay to heart in thinking of the Mystery of the Holy Catholic Church is that Christ and His Church are one.

We have not far to look in order to see how lamentably this great truth is overlooked in its practical bearings in everyday English thought.

Many years ago, when first the reaction against popular Protestantism set in in this country, and the Divine character of the Church was once more brought into prominence, Protestant objectors to Catholic truth thought they would exalt Christ by belittling the Church. It was said in those days: " The High Church put the Church above Christ; but the Low Church put Christ above the Church." And Catholics were supposed to be impaled on the horns of a dilemma when Protestants asked them the question: " Do you belong to Christ because you belong to the Church, or do you belong to the Church because you belong to Christ ?" But the solemn tomfoolery of such an egregiously silly question was only possible because men had come to think of Christ as one thing, and of the Church as another. These good men had forgotten all about the Vine and the branches. Who would be such a fool as to ask whether these are the branches because they belong to the Vine, or whether they belong to the Vine because they are branches ?

The first thing, then, that we learn about the Mystery of the Holy Catholic Church is that Christ and His Church are one.

The next truth that the Holy Ghost labours to teach us is that the Church, being the Body of Christ, is wholly indwelt by the Holy Spirit, the Spirit of Christ.

The unity of the Church is not the unity of sticks bound together in a faggot, a merely fictitious and accidental unity. It is the unity of a common life. It is from within, not from without.

Think steadily of the wonderful words of Psalm cxxxiii.: " Behold, how good and joyful a thing it is, brethren, to dwell together in unity. It " (the dwelling together of brethren in unity) " is like the precious ointment upon the head, that ran down unto the beard; even unto Aaron's beard, and went down the skirts of his clothing." The indwelling of the Holy Ghost in the Body of the Church, and His abiding presence with any individual man is the direct outcome of the Oneness of the Body with the Head. Never was the Holy Ghost promised to an individual *as such*. " The Spirit of the Lord shall rest upon Him "—*i.e.*, upon Jesus Christ. " He saw the heavens opened, and the Spirit of God like a dove descending upon *Him*."

Nowadays " individualism " is supposed to be the watchword of what men are pleased to call " Christianity." Men have somehow or other drifted into the idea of men individually making their terms with God, and of the Holy Spirit dropping, as it were, on this man here and on that man there. No such thing ! There is One Person on Whom the Spirit of the Lord rests, and the One Person is Jesus the Son of Mary. If any other man receives the Spirit of God, it is because he is incorporated into the mystical Body of Christ. So St. John speaks of the cleansing power of the Precious Blood. " If we walk in the light, as He is in the light, *we have fellowship one with another*, and the Blood of Jesus Christ His Son cleanseth us from all sin." It is not the Precious Blood casually dropped upon an individual here, and an individual there, cleansing them as isolated individuals, but the Blood of Life circulating through the members of the One Body.

" Individualism," like " Undenominationalism," is an essentially un-Christian, and therefore anti-Christian, idea. Let it go, with all other anti-Christian ideas, whence it came !

The One Body, then, is wholly indwelt by the One Spirit. You cannot locate the Spirit in any one part of the Body. You cannot say of your soul that it is in your head or in your heart. "The eye cannot say to the ear, I have no need of thee, nor again the head to the feet, I have no need of you." You cannot locate the Holy Ghost in the Church of England, or the Church of this or that. He indwells the whole Body. And from this truth we read this immensely practical conclusion—viz., that the action of the One Body is the action of the Holy Spirit. In other words, it is *Catholicity* that is the test of truth, both in Faith and in worship. Catholicity! What do we mean by that ? The word, of course, means universality. The test of the truth in faith and worship is that that faith and worship be universal in the Body.

"But," a person may say, "anyone may destroy that universality by refusing to accede to a certain dogma or practice." In the old Scandinavian mythology, it was said that Baldur the Beautiful, having been killed, might be restored to life if all creatures would weep for him. One creature, old Thaukt, refused to weep. Is faith and worship to be thus left at the mercy of any individualist in the Body who will persist in following his own way ? Certainly not.

The old maxim of Vincent of Lerins is " Quod semper, quod ubique, quod ab omnibus." " Quod semper !" Not only that which is now held in common by all— what, for instance, Catholics and Unitarians can agree upon—but what has *always* been the universal belief of Christendom.

A new religion, or form of religion, stands self-condemned because it is new. It matters not whether its adherents are numbered by tens or by millions. It is not a question of Parliamentary majorities. The point is that you can place your finger upon the spot at which that organism began as a separate organism, the point at which it diverged from the main Body; and at that point it was individualism asserting itself against the body. So it is, as a simple matter of historical fact, with all the Protestant sects. Whatever they may have to say for themselves (and they may, no doubt, have much to urge in their defence), however they may seek to justify their action (and they may, and probably have, just cause of complaint), the fact remains that they did separate themselves from the Church and start a new organism. If we ask any of them, " When did your particular form of faith and worship begin?" he cannot say, " It was always so from the beginning." He may say that this form is better, or purer, than that of the Church, but he cannot say that it was always there.

The Protestant will tell us that the Revolution which in the sixteenth century produced modern Protestantism was rendered necessary by the corruptions of Rome. But the Holy Eastern Church protests emphatically against the corruptions of Rome, and yet stands exactly where it always did: its faith and worship are just what they always were. It is not necessary to create a new organism in order to reform abuses.

It is not enough, then, for a new religion to be able to show (even if it can do so) that it commands the sympathies of a majority in Christendom to-day. That does not give it Universality. It has got to show that its particular tenets and particular form of worship were *always* the tenets and form of worship of Christendom. If we can show that a particular mode of faith

or worship was, at any time in the Christian history,
new, we have proved that it is not universal.

"Yes," but a Protestant may say, "our faith and
worship were not new in the sixteenth century. We
were merely returning to the purer faith and worship
of primitive Christianity." Or a Presbyterian, in support of his peculiar position, may prove, if he please,
up to the hilt, that there were Presbyterian ordinations
in the first fifty years or so of Christendom. "But,"
we ask in return, "what then was the Holy Spirit doing
for those fifteen centuries that lay between these first
fifty years or so (even supposing you have proved your
point as regards them) and the sixteenth century?
Did the Body of the Church disappear for fifteen centuries? If, confessedly, your form of faith and worship
had disappeared for fifteen centuries, it is clearly not
universal; and if, in order to make out your case, you
have to make a leap of fifteen centuries, what becomes
of the One Body and the One Spirit?"

We may say, then, of all these new organisms in
what is grimly called "the Christian world" that what
is new in them is not true, and what is true in them is
not new. If you ask a Protestant where his peculiar
religion was one thousand years ago, I fancy that, like
the beaver in "The Hunting of the Snark," he will
"seem unaccountably shy." We Church-people, too,
can go back to primitive Christianity, but we can do
so quite comfortably. We have not got suddenly to
jump fifteen centuries. We can move about in the
atmosphere of the fourth, or eighth, or twelfth century,
for instance, quite as comfortably as we can in the
atmosphere of the twentieth, for our watchword is: "I
believe One Catholic, Apostolic Church"—"Quod
semper, quod ubique, quod ab omnibus."

Catholicity

Our second great principle, then—viz., that the Church, being the Body of Christ, is wholly indwelt by the Spirit of Christ, leads us to the negative conclusion that if a form of faith or worship can be shown to be new, it is not of the Spirit of God.

But now we must draw the positive conclusion from this second great truth about the Catholic Church. And that is, that whatever of faith and worship can be shown to have been the faith and worship of undivided Christendom, is binding on the consciences of Christians. Its Catholicity constitutes its authority. And I should like to divide this positive conclusion into two heads—

1. That no man must have any scruple as to the lawfulness and rightfulness of anything that is universally accepted in Christendom.

2. That every individual Christian must conform his faith and practice to the faith and practice of undivided Christendom.

1. No man is to have any scruple about a Catholic practice.

It might sometimes happen that a timid soul (such an one as the Apostle would call a " weak brother ") might feel the tremendous force of the institution and of the command respecting the Sabbath, and might be led to think that there is a good deal of force in the argument of those fanatics who call themselves " Seventh Day " this or " Seventh Day " that—who imagine, that is, that they are bound to keep the seventh day—*i.e.*, Saturday—rather than the first day —*i.e.*, Sunday. Or we may have known instances of people who feel uncomfortable about " clean and unclean " meats. Or a female member of the crazy " Hatless Brigade " may think it her duty to worship with her head uncovered. There are to be no scruples

E

about these things. Universal Christendom has discarded the Sabbath and keeps the Lord's Day. This is, therefore, the Mind of the Holy Ghost. Undivided Christendom has abrogated all distinction between clean and unclean; these, then, are abrogated by the authority of the Holy Ghost. And St. Paul made very short work of females of the " Hatless Brigade." He simply said: " We have no such custom, neither the Churches of God," and there was an end of the matter. He brought forward against them the authority of the Holy Ghost.

Or, to come to what is constantly meeting us now, we often find people asking, " Is this primitive ?" To take a homely instance from one of the " burning questions of the day "—*i.e.*, the " ceremonial " use of incense. When those unfortunate things known as " the Lambeth opinions " came out, a learned man of my acquaintance wasted a good deal of time in laborious research, and, as a result of these misdirected labours, gave to the world his conclusion that there may possibly have been " still " use of incense in the first century. But what has that got to do with the matter ? Christians " may possibly " have observed the Sabbath in the first forty or fifty years of Christendom. That has nothing to do with the matter. What the silly man had got to show was, why there has never been a " still " use of incense ever since ! When, therefore, we are implored to adopt a " still " use of incense—*i.e.*, not to use it in the way in which Christians *do* use it— viz., censing persons and things—our answer is the answer of St. Paul to the female " Hatless Brigade ": " We have no such custom, neither the Churches of God."

We often find people casting about for a reason for

certain ritual observances. They will ask us, for instance, why we use incense for the purpose of censing
persons and things. What is our answer? We should
say (should we not?) that it is the way in which
our fellow-Christians, East and West, always use it,
and that that is all-sufficient for us. And if, as
sometimes happens, we are implored to use it in
some other way we should answer (should we not?)
" We have no such custom, neither in the Churches of
God." And there would be an intelligible end of the
matter.

What an infinity of trouble and of worrying anxiety
Christian men and women would save themselves if
they met their scruples with the simple answer that
Catholicity is the test of truth, because there is One
Body and One Spirit !

2. Every individual Christian is bound to conform
his faith and practice to the faith and practice of undivided Christendom.

The question is not, " Does this seem to me to be
right and justifiable?" but " How has undivided
Christendom always dealt with this matter?"

Let us illustrate this position by another more or
less " burning question "—viz., the power of absolution
vested in the priesthood, and the manner in which it is
exercised?

Many professing English Churchmen find it impossible to bring themselves to believe that the priest has
the power of absolution. When such people are confronted with the plain words of the Prayer-Book on
this matter, they probably say: " That is the part of
the Prayer-Book that I do not like."

Now, we can all see the impudent absurdity of the
man who said: " Oh, that is where Paul and I do not

agree "; but this " not liking that part of the Prayer-Book," when we come to sift it, is really as impudent and as absurd.

Go back a thousand years to undivided Christendom. Is there the smallest doubt as to the faith and practice of undivided Christendom on this subject ? Look at the East and West to-day. Is the power of the keys a Roman accretion ? Certainly not ! It is as implicitly believed in and used in the East as it is in the West. There is no question at all as to the belief and practice of undivided Christendom as regards the power of the priest to absolve from sins. What is the meaning of this unanimous belief and practice ? It means that this is the Mind of the One Spirit expressed in the One Body.

But many Englishmen who do not deny what the Prayer-Book tells us to say twice a day—viz., that " God hath given power and commandment to His Ministers to declare and pronounce to His people, being penitent, the absolution and remission of their sins," seem to think that the Church of England has instituted a new order of things—viz., that absolution is to be conveyed by a general declaration in the public service, following upon the general confession.

But, of course, the question at once arises whether there is any precedent for this in universal Christendom. As a simple matter of fact, was such a thing ever heard of in undivided Christendom as that the public declaratory absolutions in the Eucharist and the Divine Office should take the place of the judicial absolution given in Sacramental Confession ? No one can attempt to argue such a thing for a moment. Everyone knows, or ought to know, that these general confessions and declaratory absolutions occupy exactly the same place in the Roman Catholic Service Books that they do in the Church of England Prayer-Book. The English Prayer-Book was doing no new thing at all when it placed those confessions and declaratory absolutions where they are. If anybody says, therefore, " It is true that in undivided Christendom people had to go to Confession, but in the English Prayer-Book ' nous avons changé tout cela,' " he is stating a falsehood, because the Prayer-Book has put these things just where they are in the Roman Service Book to-day. And if for a moment it could be granted that he was speaking the truth, then we should have had the Church of England unchurching herself by introducing a new religion, as against the universality of undivided Christendom. Yet we find that this absurd idea is gravely put forward in some Anglican books of instruction !

The rule of faith, worship, and practice, for every individual Christian is the consensus of undivided Christendom. This is so because there is One Body and One Spirit, and because, therefore, the action of the Body of Christ is the action of the Spirit of Christ. To the countless vagaries of individualism we oppose the authority of Catholicity.

We sum up, then, the principles as regards the Holy Catholic Church at which we have now arrived:

1. The Holy Catholic Church is not a human institution, but a Divine Mystery.

2. The Mystery of the Holy Catholic Church is that it is one with Christ. It is the Body of Christ. To think of Christ as apart from the Church is to think of Him as He is not, and never was, in the mind of God.

3. The Holy Catholic Church, being the Body of

Christ, is wholly indwelt by the Holy Ghost, Who is the Spirit of Christ.

The consequences of this truth are—

(1) That it is only through the One Body that the One Spirit acts or expresses Himself.

(2) That the action of the Whole Body is the action of the Spirit that indwells it.

(3) That, therefore, universality—" quod semper, quod ubique, quod ab omnibus "—is the authority of Jesus Christ in faith, worship, and morals.

(4) That, therefore, it is the duty of every individual Christian to believe as his fellow-Christians have always believed; to worship as his fellow-Christians have always worshipped; and to live according to the standard that his fellow-Christians have always acknowledged.

And, this being so, we have, in this instance, as in others that I have previously brought before you, to face the alternative. What is the alternative to accepting the Divine authority of Jesus Christ as given us in His Body and His Spirit ?

It is, of course, that we must be prepared to take the consequences of our disobedience. If it were merely a question of playing a game or of following out a logical sequence, we might stand on one side and say that, after all, it does not matter much. But if it is the question of accepting or rejecting a Divine revelation, it is quite another matter.

When, therefore, we are bidden by our Creed to believe in the Holy Catholic Church, it is an essential part of God's revelation in CHRIST that we deny or despise at our peril.

Two great considerations arise out of belief in the Holy Catholic Church:

Catholicity

First, the tremendous responsibility placed upon every individual Christian by the fact that Catholicity —*i.e.*, Universality—is the test of truth in faith, worship, and morals.

If any individual finds himself believing or worshipping in any way differently from the way in which undivided Christendom has always believed or worshipped, the burden of proof lies with that man. It is he who has to show that he is right in this individualism.

It is astonishing how, in these days, when holy fear is conspicuous by its absence, no one is afraid to " do that which is right in his own eyes." Yet this is just the expression that is used in the Holy Scriptures to describe a wrong state of things. A certain thing seems to a person to be right, or, at any rate, justifiable. At once he flies off after it, with no thought of judgment to come.

But since, as we have seen, Catholicity or Universality is the test of truth in faith, worship, or morals, we cannot justify any peculiarity in faith or morals; while any peculiarity in worship can only be justified as regards unimportant matters where such divergence is recognized as justifiable by the practice of undivided Christendom.

And this is really the rock on which we stand in the storms and tempests and turmoil of life. Protestant innovators, inventors of new religions, higher critics, etc., are very glib, and have plenty to say for themselves; and by individualist appeals to Scripture or to natural reason they puzzle unlearned and simple souls. It is quite a mistake to argue with people of this sort. Do let us set our feet firm on the rock, and say: " We have no such custom, neither the Churches

of God." In an age when no one is afraid of consequences—a shallow and irreligious age—let us stir up
the gift of holy fear that is within us, and at least have
the modesty to think that if I or Mr. So-and-So think
such-and-such things, and undivided Christendom
clearly does not, it must be I or Mr. So-and-So that is
wrong.

A notable instance of the utter want of humility that
lies at the bottom of all individualism is to be found
in the rise of Irvingism—a new and noxious sect that
sprang out of Scotch Presbyterianism some fifty or
sixty years ago. One of these sectarians, describing
to me their start, said that " certain people were pray-
ing for an outpouring of the Holy Spirit; and the
answer," he said, " came in a way they did not expect."
This " manifestation " was sent to the English Arch-
bishops and Bishops, and to the Pope, and the Emperor
of Austria, " and *people of that sort* (*!*). And they none
of them took any notice of it." Well, if neither the
English Episcopate nor the Roman Episcopate saw
anything Divine in this " manifestation " that was
vouchsafed, I believe, to thirteen people, how strange
that those thirteen people could not have thought:
" Perhaps, after all, we were mistaken "; but no! the
immediate conclusion was: " We had to go on
without them "; and another abominable sect was
founded.

Let us, then, one and all, " enter into rest " in our
spirit by acting firmly and unhesitatingly upon the
great fact that Universality is the test of truth; and
to that great authority let us cheerfully sacrifice whims,
" views," and " opinions." And what is this, after all,
but what the HOLY GHOST bids us do when He tells us
to " cast down imaginations and every high thing

which exalteth itself against the knowledge of GOD, and to bring into captivity every thought to the obedience of CHRIST " ? And is it not significant that in the same breath He should bid us to " have in readiness to revenge all disobedience " ?

Then, secondly, our belief in the Catholic Church will make us see that the life of ceaseless worship which is the distinguishing mark of the Church, as against the sects, is the outcome of the tranquillity of soul that can only come from settled convictions.

St. Paul tells us that we are *not* to be perpetually laying again the foundations. But this is exactly what Protestantism, in its ceaseless flux, is always doing. No one can begin to worship till he is *sure of his ground.* The Church is absolutely sure of her ground; therefore she is free to devote herself to the life of worship. If a man is to have one foot in the grave before he has quite made up his mind about the Holy Trinity, the Incarnation, and the One Mediation, what is left of his life in which to walk with God ? If our whole life is to be spent in laying foundations, when are we going to build ? Protestantism is not, and cannot be, sure of its ground; therefore it cannot live the life of worship. And it is just that tranquil, ceaseless round of worship that is the distinctive mark of the Catholic Apostolic Church. It is the loveliness of this tranquil life that is its great attraction. From out of the turmoil of thoughts and doubts and opinions men look across, like Balaam of old, to the peaceful camp of God, and then, if they will listen, they will hear the Spirit of God saying: " Surely there is no enchantment against Jacob; neither is there any divination against Israel; according to this time it shall be

said *of Jacob and of Israel*, What hath God wrought?"
And, again: " He hath not beheld iniquity in Jacob,
neither hath He seen perverseness in Israel; the Lord
his God is with him, and the shout of a King is among
them."

Let us, then, be quite certain of this—viz., that as
long as men allow their minds to be in a state of flux,
and as long as any doubts are harboured or cherished
there, so long they are excluding themselves from that
life of worship that can alone fulfil the end of their
being and satisfy the aspirations of their inmost
soul.

CHAPTER V

"THE CHURCH" AND "THE CHURCH OF
ENGLAND"

BEFORE we proceed to consider the tranquil loveliness of the life of worship as exhibited to us day
by day in the Catholic Church, two questions seem to
demand an answer; and the answers to these two
questions, added to the previous considerations, will
furnish us with an idea of the mystery of the Holy
Catholic Church that will form a working basis for our
realization of Prayer-Book worship.

The first of these two questions is: " Who actually
constitute the Holy Catholic Church?" In other
words: " What is it that differentiates the Church from
the rest of mankind? What is the dividing line
between the Church and the world?"

For the answer to this question we turn to the next
Article of the Creed: " I believe in the forgiveness of
sins." The Church is the body of those whose sins
have been forgiven. This great dividing line between
the Church and the world is sharply marked for us
by the Holy Ghost. Think, for instance, of the words
of St. John: " We know that we " (the members of
the One Body) " are of God, and the whole world lieth
in wickedness." Think of the words of the Catholic
Church: " All men are conceived and born in sin; and
our Saviour Christ saith none can enter into the King-

dom of Heaven, except he be regenerate, and born anew of Water and of the Holy Ghost."

When we speak of " the world," we mean all—good, bad, or indifferent—who are merely in a state of nature, in a state (to use the language of the Church) of original sin.

When we speak of " the Church," we mean all— good, bad, or indifferent—who have been delivered from original sin by a new birth, by which they were made " members of Christ," and, therefore, " children of God."

It is characteristic of the prevailing Paganism of modern English thought that nowadays it is the fashion to divide men into " good men " (meaning morally good men), and " bad men " (meaning morally bad men), whereas, throughout the Bible, men are divided into those who are, and those who are not, in the Covenant of God. In the Old Testament, it is the children of Seth, as against the children of Cain; the children of Shem, as against the children of Ham; the children of Abraham, as against all other men; and, as the Covenant develops, the circumcised, as against the uncircumcised. In the New Testament, it is " the children of God," as against " the children of this world." In modern language, " Christians," as against " heathens "; the baptized, as against the unbaptized. There are morally good and morally bad on either side of the dividing line, just as to-day there are morally good heathens, and morally bad Christians; but this moral goodness does not make the heathen a Christian; nor does his moral badness make the Christian a heathen. It is a question of a different genus, a different order of beings, a question of difference of *kind*, not of difference of degree.

And so we find that the Church, *as a whole*, has the attribute of sanctity, while the world, *as a whole*, has the attribute of wickedness. " We know that we are of God, and the whole world lieth in wickedness."

How forcibly is this inherent sanctity of the visible Church brought before us in the words of Balaam, already quoted. Balaam, speaking by the Spirit of God, says: " He hath not beheld iniquity in Jacob, neither hath He seen perverseness in Israel." And yet we know that there was abundance of individual (yes, and sometimes even of collective) iniquity and abundant " perverseness " in Israel. But the distinguishing mark of the visible Church was that its members were all in Covenant with God.

If we ask how it is that the dividing line between the Church and the world has become so blurred in modern English thought, we shall answer at once that it is because modern English thought takes no practical count of *original* sin. When modern Englishmen talk of " sin," you will, I think, invariably find that they are thinking of *actual* sins, actually committed in life. Original sin has no reality for them. And yet we can see that, from one point of view, original sin is a more formidable barrier between God and men than even the actual sins of Christians. This, I think, is very clearly shown us in the parable of the Prodigal Son, who is the divinely-given type of a lapsed Christian.

The whole point of the history of the Prodigal Son lies just in the fact of his sonship. He was his father's son all along, and therefore he had only to " come to himself," to realize, that is to say, his sonship, and at once his return home became possible. He could arise and go to his father, *because he had a father to go to*. So with the Christian who has fallen from grace. He *is* a Child of God *because he has been born so*. Consequently, he can return to his Father at any moment that he " comes to himself."

Original sin can only be forgiven by the gift of a new nature: " Except a man be born again, he cannot see the Kingdom of God." And so we are not at all surprised to find that, in the Nicene Creed, the words, " I believe in the forgiveness of sins," are rendered, " I acknowledge One Baptism for the remission of sins "; which shows us that it is original sin that the Church is thinking of in the Creed. As a matter of fact, the Church, in the Creed, does not speak of the actual lapses of Christians, because it is at least conceivable that a person born into the new life will grow in it. " Such *as are planted* in the House of the Lord shall flourish in the courts of the House of our God." " *He that is washed* needeth not save to wash his feet."

It is Baptism, then, that constitutes the differentiating mark between the Church and the world; and it is in the same Spirit by Whom Balaam spoke of Israel as a whole, that the Apostles, speaking of the baptized as a whole, call them " the Saints," " the faithful men," etc. And so in the Catholic Church the expression " the faithful " has acquired a technical meaning, a fact that is too often entirely overlooked. " The faithful " does not mean the men who are actually using, and living by, their faith. It does not connote that modern idea of an " invisible Church." It is simply equivalent to " the baptized." So in the nineteenth Article this matter is accurately stated in the words: " The Visible Church of Christ is a congregation of faithful men." Of men, that is, who have received the faculty (or " theological virtue," as it is called) of faith; in other words, the baptized.

The Church, then, consists of the whole body of the baptized. It is " the household of God." Some of this household, or family, stray away; some sheep of this one fold wander off and lose themselves; but the rebellious children are still children of their Father, and the strayed sheep is still a sheep of that fold and no other.

The first distinguishing mark of the Catholic Church, then, is that she is Holy, because her children are partakers of a new nature by a new birth.

There are other marks which, alas ! put many of our baptized brethren in the wrong, and show them to be wanderers from their true home. These are that the Church is " Catholic," and that she is " Apostolic."

Any Christians or body of Christians that cannot claim Catholicity are children who have gone astray; but they are still children of God's family by virtue of their Baptism.

So, too, any body of Christians that cannot claim Apostolicity are, in like manner, wanderers over whom the heart of their Father yearns; children always, but not submitting to the regulation of the household.

And so the nineteenth Article sums it up in a clear definition. " The Visible Church of Christ is a congregation of faithful men, in the which the pure Word of God is preached, and the Sacraments be duly administered according to Christ's ordinance, in all those things that of necessity are requisite to the same."

The Church, then, is the body of the baptized, good, bad, and indifferent. " The Kingdom of Heaven is like unto a net that was cast into the sea, and gathered *of every kind.*"

The second question to which we require an answer, in order to be able to understand about Prayer-Book worship, is: " What is the Church of England ?"

We have seen that there can no more be two Churches than there can be two Gods. If, then, we find, as we do, the " Church of England " outwardly separated from the Churches of the Roman obedience on the one hand, and of the Eastern Communion on the other, we have to ask ourselves what we mean when we speak, or think, of " the Church of England." Do we mean that the Church of England is the Catholic Church ? Was it the Church of England that Jesus Christ came to found upon the earth ? Is the Church of England the organ through which the Holy Ghost acts exclusively on the world ? We have only to state the question thus to see its absurdity.

Of course, the Church of England is not the Catholic Church, for the one simple reason, if for no other, that the Catholic Church was in the world centuries before England existed.

Well, then, that proposition being ruled out by its inherent absurdity, we next proceed to ask: " Is the Church of England an isolated, self-contained, self-sufficient body, having no responsibilities to anything or anybody, but to itself and God ?" This proposition is as absurd as the last. How can there be an isolated, self-contained, and self-sufficient portion of Christendom ? Nay, it is even more absurd to suppose that the Church of England can be a separate, self-contained unit, than to say that it, and it alone, constitutes the Catholic Church.

The latter proposition, though it reminds us of the fable of the frog and the bull, does, at any rate, recognize the fact that there can only be One Body, because

there is only One Spirit; whereas, the idea of the Church
of England as an isolated unit is quite unthinkable
on any Christian supposition at all. What becomes
of the Vine and the branches if another vine can be
set up with an independent existence ? If the Church
of England could conceivably be an independent,
self-contained unit, one thing is quite clear—that its
life cannot come from Jesus Christ.

Now, these two propositions are so ridiculous that
one would have thought that no sane person could
have contemplated them for a moment, and that,
therefore, nothing more need be said about them. But,
as a matter of fact, these gross absurdities, which are
really on a par with the whimsicality which amuses us
so much in a delightful Gilbert and Sullivan opera, are
really taken *au sérieux*, and made the basis of argument by two totally different classes of people !

Roman controversialists are not ashamed to argue
with weak-kneed English Catholics on the assumption
that the Church of England claims to be the " Catholic
Church."

A Roman controversialist had the impudence, many
years ago, to say: " How can the Church of England
be the Catholic Church, when she does not claim in-
fallibility ?"

" How can the Church of England be the Catholic
Church ?" What a question ! We had thought that
it was an axiom that the whole is greater than the part,
and had therefore thought that we need not have to
assert to any sane person that the part could not be
equivalent to the whole !

But, then, the second ridiculous picture of the Church
of England, as a separate self-contained unit, seems
to form the basis of argument of what has been aptly

F

called " Church of Englandism." There are many
people nowadays who seem to think that the Church
of England has no responsibilities towards anything
outside of itself; who seem, for instance, to think that
the Church of England can abolish auricular confession
and absolve people by congregations; who seem to
think that the Church of England can abolish Eucharistic worship and substitute a form of " service "
wholly and absolutely its own; who seem to think that
the Church of England can deal with the Christian
revelation exactly as it pleases; who gravely suggest
that the Church of England should re-edit and re-
arrange the Book of Exodus to suit its own market;
who never seem to take the rest of the Catholic Church
into account at all, but think that the Church of
England is all-sufficient to judge of things human and
divine.

Is this an exaggerated picture? No! We know
quite well that these absurdities are rife among us!
What is all this but to conceive of the Church of
England as a separate, isolated, self-contained, self-
sufficient entity? Needless to say, the Church of
England never commits any of these follies; but it is,
I fear, not uncommon for individual Bishops, Priests,
and laymen to think and to talk in this absolutely
ridiculous way.

If, then, the Church of England is neither the
Catholic Church, nor a separate, self-contained, self-
sufficient entity, what is it?

It is an integral part of the One Body; of that One
Body of Christ in which the Blood of Jesus Christ
cleanses men from all sin; of that One Body of Christ
that is indwelt by the One Spirit.

Now, let us see some of the practical consequences

of this great truth. (1) The whole life of the Church of England is just that it is an integral part of the One Body. The *whole* claim that the Church of England has on our allegiance is that it exercises the authority of the Whole Body upon us; that it thereby brings the English people into touch with Jesus Christ, the One and Only Hope of all mankind. The Church is careful to remind us of this in her constant appeal to the authority of undivided Christendom. It is on the authority of the One Body that we have the Creeds the Sacraments, and the Holy Scriptures. It is on the authority of the One Body that we keep Sunday and the feasts and fasts of the Church.

(2) Out of this great fact springs the following conclusion—viz., that what is of universal authority is of more importance than what is of merely local custom. In a word, that " Catholic " comes first, and " English " comes quite second.

(3) This brings us to the third practical conclusion —viz., that the Prayer-Book *is always to be interpreted by the Catholic standard*. If any sentence in the Prayer-Book is ambiguous, and seems as if it might be taken either in a Catholic or in a Protestant sense, it must be taken in the Catholic sense. Let me give you an illustration of this. In the Catechism we are told that the " inward part or thing signified in the Sacrament of the Lord's Supper is the Body and Blood of Christ, which are verily and indeed taken and received by the faithful in the Lord's Supper." Now, the question arises here: " What does the Prayer-Book mean by ' the faithful ' ?" Protestants will tell you that it means those who actually exercise their faith. And they do this in order to bolster up their new and peculiar idea that the Presence of our Lord

(to use a clumsy expression) is not in the Sacrament itself, but only in the heart of the faithful recipient. Of course, if the Prayer-Book stood absolutely alone, a man might argue in this way. But it does not, andcannot, stand alone. And, therefore, we *know* that the Prayer-Book is using the words " the faithful " in the Catholic sense—*i.e.*, " the baptized."

And yet, fifty-two years ago, Archdeacon Denison was condemned to deprivation by the Court of Arches for maintaining, with universal Christendom, what is somewhat clumsily called " the Doctrine of the Real Presence." In a word, the Archdeacon was condemned for refusing to regard the Church of England as a separate, isolated unit, and for continuing to believe it to be a part of the Church of Christ !

The words of the Prayer-Book, then, are always to be interpreted by the standard of Universality, because the Church of England is an integral part of the One Body.

(4) Where the Prayer-Book is silent on any matter, the old Catholic rule holds good. This, of course, settles the matter of fasting Communion. There is no hint to be found in the Prayer-Book of any departure from universal custom in this respect. Therefore, of course, it stands where it always did. We might multiply such illustrations.

(5) Any devotion or practice not essential to the faith that has the sanction of undivided Christendom, and has not been explicitly forbidden in the English Prayer-Book, cannot be said to be wrong. It may be inexpedient, but it is not wrong. The Church of England does not set itself up as a judge of undivided

Christendom. Would that all our Bishops would remember this.

Some years ago, the Judicial Committee of Privy Council based one of its precious " judgments " upon the amazing theory that " omission is prohibition." Loud was the laughter and unmeasured the scorn that greeted this judgment. Needless to say, it perished as soon as it saw the light.

We sum up the practical conclusions that spring out of the fact that the Church of England is an integral part of the Body of Christ :

1. The words of the Prayer-Book are always to be interpreted by the Catholic standard.

2. Where the Prayer-Book is silent as to any Catholic rule, that rule remains binding on the consciences of Englishmen.

3. The utmost that the Church of England can say as regards any non-essential devotion or practice that has the sanction of undivided Christendom is that it is not expedient under present circumstances. It cannot say that it is wrong.

Bear these principles well in mind, and you will come at once to something widely different from the loose and absurd " Church of Englandism," that is so rife among us now.

In conclusion, we must remember that a divided Christendom is wrong. We must all labour and pray for the restoration of the visible unity of Christendom. Labour, by rigorously ruling ourselves by the Catholic standard of faith, worship, and morals; and pray that our Lord will, in His own time and in His own way, restore to us that outward visible unity which (to use the well-known words of Cardinal Newman) " we have loved long since, and lost awhile." The following prayer is being said by thousands of Catholics daily for the reunion of Christendom :

" O Lord Jesus Christ, Who saidst to Thine Apostles, Peace I leave with you, My peace I give unto you, regard not our sins, but the faith of Thy Church, and grant her that peace and unity which is agreeable to Thy Will, Who livest and reignest with the Father and the Holy Spirit, ever One God, world without end. Amen."

CHAPTER VI

THE CONTINUAL REMEMBRANCE

AT last, after all our preliminary investigations, we are free to contemplate the actual living fact of the daily worship that is the very life of the Church.

We have tried to see what we mean by worship.

We have tried to see what we mean by " The Church."

We have tried to clear our ideas as to what we mean by " The Church of England."

And now we step forward to see the actual realization, in everyday life, of Church worship. In a word, we come out into the domain of Church History.

Canon Scott Holland, in one of his brilliant and delightful speeches, reminds us that we are always making history ; and he points out that, at the moment, the making of history seems a prosaic and very commonplace matter. For we are making history without remembering that we are doing so. Mr. Jourdain, in " Le Bourgeois Gentilhomme," was so delighted to find out that he had always been talking prose without knowing it. The discovery that it *was* prose, seemed to invest his speech with a new dignity and a new interest. So it invests ordinary everyday life with a new interest if we remember that it is making history.

The history of the Church, then, is going on every day round about us, and we have our part and our share in that history.

Church history ! When we speak or think of Church history, we feel that we are dealing with a very chequered thing. It is mostly a record of struggles against enemies without and within; of many intrigues and much unworthiness; of periods of corruption and decay, and periods of reform and recovery; a very agitated and often very unworthy history. But is this really the history of the Church ? It is obvious that it is only of external things like these that the written history can, in the nature of things, take cognizance. But a very little thought will show us that the real history of the Church lies much deeper, and that these things are merely like bubbles and ripples on the surface of a great stream.

For, as we have reminded ourselves, the Holy Catholic Church is a Divine Mystery. It cannot be apprehended by the merely natural faculties with which we read a history-book. Its real life, and therefore its real history, is hidden from the " natural man." " The natural man receiveth not the things of the Spirit"; and the daily life of the Church is, *par excellence*, a " thing of the Spirit." So we, in thinking of the Church history that we are all always " making," have to go deeper than the things that we read in Church history-books.

What should you think of a History of England that did not mention the English kings, or what they were doing ? Our thoughts of the daily history of the Holy Catholic Church, the Kingdom of God, must begin with the King, and what He is doing.

What should you think of a History of England that confined itself to the doings and interests of one county ? So, in thinking of Church history day by day, we must not confine our thoughts to that small

The Continual Remembrance

fraction of the Church that is "militant here on earth."
The daily history of the Church has to do with what
is going on among the faithful departed. It embraces
the dead as well as the living.

Let us, then, by the exercise of our faith, picture to
ourselves a day of Church history : to-day, for instance.
What of our King to-day? He is "sitting at the
Right Hand of God the Father Almighty," as King
of Heaven and Earth, as appointed Heir of all things,
expecting that His enemies be made His footstool.
He is "standing at the Right Hand of God" as High
Priest, "appearing" in the highest Heaven for us.
He is "in the midst of the throne, and of the four
beasts, and in the midst of the elders," the Lamb as
it had been slain, His death and resurrection forming
the triumphant plea of creation reconciled to God.
If the Heavens were to be opened to us, as they
were to St. Stephen in his martyrdom, that is what
would arrest our attention. "Behold, I see the
Heavens opened, and the Son of Man standing on the
Right Hand of God."

That is the great fact of Church History to-day, the
obvious fact round which everything groups itself and
to which all is referred.

And in His mystical Body, which is One with Him,
the Son of Man is moment by moment doing the same
thing on earth. So the first thing that would catch
the eye of faith in the daily history of the Church on
Earth is the continual remembrance of the Sacrifice
of the Death of Christ, and the benefits whereof we
are partakers thereby. From the countless Altars of
Christendom the High Priest is offering continually the
One Sacrifice, Oblation, and Satisfaction, once for all
made upon the Cross.

It has been calculated that there is not a moment in the twenty-four hours in which the Holy Eucharist is not being celebrated somewhere or other; so that if we look at the world with the eyes of faith, it is one vast temple of God and of the Lamb, where the Lamb as it had been slain ever stands " in the midst of the throne," and in the midst of His creation, having taken the sealed book out of the hand of Him that sits upon the throne, and opened the way into the very Holiest of all—*to-day !*

Now, before we go any further, just think what a vision of tranquil peace and joy we have here, if only we will exercise our faculty of faith to see things as they really are, instead of being deceived by " walking by sight," so that we only see things as they seem to be on the surface. Remember that it is just by this " faith " that all the Saints of God triumphed over circumstances. The spirit of Cain was to make the best of things as they seem to be; and this is the spirit of heathenism always and everywhere. But Abel, our father in the faith, saw beneath the surface, and saw things as they really were. So, while the heathen were just looking at life from the merely natural point of view, Abraham, Isaac, and Jacob were regulating their lives in a wholly different way, for we are told " they looked for a City that hath foundations, whose Builder and Maker is God." Just so, not to multiply examples, we Christians to-day walk by faith and not by sight, and, therefore, in an evil and disappointing world, are tranquil and joyful because we see things not as they seem to be, but as they really are; and so, like Moses, we Christians in London to-day endure, " as seeing Him Who is invisible." By catching sight of this glorious vision of the ceaseless worship of the Church, we realize the great round world as being to-day one vast temple of God and of the Lamb; and so we move about, gently and quietly, as those who live in the Sanctuary of God, and "no torment shall touch" our souls. Oh, how life is transfigured for us when we realize the perpetual pleading, in the world to-day, by the Hands of our great High Priest, of the Holy Eucharist!

Then, again, this vision of the true daily history of the Holy Church gives us an ideal at which to aim, and towards which to work. That is of course, the restoration of the Daily Eucharist throughout the length and breadth of England and her possessions.

When we reflect that there is no moment in the twenty-four hours in which the Holy Eucharist is not being offered to-day, we must also sadly reflect that this is in no way due to us English Catholics. It is owing to the faith and perseverance of our fellow-Catholics throughout the world, who have patiently and perseveringly carried out in practice what we confess in theory—viz., that the Sacrament of the Lord's Supper was ordained " for the *continual* remembrance of the Sacrifice of the Death of Christ and of the benefits which we receive thereby." If it had rested with us degenerate English Catholics, the " remembrance " would long ago have ceased to be " continual," and the world would not have been the temple of God and of the Lamb that, thank God, it is to-day.

Go and look at the notice-board of the average English parish church, and what will you find ? Something of this sort :

" Holy Communion, Sunday, at eight " (or, perhaps, at a different hour each Sunday in the month). Perhaps you will find it also on Saints' Days; perhaps, if it is rather High Church, you will find it also on Thursdays.

Where is the "continuity" of all this? Is God not worth worshipping on Monday, Tuesday, Wednesday, Friday, or Saturday? Is the Sacrifice of the Death of Christ, and the benefits whereof we are partakers thereby, not worth a remembrance on those days? Does the Lamb as it had been slain only appear for us in the highest Heaven on Sundays, Saints' Days, and possibly Thursdays? Why this appalling state of things?

And, mark you, we have put the average of what is supposed to be rather a satisfactory and high level. There are still many parish churches where even this miserable level is not reached. Some years ago, in two parishes in the West country—large country parishes, with fine old churches—there was no Eucharist on Whit-Sunday, because Trinity Sunday was going to be the first Sunday in the month!

We English sometimes boast of our "Scriptural Church," and plume ourselves upon the blessings of the Reformation, and thank our God that we are not as other men are; but we may well hide our diminished heads in shame before our great High Priest when we think that the Daily Eucharist is the exception and not the rule.

And this shameful state of things is not "Prayer-Book." We find, in the Prayer-Book, that the Collect, Epistle, and Gospel of the Sunday are to serve for the week, unless it be otherwise ordered; and in the Rubric about the Proper Prefaces we find that those Prefaces, with the exception of that for Trinity Sunday, are to serve for the festival itself, and for "seven days after." These facts seem to indicate that the Daily Eucharist is assumed in the Prayer-Book.

"But," people will say, "what about the rubric

that says there shall be no Communion unless there are a certain number of communicants?" Bishop Cosin (who, if I am not mistaken, said of this rubric, " I penned it myself ") says: " Better it were to endure the absence of the people, than for the minister to neglect the usual and daily sacrifice of the Church, by which all people, whether they be there or no, reap so much benefit. And this was the opinion of my lord and master, Dr. Overall."

So that, in the opinion of Bishops Cosin and Overall, who ought to know, this rubric was intended for the people rather than for the priest; it was not for the restriction of the priest but to stimulate the fervour of the people.

And, as a matter of fact, even in country parishes, the Daily Eucharist is perfectly possible. Archdeacon Denison, in a scattered country parish of some 700 or 800 inhabitants, had the Daily Eucharist for twenty-five years, and was most particular that there should always be communicants.

We conclude that if any parish has the disgrace of being without the Daily Eucharist (" the usual and daily sacrifice of the Church," as Bishop Cosin calls it), it is because priest and people do not care to have it so. It is possible in country parishes, and its absence is quite inexcusable in towns.

How comes it that this awful neglect of the " usual and daily sacrifice of the Church " has become the rule in England ?

It is because Englishmen have overlooked the primary purpose of the Institution of the Blessed Sacrament. Yet they ought not to have overlooked this, if they had remembered what they are taught in the Church Catechism. Englishmen have come to look upon the Holy Eucharist exclusively as a Sacrament " for the strengthening and refreshing of our souls." To meet the average English mind, the Catechism would have to be altered; for, when the question is asked: " Why was the Sacrament of the Lord's Supper ordained ?" we should expect the answer to be : " For the strengthening and refreshing of our souls," etc.; but the answer is nothing of the kind. It is not until we have had *three* questions and answers about the Sacrament of the Lord's Supper, that the strengthening and refreshing of our souls is mentioned at all.

What is the Catechism answer to this primary question ? " For the *continual remembrance* of the Sacrifice of the Death of Christ, and of the benefits which we receive thereby."

Pause on that word " remembrance."

In our English version of the Bible, it is the very word used by our Lord Himself, the original Greek being " anamnesis." " Do this," said our Lord, " εἰς τὴν ἐμὴν ἀνάμνησιν," which, literally translated, means " for My memorial."

In modern English the word " remembrance " is used in what I may call a " subjective " sense. It denotes an act of our own memory. In the well-known little story, " Harry and Archie," the dying mother says: " Water my geranium when I am gone." In the watering of the geranium the daughter will remember her dead mother. It will be in this sense done " in remembrance " of her mother. So in those sickly vulgarities called " Memorial Services," when the favourite hymns of the deceased are sung, you are encouraged to remember that they are the favourite hymns of the deceased. In this sense they are done

" in remembrance " of the departed friend. But the Greek words translated " in remembrance of Me," have what I may call an " objective " force. They do not imply that while we are doing a certain act we shall remember a certain person, but that the performing of a certain act will make a memorial before God of a certain Person. Thus the Lord had respect unto Abel and his offering, because it presented before Him the Sacrifice of the Death of Christ, and all that that Sacrifice involved. So the Holy Eucharist does, in the perfect way, what the true sacrifices of the Old Testament did in the partial way. It makes before God the " Continual Remembrance " (anamnesis) " of the Sacrifice of the Death of Christ, and of the benefits which we receive thereby." It is the exercise upon the earth of the High Priestly Mediation of our Lord at the Right Hand of God. It is the perpetual, or " continual," presentation and pleading of the One Sacrifice once offered.

Now, it is this primary aspect of the Holy Eucharist that Englishmen, in spite of the teaching of the Catechism, have come almost entirely to overlook.

This " sacrificial " aspect of the Holy Eucharist is the direct consequence and outcome of the fact laid down in the Catechism (to take one instance among many in the Prayer-Book) that the " inward part or thing signified " in the Sacrament of the Lord's Supper is " the Body and Blood of Christ which are *verily and indeed* taken and received by the faithful in the Lord's Supper "; the fact, that is, that it is the Sacrament itself, objectively considered, that is the Body and Blood of Christ; the truth that we clumsily describe as " the Real Presence."

Of course, if there is no " Real Presence " there is

no " anamnesis." If the Blessed Sacrament be, as apparently all Protestants nowadays think, mere bread and wine, it can only be a " remembrance" in the subjective sense in which people think of the deceased when they hear his favourite hymn, or in which the daughter would especially remember her mother when she watered the geranium. And it is because Englishmen, in neglect of the Church's teaching, are not sure of their ground as regards the Blessed Sacrament, that the primary aspect of its institution, taught us so emphatically in the Prayer-Book, has faded into the background, if it has not altogether ceased to exist in their mind.

In the Holy Eucharist, then, which, as we have seen, is being offered without intermission throughout the Catholic Church, " the continual remembrance," " the usual and daily Sacrifice of the Church," we have the Lamb *as it had been slain*, standing in the midst of the Throne and of the four beasts, and in the midst of the four-and-twenty elders." It is the " perfect" worship of the Catholic Church, of which the true sacrifices of the Old Testament worship were the partial expression. It sums up and completes all true human worship in all time. And, in one of the old liturgical prayers, we find this truth expressed in this way : " Wherefore, O most gracious Father, we Thy humble servants, together with all Thy holy people, having in remembrance the Blessed Death and Passion of our Lord Jesus Christ, as well as His Glorious Resurrection from hell and Ascension into Heaven, do offer unto Thy Divine Majesty, of these Thine Own Gifts bestowed upon us, a Pure Victim, a Holy Victim, a Spotless Victim, even the Holy Bread of Eternal Life and the Cup of Everlasting Salvation. Upon which may it please Thee to look with a favourable and gracious countenance, and to accept them, as Thou didst accept the Sacrifice of Abel, the Sacrifice of our Patriarch Abraham, and that Pure Offering which Thy High Priest Melchisedek offered unto Thee."

How splendid is this vision of the ceaseless worship of the Church, as setting forth, day by day, and hour by hour, creation brought back to right relations with God, through the One Mediation of Jesus the Son of Mary. In the light of this glorious vision think, if you can, of " reading prayers to a congregation," of " giving them a bright and hearty service," of " Holy Communion on Sundays and Saints' Days," etc., and measure, if you can, the depth of degradation to which average English thought has sunk.

Four considerations seem to me to arise out of our realization of the great truth of Church worship:

1. We must rescue the word " Service " from the wrong uses to which it is put.

The word " Service " is the translation of the Greek " leitourgia," the word used for the Office of the Holy Eucharist. And so when we use the word in its Greek form and speak of a " Liturgy," we mean a form in which the Holy Church, at some time, or in some place, offers the Holy Eucharist. Thus, we have the " Liturgy " of St. Basil or St. Chrysostom, the Roman " Liturgy," the Mozarabic " Liturgy," etc. When we think of the word " Service " and whence it is derived, we see at once how absurd it is to talk of a " Mission Service " or a " Lantern Service."

So, too, how absurd, in the light of history, is the notice so often to be found outside English churches:

" Holy Communion at 8."

" Morning Service (in large letters), 11."

" Evening Service at 7."

And how pathetically absurd it becomes when we are told that on certain Sundays we are to have—

" Holy Communion after Morning Service."

I plead, then, that we should be careful in our use of the word " Service," and not call anything a " Service " unless it *is* " Service."

One word as to the various names given to the Holy Service in Christendom. It is called in the East " the Mysteries," or " *the* Service." It is known in the West as " the Mass."

It is called in the Prayer-Book " the Lord's Supper."

But, whatever it is called, it remains the same. Names cannot alter things.

A rather silly expression has grown up in England to denote the Holy Service. People speak of a " Celebration."

When people used this expression in Dr. Littledale's hearing, he was wont to say: " A celebration of what ?" You " celebrate " Mass, or you " celebrate " the Holy Eucharist; but you also " celebrate " a wedding, or " celebrate " an anniversary. The word " celebration," standing by itself, is meaningless. And, inasmuch as the word, taken by itself, is silly, and life is too short to go about saying " a Celebration of the Lord's Supper " every time we want to speak of the Holy Service, English Catholics have, very sensibly, fallen back upon the word " Mass "; of which Archbishop Benson said: " Mass is a good old-fashioned term, and we ought not to be ashamed of it."

But whatever expression you may elect to use, do be careful about the use of the word " Service." A little plant will often split a rock; and the very fact of our being jealous for the right use of the word "Service," will very likely contribute to the splitting of that great inert mass of misconception of Church Worship that sits like a very incubus on us here in England.

2. Whenever any priest who has due jurisdiction is celebrating the Holy Mysteries, our faith in the Church as one organic whole forces us to see, in that Service, the worship of the whole Church focussed at that point. It is not the Service of that handful of people assembled there, but the whole Church worshipping God. Think for instance, of the first Post-Communion Prayer in our English Liturgy : "O Lord and Heavenly Father, we Thy humble servants," etc. Who is meant by " we "? Not that handful of people who happen to be in the church at the moment, but the whole body of the baptized. For the Sacrifice is that pleaded by the One Great High Priest, and must, therefore, be commensurate with the whole Body of Christ. And the Church is careful at the end of that same prayer to put it more forcibly still: " We and all Thy whole Church." " All Thy whole Church " ; not that fraction of it that is at that moment " militant here on earth," but that great majority of it, the faithful departed, the dead, as well as the living, or, to put things in their right precedence, the dead and the living; the living, as well as the dead.

How splendid is this vision of the whole Church worshipping God at every moment, in every place ! How absolutely different to the idea that underlies " reading prayers to a congregation." And let us just note that when prayers are asked in the Church for any specific object, it is " the prayers of the Church " that we should ask, not " the prayers of the congregation." For it is, indeed, the prayers of the Church, the Sacrifice of the High Priest and His whole Church, that are going up before God in every Eucharist. How boundless will the power of prayer seem when we realize it as " the prayers of the Church !"

But our vision keeps widening. From the thought of the Church as one solid whole, we pass to that fact, so often brought before us in the Bible, of the solidarity of creation.

It is not only men who are affected by, or interested in, the Church. The Vision of the Catholic Church is instruction to Angels. To Angels, " the Principalities and Powers in heavenly places," is made known " by the Church" the manifold Wisdom of God. They, too, stand by the Grace of the Incarnation; for it is expressly said of Michael and his Angels: " They overcame by the Blood of the Lamb."

And as of the Angels, so, too, of the lower creation. We are told that " the *whole creation* groaneth and travaileth in pain together until now." We are told that the lower creation, " the creature itself," " waiteth for the manifestation of the sons of God." We are told that " the creature itself shall be delivered from the bondage of corruption into the glorious liberty of the children of God." And so, in every Eucharist, we have the whole creation brought into relation with God; and as our great High Priest pleads, in heaven and on earth, moment by moment, His all-prevailing Sacrifice, we see the accomplishing of the Will of God— viz., to reconcile, by Jesus Christ, " all things unto Himself; by Him, I say, whether they be things on earth, or things in Heaven."

And in this connection we cannot help remembering the words in the Revelation in the vision of the Lamb:

The Continual Remembrance

" And *every creature which is in heaven, and on the earth, and under the earth, and such as are in the sea, and all that are in them*, heard I saying, Blessing and honour and glory and power be unto Him that sitteth upon the Throne, and unto the Lamb for ever and ever."

The " continual remembrance " in the Holy Eucharist is the ceaseless worship of the whole creation of which man, renewed by the Incarnation, is the High Priest.

3. The ceaseless Eucharistic worship, the " continual remembrance of the Sacrifice of the Death of Christ," is the very well-spring of spiritual life.

We cannot but be struck with the comparatively low level of spiritual life in the Church of England. To keep from actual sin seems to be the highest aspiration of the average English Churchman. The higher flights of the spiritual life, such as the counsels of perfection, the prayer of contemplation, the various forms of self-crucifixion that are summed up in the word " asceticism " (the " ascetic "—*i.e.*, " practical " carrying out of our Baptismal vow), these and other kindred things are like a sealed book to the average English Churchman. He cannot appreciate them, he cannot understand them. It is the vision of these things that draws and attracts so many towards Rome. How comes it that we have, to so large an extent, lost these things? We answer at once: " Because we have lost the Daily Eucharist." And is it not significant that, directly the Daily Eucharist is even partially revived among us, these fair things begin to reappear ? With the partial revival, even, of the Daily Eucharist, there has appeared among us the partial revival of monasticism, the attraction of the virgin life, the higher standard of prayer, as witnessed in the practice of Meditation and in the Retreats that are now becoming so numerous, the great revival of Sacramental Confession, and all the many forms of self-denying activity now to be seen amongst us. These are fair flowers that grow naturally on the soil of Calvary; and it is one great proof of the truth of our Holy Orders that the Daily Eucharist among us should be producing the same effects as it has done throughout the Catholic Church, both East and West.

And, seeing these things before our eyes, we may say, like Samuel, in the partial recovery of fervour in Israel: " Ebenezer, hitherto hath the Lord helped us," and thank God, and take courage to go steadily on in the road of Catholic Revival.

4. The continual remembrance of the Sacrifice of the Death of Christ is the sanctification of all prayer, and of all work.

For Christian working men and working women, how splendid and encouraging is the thought of the perpetual pleading of the Sacrifice of the Death of Christ in the ceaseless worship of the Catholic Church! While you are toiling, the Church never ceases her prayer. And that all-prevailing pleading of the Sacrifice of the Death of Christ makes all the prayers you can say efficacious; and it makes all your labour, if only you " abide in" Christ, a bearing of His Blessed Cross. " Labour is sweet, for Thou hast toiled; and care is light, for Thou hast cared."

And so, in daily life, we, here in London, have realized for us that old truth that was exhibited so signally in the battle at Rephidim. The host with Joshua went to the battle; but Moses, Aaron, and Hur went up to the top of the hill. " And it came to pass that, when Moses held up his hands, Israel prevailed." His mediation, partial as it was, was their success. And does not the past history of our low spiritual level in England (commensurate as it is with the cessation of the Daily Eucharist) teach us the truth of the reverse side of the picture? "When he let down his hands, Amalek prevailed." So it is for the truest interests of one and all that the Daily Eucharist should become the rule throughout the length and breadth of England; and we may well take on our lips and in our heart the words of the old prayer: "O God, Who, in a wonderful Sacrament, hast left unto us a perpetual memorial of Thy Passion, grant us so to venerate the Sacred Mysteries of Thy Body and Blood, that we may always perceive within ourselves the fruits of Thy Redemption; Who livest and reignest, one God, world without end. Amen."

CHAPTER VII

THE DIVINE OFFICE

HAVING caught a glimpse of the ceaseless pleading of the Sacrifice of the Death of CHRIST as the very core and centre of daily Church history, we must now betake ourselves to another glorious vision of Church history—viz., the continual recitation of the Divine Office.

When we have grasped the general idea of the worship of the Church in the Eucharist and the Divine Office, we shall then be in a position to think of the Eucharist and the Divine Office more in detail, and to see how the universal principles of Church worship are carried out for us in the English Prayer-Book.

What do we mean by the Divine Office ? We mean the dividing up of the day by what are called " the hours of prayer." This may, no doubt, to a certain extent, have been taken over by the Church from Judaism.

We read, for instance, that " Peter and John went up into the temple at the hour of prayer, being the ninth hour." But the Church put the true meaning on to the hours of prayer, and the hours of prayer divide up every day as a distinct Commemoration of the Passion of our Lord; so that each day in Church history is modelled upon the first Good Friday, and the hours of prayer, in their way, become a continual remembrance of the Sacrifice of the Death of Christ. All over the Church this same instinct is found; and so the hours of prayer represent the Mind of the Holy Ghost for the everyday life and history of the Church.

Thus the day was divided up into " seven hours of prayer," as follows:

1. Matins and Lauds—Matins being said at midnight or soon after; Lauds at the first streak of dawn, commemorating the earliest hours of that awful Friday. These are commonly called " the night hours."

2. Prime, said at six, commemorating our Lord going out to His Passion in the early morning.

3. Terce—the third hour, at nine—commemorating especially the Descent of the Holy Ghost, but also referring to the words, " It was the third hour, and they crucified Him."

4. Sext—the sixth hour (twelve o'clock)—when the darkness came over the land.

5. Nine—the ninth hour (three o'clock)—when our Lord died.

6. Vespers—the evening hour—commemorating His being taken down from the Cross.

7. Compline—usually said about 9 p.m.—commemorating our Lord's burial.

So we have, besides the ceaseless pleading of the Holy Eucharist, this lovely vision in the everyday life of the Catholic Church of the seven hours of prayer.

We shall consider later on the way in which the hours of prayer have been simplified and condensed for us in the English Prayer-Book. Meanwhile, let us catch the general vision of the Church dividing up every day of her history, according to the hours of the Passion of our Lord.

Prayer-Book Ideals

We notice, first, that all priests and deacons (and where the minor orders survive, all subdeacons) are bound to recite the Divine Office every day, according to the form in which it is imposed upon them by authority.

An undergraduate, many years ago, was attending the lectures of the Divinity Professor at Oxford to qualify for Holy Orders. The then Regius Professor said that the Bible was to be every day in the hands of the English clergyman, as the Breviary (or Hours of Prayer) is in the hands of the Roman priest. Well, in a sense this may be true, inasmuch as the Lessons in the Divine Office are taken from the Bible; but if that is what the Regius Professor meant, he had better have said so ! For I find in the Prayer-Book the following directions : " All priests and deacons are to say daily the Morning and Evening Prayer, either privately or openly, not being let by sickness or some other urgent cause." So that the Prayer-Book evidently contemplates the Hours of Prayer being in the hands of the English clergyman, as they are in the hands of the Roman priest. The remark, therefore, of the Regius Professor was a mere bit of Protestant clap-trap !

A great many years ago (before the Lectionary was altered into its present form) a Priest visited a learned Doctor of Divinity who was a great Oriental student. The Doctor said: " I have read two chapters of the Bible to-day," meaning, of course, that he had studied them as a great student. The Priest replied: " Well, Doctor, then you have just done half your duty," meaning that if he had said his Office, he would, as the Lessons were then arranged, have had to read *four* chapters !

The Divine Office

When we think of the clergyman's day, we think of him going into his schools, tearing about his parish, visiting here and there, looking after the sick, administering relief, getting up entertainments, looking after clubs, and what is called " social work," etc. How seldom do we think of him (and, alas! that it should have to be said, how often does he not think of himself!) as primarily bound to recite the Hours of Prayer! Yet this is his *first obligation!*

So we arrive at this beautiful vision of the Hours of Prayer being recited daily by all priests, deacons, and subdeacons.

But now we must think about " Quires, and places where they sing."

In the rubric in Morning and Evening Prayer that comes immediately after the third Collect, you will find that " in Quires and places where they sing" certain things are to be done. Now, every church has something that is called " a choir," and this choir naturally sit together in a particular place. Do the gentlemen or ladies who furnish the music in any church constitute what the Prayer-Book calls a " Quire"? And does the chancel or the organ loft in which they sit constitute what the Prayer-Book calls a " place where they sing"? Certainly not. " Quires and places where they sing" is a technical term, denoting churches that are on a wholly different footing from the parish church.

" Quires and places where they sing" are foundations for that specific purpose, such as cathedral and collegiate churches, and monastic churches.

The purpose for which these churches are founded is wholly different from the purpose of the parish church. The clergy of those churches are relieved from all cure of souls. These magnificent foundations exist for the solemn singing, in perpetuity, of the Divine Office.

Now, let us go into one of our beautiful cathedral choirs, and look about us. We see at once that here is an entirely different conception from that of the parish church. The Choir belongs to a body corporate that is called "the Chapter." Each stall in that Choir is an official place. It has been founded and endowed with its own prebend. It is the property, for the time being, of the particular prebendary who has been solemnly instituted and inducted to it, and it is his freehold.

There are four "personæ," or principal officials, in the Cathedral Chapter—(1) the Decanus, or Dean, whose stall is always on the right as you enter a Choir; (2) the Cantor, or Precentor, whose stall is always on the left as you enter a Choir; (3) the Chancellor; (4) the Treasurer.

Pass up the Choir, and you will come to the places of the singing men and boys. Here you must put away all idea of what is called a "choir" in a parish church. That rests to a large extent upon voluntary effort—one has to scrape it up as one can. But the office and work of a "Quire or place where they sing" is much too serious to be left at haphazard in this kind of way. The singers are always what is called "on the foundation."

In some cathedrals—as, for example, at Wells—the "Vicars Choral and Priest Vicars"—that is to say, the singing men and the Priests who actually sing the office—are a separate corporation. They have their own property, and, to a certain extent, manage their own affairs. The organist and the singing boys also are

The Divine Office

" on the foundation," the singing boys being under the special supervision of the Chancellor, and being educated in the Scholæ Cancellari. By a more modern arrangement, the Chapter is divided into " the Chapter," consisting of the Dean and four Canons, and " the Great Chapter," consisting of the Dean and all the prebendaries. In former times, the prebendaries could be called into residence at any time, like the " courses " in the Temple at Jerusalem.

Some seventy years ago the utilitarian temper of the English mind showed itself in the establishment of the Cathedral Commission, which, regarding the cathedral clergy as so many idle cumberers of the ground, made a clean sweep in the cathedral foundations. Four stalls only were allowed to retain their endowments, the rest being summarily robbed of theirs. No doubt there may have been room for readjustment of endowments that had largely increased in value, but, as usual, the pendulum of reform swung too far, and the spiritual conception of " Quires and places where they sing " made no appeal to the worldly spirit of the time. So now it has come to pass that it is with very rare exceptions that we can fill our places in our Choir. You may judge what spiritual refreshment it would be to retire for a while out of the rush and stress and turmoil and the many pettinesses of parochial life, to take our part in the regular solemnity of the Divine Office, as sung in our Choirs; but, like the Levites of old in an evil time, our portions are not given us, and therefore we are scattered from the temple. Still, thank God, the main foundation stands, and the Divine Office goes on its majestic way, the Dean and Canons remaining to represent the Chapter day by day.

And, as with the cathedrals, so with those kindred

foundations, collegiate churches, of which the noteworthy examples that remain are the collegiate chapels of our Universities and great public schools, which also are " Quires and places where they sing."

Pause a moment here, and think what a great spiritual fact, here in England, has been the continued existence, through darkest times, of these " Quires and places where they sing "; how they have testified, as they testify to-day, to the great truth that the first great work of the Church, day by day, is to look to it that no day passes that the Church does not seize upon and appropriate to God by the solemn recitation of the Hours of Prayer. It is our cathedrals and collegiate churches—sneered at by the world as places of idleness, where the clergy are set free for this most spiritual work, utterly misunderstood by the world (as, of course, one would expect them to be)—that have kept alive for us here in England that most heavenly conception of the Hours of Prayer, and have saved us from dropping to the level of the Protestant sects, unable to conceive or appreciate the life of worship.

May God preserve our " Quires and places where they sing " ! For at the present time a danger threatens them from a new quarter—a danger that is all the greater because it looks so specious. In these days of what is called " religious activity " there are indications that the Cathedral Chapters are coming down from their lofty ideal, and are seeking to justify their existence before an unbelieving world. In these days of statistics and of measuring success by numbers—a spirit wholly foreign to the Spirit of Christ—we see a desire among the cathedral clergy to tout for congregations, so that they may seem to the world to be " doing something." This is notably apparent in the vulgar practice of what are called " popular services " in the naves of our cathedrals on Sunday evenings. It is seen in the feverish desire to pull down our screens, so that the " congregation in the nave " may see the altar, etc.

But what has a "Quire " to do with a congregation ? In ordinary cathedral towns it merely means that the people are being enticed away from their parish churches, from the clergy who have the cure of souls to the feet of the cathedral clergy, who have *no* cure of souls.

It was said of a Dean, now dead, that his one idea seemed to be to turn the cathedral into a large mission chapel. It was said of another Dean that he complained that he got " rusty " if he did not preach four times a week; so he was constantly assembling congregations in the cathedral, where he could have a harmonium and hymns, and save himself from " getting rusty." Why cannot the cathedral clergy rise to the height of their great vocation ? It reminds one of the witty saying of Mark Twain about the guide at Genoa —viz., that he " bustled about as if he had swallowed a spring mattress !" We are done to death with all this busy fussiness. For God's sake, in a shallow, superficial age, when no one has time to think, or study, or pray, let us look to it that there should be clergy who have nothing to do with parishes or " congregations," but can peacefully and tranquilly lift up the standard of Christ's sufferings in the hours of prayer.

But we have not done yet with the " Quires and places where they sing." There remain the monastic and conventual churches of the religious orders. Thank

God, with the partial revival of the Daily Eucharist, we have been privileged to see the partial revival of religious orders here in England; while elsewhere in the Catholic Church, both East and West, they have never ceased to exist.

The religious orders (whether for men or women) are divided into two classes : (1) The cloistered orders; (2) the active orders.

We in England are more used to the active orders, though, thank God, we are not without examples of the cloistered orders too; but whether in a cloistered or an active order, the Hours of Prayer are the very heart and centre of their life. Thus all monastic churches and convent chapels are "Quires," where the Hours of Prayer are solemnly recited day by day.

We see the Sister of Mercy going on her rounds in and out of the homes of the poor, the sick, and the sad; and perhaps we think that this is the beginning, middle, and end of her daily life. We forget that it is of the essence of her devoted life, that it is in an especial manner "hid with Christ in God," in the continual recitation of the Hours of Prayer.

While we are thinking of monastic churches, let us catch a glimpse of the "night hours" in a monastic church as they are to-day. Let us go in spirit to the famous monastery of La Verna in Tuscany.

We are in a wild, hilly country, out of which towers the peak of a mountain. This is the mountain-peak given by the Knight of Chiusi to St. Francis and his brethren. High up, near the top of the mountain, is a precipice, and on the edge of this precipice, wedged in between it and the peak itself, stands the monastery

The Divine Office

of La Verna, inhabited at the present moment by about eighty friars.

Anyone who has had the privilege of staying in the monastery will know how thrilling it is in that great solitude, right away from the haunts of men, to hear the great bell boom out, at midnight in winter, or at one o'clock after Easter, to sound the beginning of a new day of Church history.

We go into the great church. The Quire is behind the high altar. There a light shines on the great book on the lectern and from thence are heard the voices of the friars reciting Matins and Lauds. The nave is dim, only lit by the sanctuary lamps in front of the altars; and there you can dimly see the lay brethren, who, while the choir brothers are reciting the Office, are quietly going round the fourteen stations of the Cross, all moving into the Quire for the *Te Deum* at Matins, and for the *Benedictus* at Lauds. *Te Deum* and *Benedictus!* Just as we find them in our English Prayer-Book Morning Office!

Now here (as in countless other monastic churches) you see the Catholic Church, while the world is wrapped in sleep, and before it has been able to spoil the new day by any act of sin, seizing hold on that new day and consecrating it to God and to the Lamb, in the Divine Office. Is not our everyday Church history a wonderful, heavenly, and beautiful thing? Is the round world, after all, so bad as it looks? No! Look beneath the surface, and you see that it is redeemed unto God and the Lamb, and, by the ceaseless worship of the Catholic Church, is one vast Temple of God!

So much for (1) the private recitation of the Hours of Prayer by all priests, deacons, and subdeacons;

97   H

(2) the solemn recitation of the Hours of Prayer "in Quires and places where they sing."

There remains, here in England, the daily recitation of the Divine Office in our parish churches or chapels; for we read in the Prayer-Book that "the curate that ministereth in every parish church or chapel, being at home, and not being otherwise reasonably hindered, shall say the same" (the Morning and Evening Office) "in the parish church or chapel where he ministereth, and shall cause a bell to be tolled thereunto." And how sweet and restful to hear this daily bell, whether it be in the street of some bustling town, or in some far-away country village, reminding us that God has reconciled the world to Himself by the Passion of His dear Son.

So now we have this lovely vision of everyday life in the Catholic Church. These things are going on to-day. In another four or five hours, when we are asleep, and when the restless, feverish life of the world is still for a while, the Church will seize upon to-morrow, before the world can get a word in edgewise, and consecrate it to God and to the Lamb. To-morrow will be marked by the hours of the Passion of our Lord :

1. By all priests, deacons, and subdeacons.
2. In Quires and places where they sing.
3. In our English parish churches.

But, alas ! how far has average English Church life sunk below this splendid ideal !

What about the general run of our parish churches ? Is the Daily Office even now the rule, or the exception ?

The following notice was given out one Palm Sunday in a large country parish : " Friday next being Good Friday, there will be no service in this church on

The Divine Office

Wednesday evening." Another notice ran thus:
" Thursday next being Ascension Day, the usual
Wednesday evening service will be on Thursday morning!" We laugh, of course; but how inexpressibly
sad to think that things should have been brought to
such a pass as this! Hardly less silly than this is the
notice you will often find on the doors of " moderate "
parish churches: " Evening service on Wednesday at
seven; morning service on Friday at eleven." If this
merely meant that on those two days the Divine Office
was recited at a different hour, well and good; but
you know that it means nothing of the sort. We do
not ask if these things are religion—they certainly are
not that—but are they common sense? Where is
the common sense of taking the Continual Office of the
Church on one day in the week, torn from its context
and its continuity, and thus making it unmeaning
and ridiculous?

There is more common sense in the Protestant meeting-house, with its occasional meetings for extempore
prayer, hymns, Bible reading, and sermon. It is, at
any rate, an intelligible sort of family prayer, though,
as we have seen, it is all wrong from the point of view
of worship. But this " moderate church " one day
in the week Matins or Evensong is simply ridiculous;
it is using the Office as it was never intended to be
used.

How has this state of things come about?

The answer is not far to seek. When Englishmen
cast away the " continual remembrance," the " usual
and daily sacrifice of the Church," the Divine Office
was sure to follow suit; and though, by a miracle of
grace, it has been preserved in the Quires and places
where they sing, even under the shameful circumstance

of its divorce in those places from the Daily Eucharist, we are not at all surprised to find it thrown away in the parish churches. "Facilis descensus Averni." You cannot with impunity play tricks with Divine things.

One thought in conclusion. It has probably seemed to us such a simple thing to go to what we have ignorantly and stupidly called "Evening Service." It seemed a sort of thing that any fool could do. We thought Holy Communion was for the select few, the élite of the Household of God; while Matins or Evensong was quite plain sailing, and committed us to nothing at all.

Fools that we were! The vision of the Divine Office will probably have borne in upon us the great truth that it requires even greater insight into things spiritual to recite the Hours of Prayer intelligently than to grasp the Mass and the Sacraments. Our Lord's own service, as we should expect, is simple enough for babes, while the wisest can never fathom the depths of the Divine Mysteries. So, too, it is with the Sacraments ordained by God Himself; but the Divine Office is not so simple or so easy of apprehension.

And this we shall find to be the practical experience of the Church throughout the world. It is the Lord's own Service and the Sacraments that attract the little ones of His flock. Some years ago, in a mission chapel in a "slum" district, eighty people were assembled for the Mass of Ash Wednesday at six o'clock in the morning. All these people use Sacramental Confession habitually, and forty of them made their Communion on that morning. This is the religion of the simple and unlearned; but if any of us think it is a simple thing to walk into a Church to Matins or

The Divine Office

Evensong on a Sunday, it is because we do not understand what the Divine Office is.

We shall see this more clearly when we have considered, as we are about to do in our next chapter, the laws of Divine worship as given us in the first three Commandments.

CHAPTER VIII

THE LAWS OF WORSHIP

WE have caught the vision of the daily history of the Catholic Church in her ceaseless worship, the continual remembrance of the Sacrifice of the Death of Christ in the Holy Eucharist, and the continual commemoration of the Hours of the Passion of our Lord in the Divine Office.

Let us now try and see the relation in which each individual Christian stands to this ceaseless worship; in other words, let us consider the responsibility that attaches itself to every Christian in respect of the worship of the Church.

It is a fact that we should do well to lay seriously to heart, that four out of the ten Commandments (that is to say, almost half) relate to worship.

In these evil days, when Christians are being urged on all sides (and that by those who ought to know better) to cast away religion and substitute for it a more or less shifting moral philosophy, English Christians have come, to a large extent, practically to ignore the first table of the Law, and to confine what energies they are pleased to give to such matters to the second table exclusively. It is, then, of paramount importance that we should, at this stage of our inquiry, think seriously about the first table of the Law.

The Laws of Worship

Let us, then, try to consider somewhat of the awful import of the first three Commandments.

We shall find that these three Commandments bind us to three great principles:

1. That every man must worship the One True God.

2. That every man must worship the One True God in the right way.

3. That every man must be in the right disposition when he comes to worship God.

Let us think of these three great principles as applying to, and binding upon, every Christian, without any exception; for we have each one of us accepted the Ten Commandments as the standard of judgment by which we stand or fall. When one sees, as one does, Christians searching about, as it were, for a moral basis, questioning this, that, and the other, of the received standards of faith and morals, seeking, in these last days, to lay again the foundations, one says to oneself, " What has become of their Baptismal profession ?"

Now, put aside for the moment the awful binding force of a vow solemnly taken before God, of a covenant solemnly entered into between God and man, and look at it from the lowest ground of mere common sense. Is it in this way that men can deal in any other department of life ? Think of political and social life. Does each succeeding generation start afresh, as savages, from the beginnings of civilization ? Certainly not. Civilized life would be impossible under such circumstances. Or, again, given social and political life at its present standpoint, can any individual citizen refuse to obey the Law until he has for himself laid the foundation, and studied and personally approved of the whole code of jurisprudence ?

Let any English citizen advance such a claim and try to act upon it, and he will speedily be relegated to a gaol or a lunatic asylum. Many years ago there lived in the West Country a man who tried to shuffle out of paying his rates and taxes by an appeal to his conscientious objections. He could not pay the taxes because they went to support the Army, and he did not approve of war; he could not pay the poor-rate, because So-and-so received relief, and he did not approve of So-and-so. Does anyone dream of taking such a man *au serieux* ? So when crazy fanatics break the law in the name of " conscientious convictions," and proceed dramatically to harangue the magistrate on the subject of their convictions, the obvious answer is that which was made to such people the other day— viz., " Twenty shillings, or a fortnight." So, too, in the department of Art. Is each poet, painter, or musician, to recognize no obligation in the canons and laws of his art, but to start, *de novo*, as from a state of savagery ? The case has only to be stated for us to see at once its inherent idiotic absurdity.

To put it, then, on the mere ground of common sense, we would ask how it can be supposed that individual citizens of the Kingdom of Heaven, individual members of the Household of God, are to be free to repudiate all obligations of their citizenship, and to begin, *de novo*, to lay foundations, and to concoct a moral basis of their own. In the world we should call such people lunatics, leave them at large if they were harmless, and shut them up if they became dangerous; but these fanatics in the Kingdom of Heaven are applauded and patted on the back. They are dignified by the name of " broad-minded," " seekers after truth," etc.; but all their palaver will not exempt them from the consequences of having airily disregarded the obligations of citizenship. It is not common sense that a man should enter upon solemn obligations, and then act as if they did not exist; nor will he be allowed to act in this way. But over and above the question of common sense, there is still, let us hope, sufficient moral fibre left in us to be able to ask: " Is it common honesty ?" What do you think of a man or a nation that repudiates its debts ? As you think of such dishonesty, so think of these " seekers after truth " who repudiate their solemn obligations, and speak and act as if they did not exist.

But this is not merely a question of common sense and common honesty; it is a question of a creature face to face with its Creator, and in the pert flippancy of these " seekers after truth " who will make you a new code of morals to order, we merely hear the echo of the impious questions put by the father of lies: " Yea hath God said ?" Wrap it up in fine language if you will, and call it by some fine name if you like; this repudiation of the solemn obligations of a covenant is merely flat rebellion against God, and if a creature contends with his Maker, he must, and will, take the consequences. " His citizens hated Him, and sent a message after Him, saying, We will not have this Man to reign over us." Well ! They took their course, they " sought after truth," they made a new code of quasi obligations for themselves; but the parable ends: " Those, Mine enemies, who would not that I should reign over them, bring them hither and slay them before Me."

So we come to consider the solemn obligation imposed on each of us by the first three Commandments.

" Thou shalt have none other gods but Me." This is put for us in the negative form; but will atheism, therefore, be a keeping of the First Commandment? Of course not. The words " but Me " have their positive side. We are not to " have " any other gods, but we are to " have " the One True God; and, as we have seen before, to " have " God is to worship Him. Adoring love is the only possible attitude in which an intelligent creature can stand to his Creator. To believe in God seriously, and then to stand on one side as if that belief were a mere idle speculation is a sheer impossibility. The Israelites were only standing aloof because, as Elijah said, they were " halting between two opinions." Was it the Lord Who was God, or was it Baal? Directly that question was settled, then the worship would be paid to whichever they had decided to be God; and so, directly God, in His mercy, gave them the sign of the fire from Heaven, they fell on their faces. The idea that a man could admit the existence of God, and know what God has revealed of Himself, and then stand on one side; the idea that men can be content to give God what Canon Liddon has so happily called " a considerable amount of speculative attention "; the idea that is so prominent amongst us Englishmen to-day is altogether foreign to any serious belief in God at all.

And so the First Commandment imposes upon one and all the paramount duty of worship. Not to worship God is to perish everlastingly. It is, to say the least of it, sin, even as murder, adultery, or theft, is sin. And if a Christian has strayed away from the fold, and, by God's mercy, " comes to himself," the first sin about which he will examine his conscience will be the neglect of worship.

The Laws of Worship

Pause a moment here, and let us ask ourselves whether we realize this fact—viz., that life without worship is a life of sin. The Fourth Commandment gives us the minimum of worship that is permissible to Christians. And so the rightly informed Christian conscience will accuse a man of mortal sin if he remembers one Sunday or feast of obligation in which, through his own fault, he did not worship God. The Day of Judgment will have some considerable surprises in store for us.

When we have realized this primary obligation we are just on the ground that was common to Cain and Abel alike.

The Second Commandment imposes upon us a second obligation. Expressed in the terms in which false worship expressed itself to God's people in the old Covenant, the Second Commandment imposes upon us the necessity of worshipping God the right way. Men might make graven images of false gods—as, *e.g.*, Baal or Ashtoreth—and so be breaking at once both the First and Second Commandments. Or they might be worshipping the true God in a wrong way, as with the golden calves at Bethel and Dan.

It is this latter sin that the Second Commandment especially forbids. Men are not to worship the true God in ways of their own devising. It is no use a man saying, " I will worship the True God only," and thinking that his determination to worship no other god sets him free to choose the way in which he will worship the One True God. Given that he keeps the First Commandment, at once he comes under the dominion of the Second.

Now, the one and only approach to God is through the One Mediation of the Sacred Humanity of our Lord.

" There is One God, and One Mediator between God and men, the Man Christ Jesus." All true worship, then, must be a setting forth of that one plea; in other words, it must be a " remembrance " of the " Sacrifice of the Death of Christ."

And, as the Revelation of God in Jesus Christ gradually unfolded itself and became more clear, so did the " remembrance of the Sacrifice of the Death of Christ " become more explicit; and, naturally, as the stages of this revelation and of the worship that answered to it became more perfect, so that which was more partial was successively " done away."

Under the patriarchs this remembrance was made as perfectly as it could then be made, by the sacrifices of blood. This is what differentiated Abel's sacrifice from that of Cain.

Many years ago some children in a country school were asked why Abel's sacrifice was better than Cain's. Now the stock silly answer to this question, to which we have listened so many weary times, is: " Because Abel was a good man and Cain was a bad man," which, being interpreted, means that the sacrifice in itself was quite indifferent, the whole value of it lying in the moral attributes of the worshipper. But on this occasion the teacher, to his joy, did not get the stock, stodgy, British answer, but a little boy went right to the root of the matter and answered quite simply: " Because there was blood in it."

This simple patriarchal worship held good till the giving of the Levitical Ordinances on Mount Sinai. Then, the restriction of worship to the tabernacle of witness, the consecration of a High Priest, and the ordinance of a settled Priesthood in his sons, and the minute ordinances of the sacrifices in detail, formed a much more perfect " remembrance of the Sacrifice of the Death of Christ " than had hitherto been possible; and the Levitical worship, ordained by God Himself, became the one true and acceptable worship that men could offer to God.

The Levitical worship was to hold its sway until the descent of the Holy Ghost at Pentecost. Then " that which is perfect " was " come," and the partial memorial of Christ that had been made in the Levitical worship was to give way to the Divine Ordinance of the Host Moly Sacrament of the Altar, inasmuch as that was, in deed and in truth, the perfect " remembrance of the Sacrifice of the Death of Christ," and so became the " usual and daily Sacrifice " of the Catholic Church.

And note that each more perfect " remembrance of the Sacrifice of the Death of Christ " abrogated and put an end to the less perfect remembrance that had gone before it. For a Jew who lived after the founding of the Tabernacle to say that he would worship God in the primitive way of his forefathers would have been for him to break the Second Commandment. So to imagine that the sacrifices of the Law would continue after the coming of the Holy Ghost, divinely instituted though they were, would be to be offering to God a worship that He could not accept.

May we not, then, put it in this way—viz., that the Second Commandment binds men to make the remembrance of the Sacrifice of the Death of Christ in the most perfect way possible ? That most perfect way is, of course, the Holy Eucharist, ordained by Christ Himself " for the continual remembrance of the Sacrifice of the Death of Christ, and of the benefits which we receive thereby." To substitute anything else for the Holy Eucharist as the " usual and daily Sacrifice of the

Church " (to use Bishop Cosin's words) would be to cut across the Second Commandment. Even the Hours of Prayer, representing as they do the Mind of the Holy Ghost, can never stand alone as a substitute for the One Service ordained by Christ Himself. To put the Morning Office, then, in the place of the Holy Eucharist, and tempt people, by so doing, to neglect the worship ordained by Christ Himself, is to cut across the Second Commandment. Is it not strange that people who boast most loudly of the Scriptural character of what they are pleased to call " our Church," should be the very ones to substitute a rendering of the Divine Office (which they receive by tradition only) for the Scriptural worship of the " breaking of bread," the divinely instituted Service ?

That the Holy Eucharist should be dethroned from its place as *the* Service of Sundays and feasts of obligation is a breach of the Second Commandment. How grave is the responsibility that attaches itself to priests who, by not making the Holy Eucharist the principal worship of the day, hinder the faithful from keeping the Second Commandment! Think again of these terrible notice-boards:

> " Holy Communion at 8."
> " Morning Service at 11."

The average Englishman has been trained to expect something different from the "continual remembrance" at eleven o'clock, which has somehow come to be our sacred hour. So Matins and Lauds, with their *Te Deum* and *Benedictus*, that Hour of Prayer by which the Church consecrates the day to God, in the Quires and places where they sing, before the world can spoil it, is delayed until the absolutely ridiculous hour of

The Laws of Worship

eleven, so that we thank God for having brought us to the beginning of this new day just before midday. And all this turning of things upside down is merely in order that Englishmen may, as they think, be saved from worshipping God in His own appointed way.

And this thought leads us to the third great principle as set forth in the Third Commandment.

At bottom, it will be found that the reason why Englishmen have come to demand that Matins should be recited for them at eleven o'clock, and that this should be a substitute for the " usual and daily Sacrifice of the Church " is that while, thank God, they retain a considerable amount of awe and holy fear in respect of the Divine Eucharist, the reciting of this Office does not seem to entail any very serious responsibilities. To put it in other words, while they think that people must be very good if they are going to Communion, they need not be particularly good to " go to Church," as it is so quaintly put. " Going to Church " is regarded as a sort of third-class compartment in things spiritual; it does not involve much spiritual outlay; while the Holy Eucharist is the first-class compartment that only comes within the reach of the select few.

What has occasioned such a view as this? We answer: " They have not learned the Third Commandment."

The Third Commandment imposes upon us the obligation of a right disposition.

Not only must every Christian, without exception, worship God; not only must he worship God in the true way; but also, he must himself be in a right condition each time that he comes to worship God; for " the sacrifice of the wicked is abomination." A man takes God's Name in vain every time that he presumes to " go to Church," or even to say his prayers, not being at the moment in a state of salvation; that is to say, his sins not being forgiven. We recognize the fact that a man's sins must have been forgiven before he can presume to approach the Holy Table. Why, then, do we think that he can say Matins if his sins have not been forgiven ? If he is not good enough for Communion, can he be good enough for praise ? Certainly not. What can taking God's Name in vain mean if it does not mean reciting one of the Hours of the Passion of our Lord, at the very moment that the worshipper is, by obstinate continuance in sin, trampling under foot the Blood of Christ ? It is terrible to think how easy it is to break the Third Commandment.

The ceaseless worship of the Church in Eucharist and Divine Office, that glorious daily history of the Church of which we have caught a glimpse, imposes upon every Christian the imperative necessity of being habitually in a state of grace.

Two practical considerations present themselves here:

(1) Think of the absurd and wholly unauthorized division of professing English Churchmen into " Communicants " and " Non-Communicants." At the very outset we notice that this division is only possible through a gross and absurd misuse of the English language.

The " Communicants " are the people who, at any given Service, actually make a Sacramental Communion. If any silly person were to ask, " Are you a Communicant ? " we should, I hope, answer, " Sometimes I am, and sometimes I am not."

There is no such thing as a class of Christians who are called Communicants. This conception is a wholly wrong one. You will not find a hint of it in your Bibles or in your Prayer-Books. It is a mere idiotic expression of these last days.

And do we not know how this idea of " being a Communicant " acts in ordinary everyday life ? A man prepares, with considerable care, for his first Communion. He thereby, in the average English mind, " becomes a Communicant." It is spoken of as if he had taken a certain degree at the University, or had passed through a certain initiation in a Masonic Lodge. He has, as these people think, attained to a sort of " freedom of the city " as regards Communion, and, of course, is to be considered as always fit for Communion, because he " is a Communicant " ! What an extraordinary perversion of Christianity have we here ! And the result of this absolutely un-Christian conception is that the man will not think it necessary to prepare so carefully for his subsequent Communions as he did for the first; for he considers that he has passed into the stage of " being a Communicant," and therefore must always be fit for Communion. This most pernicious and un-Christian idea is the exact reverse of the truth. A man is not fit to go to Communion because he " is a Communicant "; on the contrary, he will, on any given day, " be a Communicant " because on that day he is in a state of grace, and therefore fit for Communion. And yet, in these abominable statistics that we are constantly being asked to fill up, we are asked, " How many Communicants have you on your Communicants' Roll ?" What nonsense ! What constitutes a " Communicant " ? Are we supposed to put on to this blessed " Communicants' Roll " anyone who has ever made their Communion in their life ? What does the question mean ?

And what shall we say about " Non-Communicants " when the Word is used to denote a permanent class of Christians ? In ordinary sensible English, " Non-Communicants " are the Christians (presumably in a state of grace) who, at any given Service, do not make a Sacramental Communion. It is in this sense that we speak of " Non-Communicating attendance." But this is not what the average Englishman means when he talks of " Non-Communicants." He means Christians who never communicate. But these are simply Christians who are living in sin. You might as well talk of " murderer Christians," or " thief Christians," as talk of " Non-Communicants " as the word is ordinarily used.

Now all this hideous perversion of the truth has arisen from a total disregard of the Third Commandment. Englishmen have got the idea that they are fit to " go to Church " though they are not fit for Communion. But if they are not fit for Communion, that simply means that they have not repented of their sins; and that means that they are in a state of damnation, and can no more say their prayers or " go to Church " than they can go to Communion. Do let us be quite clear as to the obligation of the Third Commandment. If a man is what Englishmen mean when they call him a " Non-Communicant," he is taking God's holy Name in vain every time he says a prayer or " goes to Church."

(2) Think of the extraordinary vision of the holiness of everyday life in the Catholic Church that is revealed to us by the Third Commandment.

Here is the ceaseless worship of the Church, the earthly exercise of the High Priesthood of Jesus Christ. And here are the people of God supposed by God to be ready, at any given moment, to take their share in that ceaseless Heavenly worship. No room for sin in the Catholic Church! It is quietly assumed that the true worshippers, once purged, should have no more conscience of sin; it is quietly assumed that the Christian, at any given moment, will be found to be " holy "; that the normal description of the life of the baptized will be that truly their fellowship is with the Father, and with His Son Jesus Christ.

And this is why the standard of the Christian life rises or falls in exact proportion to the observance or neglect of Christian worship.

It ought to impress us with a wonderful sense of happy responsibility to know, from the Third Commandment, that we are under a positive obligation to live *habitually* in fellowship with the Father and with His Son Jesus Christ.

CHAPTER IX

THE LITURGY

WE have now reached the point at which we may consider the actual structure of " The Liturgy " —the actual form, that is, in which the Church to-day offers the Holy Eucharist. But before we pass to think of the actual Liturgy, it will be well to clear our minds about what is called " non-communicating attendance."

We will begin by ruling out certain things that we do *not* mean when we speak of " non-communicating attendance."

1. We do not mean that it is possible that there could be a Eucharist without Communion. The Communion is as essential a part of the Eucharist as the Consecration itself. For the Eucharist is the complete setting forth of the two ideas of Sacrifice as expressed by the Burnt Offering and the Peace Offering respectively—viz., (1) that an acceptable Sacrifice must be wholly offered to God, and (2) that the worshipper must himself become acceptable by being identified, in the eating of the Sacrifice, with the Acceptable Victim. These two ideas, which together complete the idea of Sacrifice, meet in the Holy Eucharist. The Communion is as essential as the Consecration. Consequently, Catholic Christians are amazed and horrified at a report that a certain English Bishop

proposed airily to solve the difficulty of celebration for
the sick by giving what he called a " dispensation "
(save the mark !) to his clergy to celebrate for the sick
without communicating themselves ! Truly the ignorance of Church of Englandism is only matched by its
impudence.

2. When we speak of " non-communicating attendance " we do not mean that people who are out of a
state of grace are fit to worship God though they are
unfit for Communion. Most certainly not !

In the primitive Church, at a certain point in the
Service, the unbaptized and excommunicate were
turned out of church, the Deacon saying, " Holy things
for the holy." Our Lord had said: " It is not meet to
take the children's bread and cast it to dogs"; and it
would have been thought a terrible profanation that a
heathen or an excommunicate person should have been
present at the Holy Mysteries; and so they were turned
out of church after the first part of the Service. If a
primitive Christian were to walk into a " moderate "
London church and see a large congregation troop out
of church after the Church Militant Prayer, he would
think they were the unbaptized and excommunicate.
He would think that we had a very large proportion
of these unsatisfactory people in our London churches;
and perhaps he would wonder why they did not look
more ashamed; but that is what he would naturally
suppose.

3. When we speak of " non-communicating attendance " we do not in the least mean to imply that every
Christian is bound to communicate every time he
attends Divine Service. Three Communions in the
year are all that are absolutely ordered in the Prayer-
Book, and Easter is the only feast at which Communion

is of absolute obligation. Frequent Communion is the highest privilege and blessing of the Christian life; but to insist on frequent Communion as an imperative duty is to cut clean across the Prayer-Book, and is to interfere most unwarrantably with Christian liberty.

Well, then, when we speak of " non-communicating attendance," we do not mean to imply that the Eucharist is possible without Communion; nor do we mean that people in a state of sin can worship God.

What do we mean ? We mean that faithful Christians may, and ought to, join in the worship of the Church at such times as they are not actually going to make a Sacramental Communion.

Now here, as elsewhere, the burden of proof lies with the people who have invented a new religion. It is not for us to prove that we have a right to join in the worship of the Church; it is for the Protestants and "moderate" people to prove that they have a right to turn us out. There is not a hint in the Prayer-Book about Non-Communicants going out of church. Nay, the Sanctus and Gloria are ordered to be sung quite as much as the Creed. What is going to happen, then, if the choir go out after the Church Militant Prayer ?

Not a word is said about anyone withdrawing, while it is clearly contemplated that the choir are present.

Many years ago, a well-known Bishop of that day, officiating at the consecration of a church, said in the pulpit: " After the prayer for the Church Militant a pause will be made that those who are not going to communicate may withdraw." In giving this notice he was, of course, merely making a rule of his own in contradiction to the Prayer-Book.

Whatever there may be to be said for this practice

of turning out the faithful in the middle of Divine Service, one thing is quite certain—viz., that it is not " Prayer-Book " worship. If anyone, be he Bishop, Priest, or layman, says that those who are not going to communicate should leave the church in the middle of the Service, we flatly refuse to go; and our answer to such an ignoramus is: " We have no such custom, neither the Churches of God." To turn (or try to turn) the faithful out of the church in the middle of the Service, is a mere bit of Protestant impudence, and Christians have tamely submitted to this tyranny because they have never faced and floored their bullies by the simple little question, " Why ?"

A good many years ago, the Holy Eucharist was to be celebrated in an English cathedral on a given Sunday, after the Morning Office. The singing men and boys had not realized this fact, and when they saw the Canon go to the altar after the sermon, they " fled incontinent," as if, as the *Church Times* remarked, they were afraid that there was going to be a sort of Thyestean banquet, in which they would be gobbled up ! We do not, of course, ask if this is religion. Of course it is not; but is it decent ?

Let us put the matter in a very elementary way. Let us ask those who object to " non-communicating attendance " a simple question. Let us say to them: " On the days that you do not communicate, do you think that you make a better remembrance of the Sacrifice of the Death of Christ by lying in bed, or by walking in the park, than you would by assisting at the Divine Service ? Do you seriously think that you are more acceptable to God when you go out of church in the middle of the Service than you are when you stay to the end and receive the blessing ? If you can seriously think this we can say no more to you; but we will say that you must have a very queer idea of God, and a very odd idea of what you are pleased to call religion !

But all this is merely negative. We can easily establish our right not to be excluded from the worship of the Church; but what Englishmen want to know, and what you will want to know, is the positive side —viz., " How are we to assist at Divine worship on days which we do not make a Sacramental Communion ?" This will become more apparent when we consider the structure of the Divine Service.

When we take our Prayer-Book in our hands to examine the Liturgy as there given to us English Christians, we begin by asking ourselves why the Service takes the exact shape that it does.

If we allow ourselves to try and think of the Church of England as an isolated, self-contained, self-sufficient, irresponsible entity, we cannot account for the structure of our Liturgy. If we think of a certain number of gentlemen sitting round a table to invent a " service "—an altogether new departure with no connection with anything that went before—it will, of course, seem quite inexplicable why the Service should have taken this form rather than any other. But the Church of England is not such an isolated, self-contained body as " Church of Englandism " would have us to suppose it to be. The Divine Service in the English Prayer-Book takes the form that it does because Divine Service had always taken that form. Not only have Christians always had the same worship, but, in its main lines, they have always worshipped in the same way.

When we come to examine the Divine Service we

The Liturgy

shall find that the main framework of every Liturgy is the same. In different parts of the One Church this main framework has been embellished and " clothed upon " in different ways; but the skeleton, or framework, is the same.

That skeleton, or main framework, on which the service is built, is as follows:

1. The Kyrie.
2. The Collect, Epistle, and Gospel.
3. The Offertory.
4. The Preface and Sanctus.
5. The Consecration.
6. The Communion.
7. The Blessing.

If we look at our English Prayer-Book we find these things there in this order. If we cross the water and attend Divine Service according to the Roman rite, we find these same things in the same order. If we go to the East, and attend Divine worship according to the Eastern rite, we find these same things there, in the same unvarying order.

Now perhaps, if we have found ourselves at High Mass in some Continental church, we may have thought that we understood nothing about it and we may have rather plumed ourselves on being superior kind of people, who of course know nothing of such outlandish worship. One certainly sees English Churchpeople in foreign churches looking on in an unconcerned kind of way, as if the worship were something that had nothing to do with them, standing as spectators, much as they might watch the dancing dervishes in Constantinople or Cairo; and if English travellers find themselves in a Russian or a

Greek church they would think the service even more queer and unintelligible than the Roman High Mass.

But if English Churchpeople would take a little trouble to understand their own Liturgy, and would, in the light of that knowledge, try to learn something about the Roman and Eastern Liturgies, things would fall into their proper places and become quite simple and intelligible. A very little investigation would suffice to show us that Romans, Easterns, and Anglicans are not only doing the same thing when they worship God, but are actually doing the same thing in the same way. We should find both in the Roman and Eastern Mass, as we find in the English Liturgy, these seven things:

1. The Kyrie.
2. The Collect, Epistle, and Gospel.
3. The Offertory.
4. The Preface and Sanctus.
5. The Consecration.
6. The Communion.
7. The Blessing.

And finding these things in their unvarying order in the more ancient Liturgies of Eastern and Western Christendom, you would begin to see why they occupy the place and the order that they do in our modern English Liturgy.

What a long way we should have gone towards the right understanding of our own Service if we would try a little to begin to understand something about the Divine Service according to the Roman and Eastern rites! And what a bond of unity, in the unhappy divisions of Catholic and Apostolic Christendom, should we find in the fact that not only are we all offering to

The Liturgy

God the same worship, but that we are all offering it in the same way!

We find, then, that our English Liturgy is built, as, of course, it must be, on the main lines of Divine Service common to Catholic Apostolic Christendom.

Now we will glance for a moment at those features in our English Liturgy which are distinctively English and local. And, inasmuch as the whole is greater than its part, we will remember that what is Catholic (*i.e.*, Universal) is of more importance than what is merely local.

We notice that in our Liturgy the Commemoration of the Living (the prayer for the Church Militant), which in the other Western Service Books is the first part of what is called " the Canon of the Mass " (of which the Consecration forms the middle part), is separated from the Prayer of Consecration by (1) the Communicants' Confession and Absolution, and (2) the Preface and Sanctus; while the last part of the Canon (embodied in the prayer, " O Lord and Heavenly Father," etc.) is separated from the Prayer of Consecration by the Communion of the Priest and people, and the Lord's Prayer.

Then, secondly, we notice that the part of the Service that especially concerns the Communicants— viz., the Exhortation, Confession, Absolution, and Comfortable Words—is inserted between the Church Militant Prayer and the Preface, instead of coming, as it would in the other Service books, after the Consecration, at the time of Communion itself.

Now this alteration in the position of things, though it left the order of the main framework untouched, may have arisen partly from the desire (as evinced by Bishops Cosin and Overall), to stimulate the faithful to more frequent Communion; but it would be idle to attempt to deny that it was owing to the strong pressure of the new foreign Protestant ideas that made itself continuously felt in our past Reformation history— viz., the desire to confine the commemorative aspect of the Holy Eucharist to the subjective act of the memory, and to view the Holy Eucharist almost, if not quite, exclusively as the Sacrament for the strengthening and refreshing of our souls.

What Protestantism led to, when applied to the Blessed Sacrament, may be seen in the speculations of Zwingli and Swiss Protestantism, and in the decay, all along the Protestant line, of the idea of worship and of Sacramental teaching. And this, of course, as we can well see, is the direct and inevitable result of the audacity and impatience that led men, in their zeal for reform, to sweep away the Apostolic Episcopate, and therewith all Divine authority. And it is surely a sign of the good Providence of God that, in parting company with the Apostolic Ministry, they invariably lost their faith in the Eucharistic Sacrifice and in the " Real Presence," so that they have been saved from offering to God a Sacrifice that they have not got, and from adoring a Sacramental Presence that is no longer theirs.

But, as we all know, the Reformation in England was saved from the disasters to which the foreign Reformation fell a prey, and proceeded along more sober lines, making its appeal to the consensus of undivided Christendom, and therefore retaining at all hazards the Apostolic Ministry, and with it the reality of the Blessed Sacrament and of Catholic worship; so that, to come to the present instance, though some of the local arrangements in our Liturgy are, as one would expect them to be, tinged with the reforming trend of thought, nevertheless, in the main structure, the Catholic Liturgy remains untouched, and so we English Christians find ourselves at home, on familiar ground, in the Liturgies of Eastern and Western Catholicism.

We are not concerned to prove, or to try to show, that the modern English Liturgy is the most perfect Liturgy of Christendom, nor are we bound to prefer it, from an historical and Liturgical point of view, to the more ancient Liturgies. It is not a question of likes or dislikes. We do not conform to the English Liturgy because we like it best, but because it comes to us with the authority of the Church. It is most important that we should remember this, because foolish people get into the way of thinking that if the Roman Liturgy appears to them (as I dare say it very well may) to be a more perfect Liturgy than the English one, they must go over to Rome. It is a question of authority and of sufficiency. It may be matter of regret that in the English Service the old order should have been altered in those particulars that I have mentioned, and that thereby, possibly, the primary aspect of the Holy Eucharist as the remembrance of the Death of Christ should have been somewhat obscured ; but the fact remains that the English Liturgy is, in its main structure, identical with the Liturgies of Eastern and Western Christendom, and the other fact remains, that there is no hint whatever of the English Liturgy being for the exclusive use of the Communicants of the day, but quite the reverse.

We must bear in mind that the English Prayer-Book is the result of the struggle between Church authority on the one hand, and Protestant boldness on the other. The Church in England, while holding fast at all hazards to things that are absolutely essential to the continuity of the Holy Church, has tried to meet and appropriate to itself all that was right and good in the reforming movement. And if in this attempt our Liturgy has lost some beautiful things that are to be found in other Liturgies, we may surely look upon this as the price paid for the great vantage-ground possessed by the Anglican Communion in the Holy Church, which, we must see, gives us so great a part to play in the ultimate reunion of divided Christendom.

We do not, then, dogmatically assert that the English Liturgy is perfect, nor even that it is the best among existing Liturgies. That is a matter of taste on which every Christian has a right to his own opinion. It is a Catholic Liturgy, identical in structure with all other Catholic Liturgies, and we English Christians know that not only are we offering the same worship as undivided Christendom has always offered, but we are offering it in the same way as our fellow-Churchmen all over the world.

We are now in a position to say one word on the positive side of what is called " non-communicating attendance." We have seen that there is everything to be said for it on the negative side. Let us now think of it as a positive duty.

We go back in thought to the great laws of worship as given us in the first table of the Law.

We have seen that every Christian is bound, at least on every Sunday and Holy Day of obligation, (1) to worship God, (2) to worship Him in the right way by the remembrance of the Sacrifice of the Death of Christ, (3) to be at the moment of worship in a state of grace.

Let us start from the last of these three commandments. The Church takes it for granted that when-

The Liturgy

ever we " go to Church " we are (1) Christians—*i.e.*, baptized people; and (2) that any sins we may have committed since our Baptism *have been forgiven*. This obligation is laid upon us all by the Third Commandment. If, on any given Sunday or day of worship, we have any unforgiven sin upon our soul; if we cannot show that at that moment we are in vital union with Jesus Christ, not only is worship quite out of the question, but we are, for the time being, in the state spoken of by the Apostle as " having no hope, and without God in the world."

We take it for granted, then, that on any ordinary Sunday we are in a state of grace. It is Sunday, and we are therefore under the obligation of worshipping the One True God through the Mediation of Jesus Christ; in other words, we are under the absolute obligation of taking our part in the " continual remembrance of the Sacrifice of the Death of Christ, and of the benefits which we receive thereby." We are *not* under obligation to make our Communion on that particular Sunday. How, then, do you propose to fulfil the obligation on that day of the First, Second, and Fourth Commandments ?

Here is the Divine Service: The Kyrie, the Collect, Epistle, and Gospel (with exposition of the Gospel, or sermon, on Sundays), the Offertory, the Preface and Sanctus, the Consecration, the Communion, and, crowning all, as God's answer to His true worshippers, the Blessing. Can we fulfil our obligation of making the remembrance of the Sacrifice of the Death of Christ in any better way ? If not, we are bound to fulfil it in this way.

Now if a man says, " I will go to Matins and sermon on each Sunday," the immediate answer is that whatever Matins and sermon is, it is not Prayer-Book worship. Nothing is said in the Prayer-Book about Matins and sermon. On the contrary, the ordered place for the sermon is in the Liturgy after the Nicene Creed. And we remind ourselves that children are especially to be called upon to hear sermons. Therefore the Prayer-Book expects that children will be present when the sermon is preached—*i.e.*, at the Liturgy. " Matins and sermon " is a monstrous invention of these latter days. But if it dawns upon our man that Matins and sermon has no sort of authority, he may say: " Well, never mind the sermon, I will go to Matins and Litany." The answer is that if the Divine Office is used *as the substitute for* the Divine Service, it is being used for a purpose for which it was never intended, and that to use the Divine Office in this way is to cut across the Second Commandment. But if we succeed in hunting our Englishman off Matins and sermon, and Matins and Litany without sermon, he may very likely take refuge in going to church for Matins and Litany, remaining for the sermon, and coming out after the Church Militant Prayer. But if he does this he is not only doing something for which the Prayer-Book does not give him a shred of authority, but he is putting himself in the place of the unbaptized and excommunicate.

So we are led to the horns of a dilemma. Either we must be under obligation to communicate every Sunday, which we certainly are *not*, or else we can only fulfil on ordinary Sundays our obligations to the First, Second, and Fourth Commandments, by what we call " non-communicating attendance." It is not an æsthetic pleasure that may be conceded to us, but an obligation of Christian life.

The Liturgy

Meanwhile, the great reason why all Christians (whether on that given day they are Communicants or not) are bound to Eucharistic worship every Sunday is that our fellow-Christians have always been so bound; and our answer to any proposal for " Matins and sermons," " Matins and Litany," or " coming away after the Church Militant Prayer," is the one all-sufficient answer : " We have no such custom, neither the Churches of God."

CHAPTER X

THE LITURGY (*continued*)

IN our thoughts about the Liturgy let us keep firmly hold of our main point—viz., that Eucharistic worship is the great primary duty of all Christians, imposed upon them by the first title of the Law. Men are apt to get " switched off " on to side issues, and to lose their hold on the main thing. And so we often find men who take a keen interest in the historical or archæological questions that confront them in the study of the Prayer-Book, while as regards the broad lines of worship in general they are hazy and indifferent. The Liturgy appeals to them in a British Museum kind of way. It is a valuable and interesting " specimen." But our Liturgy is not just an interesting specimen to be disputed over and chattered about, but a very serious fact which entails great moral obligations. For it is by our English Liturgy that we English Christians are to keep the first title of that law of God to which we are committed, and according to which we stand or fall for ever. It is plain, therefore, that it does not come within the scope of this book to enter at any length into the details of the Liturgy.

But while we leave the details mainly on one side, there are certain salient points among those fundamental things which are common to all Liturgies that it will be well to consider, that our grasp of the moral obligations of the English Liturgy may be strengthened. We will therefore in this chapter set before ourselves a few considerations about—

1. The Offertory.
2. The Consecration.
3. The Communion.
4. The Blessing.

1. The Offertory. We have seen that the Offertory is a part of that skeleton framework on which every Liturgy is built—that, as a matter of fact, it is an unvarying element of Divine worship.

Now, we must get out of our mind the idea of *money* when we speak of the Offertory in its Liturgical sense. In our English Liturgy it is at the time of the Offertory that alms are collected and offered, but that is merely English custom. The word " Offertory " denotes a regular portion of the Divine Service, whether money is collected at that time or not.

It is the solemn offering of the Bread and Wine for the Holy Eucharist, and the Bread and Wine thus solemnly offered are called the " oblations," or " things offered."

How absurd, then, it is to hear, as we sometimes do, people at a week-day Eucharist say, " Is there an Offertory to-day ? " meaning " Is there a collection ? " And how absurd to hear, as you sometimes do at Evensong, the priest say: " The Offertory this evening will be for such-and-such an object " !

The Offertory, then, is the solemn offering of the Bread and Wine for the Eucharist.

Now comes the question, " Whose Offertory is it ? "

And the answer to this will be found in the answer to another question—viz., "Whose Bread and Wine is it?" And that, again, necessitates another question—viz., "Who pays for it?"

We see in our Prayer-Book that the Bread and Wine are to be " provided by the Curate and the Churchwardens at the charges of the Parish." The Bread and Wine, then, are paid for by the parishioners, and are therefore the offering of the parishioners. The Bread and Wine are a first charge upon the fund for meeting Church expenses.

Up to between forty and fifty years ago this fund was provided by a rate. The Church expenses, strange as it may sound now, were chargeable on the rates. Every ratepayer in the parish then paid his share towards the Bread and Wine. This, of course, was a relic of the times when all were of one heart and of one mind; and it made the Offertory most emphatically the offering of the whole people. Now Church expenses come out of the voluntary offerings of the people. But however they are provided, the Bread and Wine for the Holy Eucharist become the first charge upon them.

The Bread and Wine, then, are the offering of the Christian people. And this takes us very deep down into the counsels of God. It does not please God, in His Infinite Wisdom, any more to create out of nothing. Is not this what is taught us by the seventh day rest of God? God works His Wonders on something that already exists. Unless the sower is willing to part with the seed, and " cast it into the ground," that seed will " abide alone." Unless the little lad will part with his five barley loaves, the five thousand will not be fed. Unless Bread and Wine are provided,

The Liturgy

there can be no Eucharist. If there is no Offertory, there is nothing to consecrate.

And yet, in each case, how absurdly inadequate does the means appear to the end! Think of the little bare grain and what is to come out of it. Think of those absurd five loaves and the five thousand hungry men. Well may they say, " What are they among so many?" So, too, think of the Bread and Wine and the Adorable and Life-giving Sacrament. And yet you cannot have the one without the other.

It is, then, in the Offertory that the people do their part, and all that they can do. They bring their oblation and contribute their share towards the Most Holy Sacrament. They must wait upon God for the rest. But, having done what they can, in accordance with the Ordinance of God, they can take their part with the obedient Angels and Archangels in the heavenly song of the *Sanctus*. Like the sower, they have sown their seed and wait upon God to give the increase. Like the little lad, they have given their five barley loaves and two small fishes for the miracle to be worked upon. They have made the holy oblation on which the Holy Ghost will work His wonders in the Consecration.

We must, then, realize the tremendous import of the Offertory. Fancy going out of Church at that point, and not being there when that poor oblation becomes that " Divine thing " in the Consecration! Oh no; that will never do. Like the husbandman, we will wait for the precious fruit of what we have sown. Like Miriam watching the cradle of Moses, we will wait to see what will come.

2. The Consecration. Here we must for a moment go down into the chill region of controversy, and try

to see what is the net result of the controversies that have raged around this Holy of Holies of our religion.

In examining the controversy, we come across the word "Presence." Now, we use this word under protest. It is a clumsy and possibly misleading expression. Nevertheless, as it has gained currency, we can hardly avoid using it. But do let us remember that it must be used with great caution.

(1) The broad line of controversy between the Catholic Church on the one side and Protestantism on the other is as to whether the "Presence" of our Lord is objectively in the Sacrament itself, by virtue of the Consecration, as the whole Catholic Church asserts, or whether it is merely subjectively in the heart of the worthy Communicant, which was the new teaching of Protestantism.

This is really the great dividing line as regards the doctrine of the Holy Sacrament. Catholics on the one side of the line, and Protestants on the other, will soon respectively draw together and understand each other; but between the Catholic truth of the Real Objective Presence and the Protestant novelty of a merely Subjective Presence there is a great gulf fixed.

Protestant controversialists see clearly that, given the Real Objective Presence, the fact of the sacrificial aspect of the Eucharist is immediately apparent. And that is why, as we have already seen, in the Protestant mind the memorial aspect fades into the background, "non-communicating attendance" is not to be tolerated, and the Eucharist is to be nothing more than the Sacrament of Communion.

To the Catholic it is the Consecration that makes the Blessed Sacrament what It is. In the Consecration the Catholic sees the operation of the Holy Ghost brought to bear upon the oblations, making them become, in a wonderful and heavenly manner, the Body and Blood of Christ.

To the Protestant the Consecration is comparatively unimportant. It is a blessing on the oblations, which remain, in themselves, as they were before, merely conveying the Body and Blood of Christ where they meet with active faith in the individual Communicant.

To sum it up in a sentence: In the mind of the Catholic Church the Blessed Sacrament is the Body and Blood of Christ, antecedently to, and independently of, the use, good, bad, or indifferent, that may be made of It.

In the Protestant mind the Blessed Sacrament is nothing in Itself, but depends (not only for Its virtue, but for Its existence) upon the state of the receiver.

To the Catholic it is the fact of the Blessed Sacrament being the Body of Christ that constitutes the horror and awfulness of unworthy Communion. As St. Paul says, the unworthy Communicant eats and drinks his own damnation because he does not discern the Lord's Body.

It is because, to the Protestant, the Blessed Sacrament is nothing in Itself, that we Catholics are saddened and horror-struck at the profanations that alas! are to be found in " Low Church " Churches—e.g., the abomination of Evening Communion, the frightful desecration of what remains of the Blessed Sacrament, the omission to cleanse the Holy Vessels, and that absolutely new profanity of wiping the Chalice for each Communicant. It is impossible to express the shuddering, heart-breaking sorrow that these things cause us. We can but weep over these abominations, and make Acts of Reparation for the frightful indignities done thereby to our Lord, and pray that they may cease utterly and for ever.

So much for the broad line of demarcation between the Church as a whole and Protestantism as a whole.

(2) The controversies that have arisen within the Church itself have arisen as to the manner of the Real Objective Presence, England and Rome being at one as to Its Reality and Objectivity.

To go into the history of the word " Transubstantiation " would be impossible at this moment.

We cannot begin to understand what the Roman definition means by " Transubstantiation " until we remember that philosophy uses the word " substance " in the exactly opposite sense to that which it bears in ordinary English. When we English speak of " substance " we mean what we can feel or weigh. But this is exactly what the philosophers did not mean by the word. " Substance " in their language meant that intangible something that makes a thing what it is. It was to things what personality is to men. We cannot at all understand the questions about Transubstantiation unless we know something of the history of Realism and Nominalism. The philosophy of " substance " and " accidents " is an attempt to explain what we mean by the little word " is." Let anyone try to think what he means when he says: " This is a man," " That is a book," and he will find it exceedingly difficult to say what he does mean. It is by no means so simple as it looks. The definition of Transubstantiation is an attempt to state in language the truth that the Blessed Sacrament " is " the Body of Christ.

Now, it is quite clear that the Article on " Transubstantiation " is using the word " substance," not in its philosophical, but in its ordinary sense, and therefore the Article and the Council of Trent are quite at cross purposes. The Article is condemning one thing, while the Roman definition is asserting quite a different thing. They are using the word " substance " in two diametrically opposite ways. It is impossible here to go into this matter at length. It will be found well explained in Bishop Forbes' book on the Thirty-Nine Articles.

Meanwhile one pithy sentence of dear Canon Liddon's will, I think, immensely help us. At one of those " reunions " of Oxford undergraduates in which Dr. Liddon and the late Bishop of Lincoln did such solid work for the Church in Oxford, some thirty or forty years ago, an undergraduate, probably thinking to " draw " Dr. Liddon, said: " Come, now, Dr. Liddon, I wish you would tell us the difference between the Real Presence and Transubstantiation, for it seems to me they mean the same thing." To which Dr. Liddon immediately replied: " Indeed, now, I should have thought, do you know, that the one is a fact, and the other an attempt at an explanation of that fact."

Yes, there you have the whole matter in a nutshell. " Transubstantiation " is an attempt at an explanation of the fact of the Real Objective Presence. It was the term in which the scholastic philosophy would express the truth, held by all Catholics in common, that the bread in the Holy Sacrament " is " the Body of Christ.

Let us study, by all means, if we will, the philosophy of substance and accidents; let us learn, if you will, something about Realism and Nominalism. But do not let anyone think they can airily settle the complicated question of Transubstantiation. Let us re-

member Canon Liddon's words about the " Real
Presence " and " Transubstantiation ": " The one is a
fact, and the other an attempt at an explanation of
that fact."

And now let us leave the dreary region of controversy,
and fix our minds upon the great fact, joyfully held
by the Catholic Apostolic Church, but rejected by
Protestantism—the simple, marvellous fact that the
Blessed Sacrament " is " the Body and Blood of
Christ; that, to put it in our own Catechism words,
the " inward part or thing signified " in the Sacrament
of the Lord's Supper is " the Body and Blood of Christ
Which are *verily and indeed* taken and received by the
faithful in the Lord's Supper."

In the Consecration we watch in the stillness of
breathless adoration the operation of the Holy Ghost
on the oblations that we ourselves have brought to Him.
All over the world the Divine instinct of the Church has
led her to the Consecration of the oblations by the
words and acts of our Lord Himself, " the same night
that He was betrayed."

And all over the world that same Divine instinct has
confined the Consecration to the Apostolic Priesthood.
Nowhere, and under no conceivable circumstances, is
it thought for a moment, in Catholic Apostolic Christendom, that a Deacon or a layman could possibly
consecrate the Most Holy Sacrament.

How awful, how sweet, and how wonderful is the
time of Consecration ! Jesus Christ, the true High-
Priest after the Order of Melchisedek, exercising His
High-Priestly functions here in our midst; and we,
unworthy creatures, privileged to be united with Him
in that supreme and wonderful moment.

If English Churchmen bear these solemn facts in

mind, they cannot surely think it well or advisable to go out of Church in the middle of the Service on days when they are not going to communicate.

One last thought before we pass on. Supposing that, as the Protestant thinks, the Consecration is not a reality, we have taken a step backwards in worship. " That which is in part " is only done away because " that which is perfect " is come. There can be no question at all that a sacrifice of blood is a more perfect remembrance of Christ's Death than mere bread and wine could be. It is because, by the Consecration, that Bread (*the* Bread, as the Bible calls it so emphatically) *is* the Body of Christ, and that Wine *is* His Blood, that we have the perfect remembrance of the Sacrifice of the Death of Christ, before Which all partial and imperfect remembrance fades away. " He taketh away the first that He may establish the second."

3. Think of the Communion. We can see at a glance that it is possible to regard Sacramental Communion under two aspects; not, of course, that these two aspects are really distinct, but that we can, and do, distinguish them in thought.

We may think of Communion—

(1) As the completion of the Act of worship. This is what we may call its liturgical aspect.

(2) In relation to our spiritual life. There is no need for us to speak now of this second aspect of Communion. Our subject is worship, and we want to see the place of Communion in worship.

By the Consecration we have made to God the offering with which He is well pleased. It is, in truth, our offering, for we brought the oblation. It is a perfect offering, by reason of the Consecration.

So far, so good. But when we have come thus far, we ourselves are still standing outside of the offering. It remains that we should, by Communion, identify ourselves with the acceptable Victim, and so become ourselves a living sacrifice, holy, acceptable unto God.

Think a moment. We hear people speaking of " giving their heart to the Lord." But is that heart an offering that God can accept ? Is not this rather to fall into the error of Cain, who thought that God was bound to accept what he was willing to give ? We need a Mediator to make it possible to " give our hearts to the Lord." The only hearts that God can accept are the hearts that are one with the Sacred Heart of Jesus Christ. The only life that God can accept is the life that can honestly and truly say, " I live, yet not I, but Christ liveth in me."

The completion of worship is the complete offering of self. Therefore, when we have a Victim wholly acceptable to God, we must identify ourselves with that Victim, and so offer ourselves to God.

And so the Eucharist, without Communion, if such a thing were conceivably possible, would not be complete and perfect worship. The Priest's Communion, then, is an essential part of the Eucharist. It is not merely the Priest as the individual man, receiving the Blessed Sacrament for his own soul's salvation. If that were all, it might be conceivable that a Priest might celebrate for the Communion of others, without communicating himself. But the Priest, as we have seen before, when he celebrates at the Altar, sums up in himself the whole Body of the faithful. He is not there merely as an isolated individual, nor is he there as the spokesman of a particular congregation; nor even as representing the Church Militant here on

The Liturgy

earth. The Church is one solid whole, and the right of each Priest to minister is that he represents the solid whole because it is in him that, at the moment, the One Great High Priest is exercising His High Priestly Mediation. "This Man, because he abideth ever, hath an unchangeable Priesthood." Thus the oblation offered by the Priest at the Offertory is the offering of the Whole Church. So, in a sense, is the Priest's Communion the partaking of the Whole Church in the Acceptable Sacrifice. And so, after the Communion, the Whole Church cries, "Here we offer and present unto Thee ourselves, our souls, and bodies, to be a reasonable, holy, and lively Sacrifice unto Thee."

On the days when we individually make our Sacramental Communion we actually partake of the Sacrifice ourselves. On the days on which we are not making a Sacramental Communion, we have our spiritual share in the Communion of the Priest, as being at that moment in vital union with the whole Body of Christ.

Do let us get rid of this dreary "individualism," and learn to view things from the point of view of the solidarity of the Holy Church. Then, instead of wondering why "non-Communicants" should attend Divine Service, we should marvel that anyone could ever have supposed that they would not. For let us again remember that when a Catholic speaks of a "non-Communicant" he does not mean a person who is living in sin by never approaching the Sacrament of Communion. He means one of the faithful, in a state of grace, who is not going to communicate at that particular Service.

And this fact ought to dispose, once for all and for ever, of the pompous nonsense that we sometimes hear talked about "non-communicating attendance" being a " substitute for Communion." Who ever dreamt of such a thing? Certainly not a Catholic Christian. We are not contrasting " non-communicating attendance " with Communion; we are contrasting it with staying away from Divine Service, or going away in the middle of it. The question is not whether a Spiritual Communion is better than a Sacramental Communion, but whether it is better than staying in bed or going out of Church. This, of course, is a poor, meagre, negative way of putting it, but it is a primary question for those who, by separating themselves from the worship of the Whole Church, seem to think they are wiser than their brethren.

4. The Blessing. A little thought will make us see something of the import of the Blessing. It is the answer of God to the Acceptable Sacrifice.

When the first Sacrifice was offered in the Tabernacle, the fire of God fell and consumed the Sacrifice. It was the token of God's acceptance of the Levitical Sacrifices. And as such the people regarded it. When they saw it they fell on their faces.

So, too, when Elijah challenged the Priests of Baal, the answer was the test, " The God that answereth by fire, let Him be God." And the hopeless impotence of the Baal worship lay in the fact that there was no voice, nor any to answer, nor any that regarded it. But when Elijah had based his Sacrifice on the Covenant that the people had forgotten, building his Altar of twelve stones, recalling the twelve tribes of Israel who, because they were children of Israel, were in a definite Covenant with God; when, that is, Elijah had offered the Sacrifice of the Covenant, then the answer of God was given; this fire of the Lord consumed the Sacrifice, and the people fell on their faces with the shout: " The Lord, He is the God."

So, too, on the great Day of Atonement in the Tabernacle. The crowning and culminating point was the return of the High-Priest from the Holy of Holies to bring the people the blessing of God on the acceptance of, and the answer to, the true and rightful Sacrifice.

And so, in the perfect worship of the Holy Eucharist, the Blessing is the crowning, culminating point. It comes as God's acceptance of, and answer to, the true worship.

Step by step the successive elements of perfect worship have been accomplished.

In the Offertory the worshippers have brought the oblation.

In the Consecration that oblation has been made absolutely perfect.

In the Communion the worshippers have become one with the acceptable Victim.

Then comes the answer of God: " The Blessing of God Almighty, the Father, the Son, and the Holy Ghost, be amongst you and remain with you for ever. Amen."

Thus the whole act of worship is crowned and completed by the Blessing.

By the Offertory, the Consecration, the Communion, and the Blessing, the obligation of the first table of the Law is fulfilled, and man, through the High-Priestly Mediation of Jesus Christ, finds himself in that right relation to God that alone can be called " life." " I am come that they might have life, and that they might have it more abundantly."

And in the light of this glorious fact, what a monstrous deformity appears that conception of worship that, alas! has such a strong hold on the average Englishman; that conception of worship that makes it possible for him to think that the Eucharist is for Communicants only; that makes him "shrink away like a guilty thing," going out in the middle of the Service as if he were unbaptized or excommunicate.

Undivided Christendom has "no such custom"; the Prayer-Book knows nothing of such a custom. Let us hope and pray that it may vanish away from among us as "the remembrance of a dream when one awaketh."

CHAPTER XI

PRAYER-BOOK OFFICES

WE have now to do with the Divine Office what we have tried to do with the Liturgy—viz., to look broadly at its structure and to consider certain salient points in it.

Let us once more remember that the Divine Office can never become *a substitute* for the Divine Service. To use it in this way would be to misuse it altogether and to break the Second Commandment.

The substituting of Matins for the Divine Service has had a very bad effect upon the Office of Matins itself as tending to depreciate it in three ways.

1. It has led people to think that those who are not fit for Communion are fit for Matins, and so has tended to put Matins in a much lower place than it really holds.

2. It has led people to think that Matins requires less spiritual insight, and is more easy of comprehension than the Divine Service; which means that people are using it without in the least understanding its real depth.

3. It has led Catholics to speak disparagingly of Matins. When first Catholics find out how they have been cheated of their rights in being deprived of Divine Service on Sundays, they, not unnaturally, perhaps,

Now, bearing in mind the source from which our Offices come, we proceed to examine their structure.

And here, just as in the Divine Service, we find that there is a skeleton framework on which the Divine Office is built which is common to the Divine Office everywhere. That common framework is as follows:

1. General Confession and Absolution.
2. The Psalter or Book of Psalms.
3. The Lessons.
4. The Canticles or Gospel Songs.
5. The Collects.

So that, in the broad lines, we are not only doing the same thing as the rest of Catholic Christendom when we recite the Divine Office, but we are doing it in the same way.

Now, the recollection of this fact of a common framework of the Divine Office ought to keep people from the extraordinarily silly mistakes that they often make.

Take one notable instance of such ignorant folly. People are constantly found who say that, in what they are pleased to call " our Church," Christians need not go to Confession because they make a Confession and receive Absolution in the public services of the Church! This is sheer nonsense, though we hear it pompously laid down by people who ought to know better. The General Confession and Absolution in the Offices have nothing whatever to do with the question as to whether people are to go to Confession or not, for this very simple reason—viz., that in the old Service Books, as in the Roman Breviary to-day, there is just such a General Confession and declaratory Absolution as you find in the English Prayer-Book—viz., at Prime in the morning, and at Compline in the evening. The reason why these Confessions and Absolutions are in the English Office is not because the Church of England wanted to start a new idea about Confession, but *because they were always there.* Whatever reason people may think they can find for excusing themselves from going to Confession, do not let them give that reason; for that only shows culpable and abominable ignorance on their part. The General Confession and Absolution in the Offices has no more to do for us with going to Confession than it has for Roman or Greek Catholics. It is amazing to what shifts Protestants are driven sometimes !

The General Confession and Absolution, then, are in the English Office as a part of the common framework of the Divine Office.

After the Lord's Prayer and opening Versicles and Responses, we pass to the Psalter.

By our English arrangement the Book of Psalms is recited steadily through each month.

In the old arrangement it was theoretically recited through each week, but this arrangement was constantly being upset by festivals, so that practically certain Psalms were being very often recited, while others were constantly being omitted.

According to the old arrangement, for instance, the faithful who went to Vespers and Compline on Sundays would practically always recite the same Psalms, five at Vespers, four at Compline; always, week by week, the same Psalms. There was a greater variety of Psalms at Matins and Lauds, but those being the night hours, were practically out of reach of ordinary people.

Here we have gained by the English arrangement, by which the whole Book of Psalms is recited steadily through month by month.

On the other hand, the daily reciting of the 119th Psalm at Prime, Terce, Sext, and Nones, was a very treasure-house of holy aspirations to devout souls. Still, on the whole, I think we have gained more than we lost by our arrangement of the Psalter.

I now pass to consider the Lessons, the third unvarying element of the Divine Office.

According to the old arrangement, there were nine Lessons on festivals, and three on ordinary days, at Matins. These nine Lessons were much shorter than our Lessons. On festivals, the fourth, fifth, and sixth Lessons were often not taken from the Holy Scripture, but were readings from the life of the Saint whose feast it was. At the other Offices of the day the Lesson would consist of one verse only.

Now we can see at once that in this way comparatively little of the Bible was read during the year; for with the Lessons, as with the Psalter, the continuity was constantly broken by the number of festivals.

By our English arrangement of Lessons the Bible is read consecutively through; the Old Testament once a year, and the New Testament twice. The Old Testament Lessons on Sundays have a sequence of their own, while the festivals for which proper Lessons are appointed are comparatively few.

It is difficult to overestimate the immense value, from a devotional point of view, of this arrangement of the Lectionary. It gives one a knowledge of the Holy Bible such as nothing else will do. Priests who have recited the Office day by day for years and years find that the Holy Scriptures are continually opening out new depths and appealing to them with new force. Therefore among the advantages of our English form of the Divine Office we put emphatically the arrangement of our Lectionary.

The Canticles. We divide the Canticles into two classes. On the one hand, in our English Office we treat *Te Deum* and *Benedicite* as Canticles, whereas, in the old Office, they would have ranked among the Psalms.

On the other hand, we have the Canticles proper— viz., the Gospel Songs. In the morning, *Benedictus*, the Song of Zacharias. In the evening, *Magnificat*, the Song of Mary.

These Canticles stand on an especial footing. In the mind of the Church they occupy a peculiar position. Where the Office is solemnly sung, it is at the *Benedictus* at Lauds, or at the *Magnificat* at Vespers, that the Altar, Officiants, and people are solemnly censed. These Gospel Songs are, as it were, the culminating point of the Divine Office. For in the old arrangement of the Hours of Prayer it was only Lauds and Vespers, that ranked as the greater hours, that would be solemnly sung with Cope and Incense. If we study the Breviary we see in a moment that these two Hours exactly correspond to each other, and stand out among the Offices of the day. Thus, *Benedictus* is the crowning point of the Morning Office, and *Magnificat* of the Evening.

Our Evening Office being a combination of Vespers and Compline, *Nunc Dimittis*, the Canticle of Compline, is sung as well as *Magnificat*, but, according to old custom, does not stand quite on the footing of *Benedictus* and *Magnificat*.

The Collects. Quite at the end of the Office come the Collects, or prayers of petition.

Now, let us notice here the great and striking difference between the Church and all other forms of Christianity in respect of the place proportionately held in the Offices (or form of Prayer) by praise and petition respectively.

In the Church, the Glory of God in the Incarnation of the Eternal Son is the ruling idea to which all else is subservient. As in the Divine Model—the Lord's Prayer—petition in respect of our needs holds quite a subordinate place. Thus in the Divine Office we find invariably that the bulk of the Office consists of Psalms, Lessons, and Gospel Songs. Then, quite at the end, come two or three short prayers of petition. And not only so, but the old traditional rule of the Church lays down the principle that the greater the feasts the fewer the prayers.

Now, contrast with this unvarying order in the Church the customs and usages of Protestantism.

In the sects that discard (as most do) any set form for their devotion, the devotional exercises consist, as we have seen, in the main, of subjective hymns and extempore prayer. No wonder that the Lord's Prayer should be omitted occasionally from their devotional exercises ! The contrast between its principle and theirs is so glaring. I remember, many years ago, a poor man in the West Country finding his way into a Baptist meeting-house. He stayed and listened awhile; but finding that the Lord's Prayer was not said, he came out, remarking, like a sensible man, that if the Lord's Prayer was not said, that was no place for him !

But the inevitable trend of Protestant thought peeps out even where a sect plumes itself on having an elaborate set form of prayer.

The Irvingite sect, as we have seen, arrogates to itself the sonorous title of " Catholic Apostolic Church."

It is very ritualistic, with vestments, lights, and incense !

But if anyone finds himself at Irvingite Evening Prayer, he will soon see that that is no place for a Catholic Christian.

Let us think about this extraordinary function. There is a certain amount of pomp and show. There is an officiant in a violet cope and seven people in albs, each with a different coloured stole, and a deacon with a red stole. Very smart ! But the " Evening Prayer " !

It seems to be mainly a congeries of petitions, sounding like tags from the Litany. In the middle of this medley comes *Magnificat* with incense, the incense (perhaps needless to say) being used as it is used in no other part of Christendom.

Quite so ! The Irvingites set to work to invent an Evening Prayer, and at once their Protestantism became apparent. For all their high-flown title, and for all their pinchbeck ritualism, they stand confessed as Protestants of the Protestant. The Christian proportion of praise and prayer are just reversed, and the magnificent idea of the Hours of Prayers has dwindled to a sort of hashed-up family prayer with a few *purpurei panni* of ritual scattered over it.

The prominence of petition would strike one at once.

The Collects in our Offices are three; the first being the Collect of the day, the two others being always the same throughout the year.

The Collect of the day ! Here arises the question on any given day, " What is the Collect of the day ?" or, rather, " What is ' the ' day ?" Ordinarily the answer to this question is easy enough. On an ordinary day, or feria, the Collect of the previous Sunday is the Collect of the day. On a Festival or holy day, the Collect for the Festival or holy day is the Collect of the day, the ferial Collect being only the Collect of the day in the absence of anything better. Festivals begin (as the rubric is careful to remind us) at the Evensong before, or " First Evensong," as it would be technically called. So far so good ! This all seems plain sailing.

But suppose two Festivals occur on the same day, what are you going to do then ? What, then, is the " Collect of the day " ? Supposing, for instance, an Apostle's day falls on a Sunday; or, suppose it falls on a Monday, so that the second Evensong of the Sunday coincides with the first Evensong of the Apostle. Or suppose that Lady Day falls on one of the days of Holy Week, or that St. Mark's Day were to fall on Easter Day, or Easter Monday. What, under such or like circumstances, will be the " Collect of the day " ?

Now, your average Englishman, in his blundering, downright way, scorns to enter into such details, and thinks it rather fine to know nothing whatever about them. He will settle it somehow or other, when the time comes, by " rule of thumb." But, however small the matter may seem, it has got to be settled somehow or other; and if the Office is worth saying at all, it is worth saying rightly and well.

Many years ago there were great searchings of heart at Oxford Cathedral, because Lady Day in that year fell on Maundy Thursday, and great were the questionings and agitations as to what was to be done. Now, one would have supposed that, inasmuch as a " Quire or place where they sing " exists for the purpose of the uninterrupted solemn recitation of the Divine Office, the Chapter officials would have made it their business to know exactly what was to be done. But no ! These good people had no principle on which to settle the matter, so they fell back upon "rule of thumb," and rather congratulated themselves on having made a neat and ingenious combination of two such totally different days as Lady Day and Maundy Thursday; and a pretty hash they must have made of it !

And not many years ago we had floods of correspondence in Church papers as to Lady Day and Holy Week, and wondrous and abstruse theories were formulated. All this is very pitiful and absurd. Surely there must be a principle on which these questions are decided, and to which they may be referred as occasion arises. Where shall we find our principle ? Surely in this—viz., that in the absence of specific directions in the English Prayer-Book as to the concurrence of festivals, the old rules and customs hold good. Those old rules can easily be ascertained from the old Service Books, or they can be found in every copy of the Roman Breviary of to-day.

Those rules are based upon a principle; the principle —*i.e.*, of the comparative rank of Holy Days. According to the comparative rank of the Holy Days that concur, the one will take precedence of the other. Thus, for instance, the Apostle's Day would take precedence of an ordinary Sunday, but would not take precedence of a Sunday in Advent or Lent; while no Festival at all could be kept in any way in Holy Week, Easter Week, or Whitsun Week, but must be kept on the first vacant day after those solemn seasons. How simple and easy things become when we get our feet down upon a principle ! And how pitiful and undignified is the spectacle of priests floundering about in a bog of perplexity, because they scorn to learn the ruling principle, and think it clever to go by rule of thumb !

Then, in connection with this matter of the concurrence of Festivals, there arises the interesting question of " commemorations "—*i.e.*, that if two Holy Days are to be kept on the same day, the greater of the two gives the " Collect of the day," while the lesser of the two is " commemorated " by its Collect being said after the " Collect of the day." Thus, if an Apostle's Day falls on an ordinary Sunday, the Apostle's Collect is the " Collect of the day," the Lessons equally being of the Apostle's Day; but the Collect for the Sunday is said immediately after the Apostle's Collect, as a " commemoration." How often it happens that priests make stupid mistakes in respect of commemorations. Perhaps they fail to commemorate the Sunday, or perhaps (which is very common indeed) they say the Sunday Collect after the Festival Collect on an ordinary weekday, which is ridiculous and absurd, because the Sunday Collect only becomes the Collect for the weekday if nothing better intervenes.

We have an interesting reminder of commemorations in the rubric as to the Advent Sunday Collect being used every day in Advent, and the Ash Wednesday Collect every day in Lent; the reason of this direction being that, according to old rule, weekdays in Advent and Lent are " greater Ferias," which can never be passed over. In the same way, Sundays in Advent and Lent are greater Sundays; so that, if a Festival falls on those Sundays it cannot be kept at all, but must be transferred to the first vacant day.

One more interesting principle may be noticed in respect of Collects—viz., the old principle that the greater the Feast, the fewer the prayers. Thus while Collects may be multiplied on ordinary days, on Festivals they are not multiplied. Three or five

Prayer-Book Offices

Collects might be said on ordinary days, but on Festivals one " Collect of the day " marks the day as being great.

How excellent, in view of the prevailing scepticism of the day, would be a commemoration of the Blessed Trinity and of the Incarnation on ordinary Sundays, the Collects for Trinity Sunday and Lady Day being used for such commemoration. Or, again, in view of the appalling divisions of Christendom, how well might such a commemoration of the Peace of the Church be made as the Collect for SS. Simon and Jude provides. And if on ordinary Sundays three Collects be thus said, how striking is the one Collect that, according to the old rule, would mark a Festival.

Most edifying and beautiful is the Divine Office when carefully and accurately recited. Most unedifying (to say the least of it) if it is delivered over to " rule of thumb."

There seems to be an idea in the English mind that accuracy as to detail interferes with spirituality. It is popularly supposed that a man is to consider himself too absorbed in the meaning of the words he is reciting to be able to stoop to think if he is saying the right words. This is sheer nonsense. Slovenliness is not synonymous with spirituality; and if a man scorns to know how to recite the Divine Office properly, this does not mean spirituality; it merely connotes crass ignorance or culpable negligence.

CHAPTER XII

PSALMS, LESSONS, AND CANTICLES

WE have seen that the main structure of the Divine Office consists of Psalms, Lessons, and Canticles, with Prayers and Collects right at the end. This is Catholic (*i.e.*, Universal), and therefore ranks in importance far ahead of what is merely " English," or local anywhere. Our English Offices naturally fall into the form they do because they exhibit the unvarying order that the Divine Office assumes throughout the Church.

In the present chapter we will set before ourselves some considerations, from the devotional point of view, in respect of the Psalms, the Lessons, and the Canticles. But first we must emphasize certain broad principles as regards the recitation of the Divine Office, which must be strangely forgotten or overlooked before it can be possible for English people to think, as apparently they do, that Matins and Evensong do not commit them to much—that anybody can " go to Church " and join in Matins and Evensong— while Communion implies a good deal. People seem to look upon the Divine Office as a sort of worship of the outer court, where people need not be so particular as they would have to be if they advanced into the inner shrine of the Eucharist. Is not this thought largely at the bottom of that substitution of Matins for the Eucharist that is, alas! so largely the rule amongst us?

Now, as against any such idea as this we must set first the consideration of the intention with which the Divine Office is recited. What is the intention with which we come to assist at Matins or Evensong? We must, of course, have some idea in our mind of what we are about. We must have some reason why we do that particular thing rather than any other thing. What is that reason?

Probably, if we had to formulate a reason why our worship should take that particular form, we should say that it is because we are Church-people, and that is the form in which the Church worships. Exactly! In other words, our " intention " in reciting the Divine Office is the " intention " of the Church.

Now, we have seen that the " intention " of the Church in the recitation of the Divine Office is the commemoration of the Hours of the Passion. The intention of the Church is that every day should be a remembrance of that first Good Friday. Matins commemorates our Lord going out to meet His Passion on Good Friday morning; and Evensong commemorates His being taken down dead from the Cross and laid in Joseph's grave.

This is the intention with which the Church recites the Divine Office, and this, therefore, is the intention with which any of us recite the Offices of the Church, if we have any intention in it at all.

Either, then, our assisting at the Offices has no " intention "—we have no meaning in the recitation of Matins or Evensong—or else they carry us into these great depths: Matins commemorating the early hours of our Lord's Passion, and Evensong the close of that Passion. If Matins and Evensong mean anything at all, they mean this.

And that being so, we see at once that this leads us to the second of our broad principles—viz., that the reciting of the Divine Office presupposes that the person who recites it is in a state of grace. And the reason of this is obvious. It is clearly nothing but a mockery to commemorate the Passion of our Lord if we are wilfully continuing to live in that very sin which it was the purpose of His Passion to "take away." If we do not care enough about sin to repent of it, we cannot care enough about the Passion of our Lord to wish to commemorate it.

Now, put these two thoughts together: (*a*) the thought of the intention of the Divine Office, and (*b*) the thought that it presupposes a state of grace; and then suddenly think of Choral Matins in a "moderate" London church at 11 or 11.30 on a Sunday morning. We should find that a good proportion of the congregation are what is vulgarly called "non-Communicants"; that is, that they are people who never go to Communion; or, to bring it down to a point, they are people who have not made their Easter Communion. Such persons, of course, are living in sin. For it is just as really sin to break the First or the Fourth Commandments as it is to break the Seventh or the Eighth. That being so, why can they possibly wish to commemorate the Passion of our Lord ? What possible meaning can such commemoration have for them ? They never thought about "intention." They "go to Church" because it is the thing to do; but they have not repented, and are not repenting of their sins. They go to Matins because it is a nice bright "choral service," and, as they think, does not commit them to anything in particular. Of course, they feel that they could not go to Communion in the state in which they are; but anyone can "go to Church." That does not commit them to anything. But what can taking God's Holy Name in vain mean, if it is not taking God's Name in vain to recite an Office in commemoration of the Passion, when, at the same moment, we are deliberately continuing to sin, our sins being unforgiven because unrepented ? Do let us knock on the head altogether that idea that a man can "go to Church" if he is not fit to go to Communion. If he is not fit for Communion, it can only be because he is out of a state of grace; but if he is out of a state of grace, he certainly cannot commemorate the Hours of the Passion of our Lord.

And this leads us to the third great broad principle as regards the Divine Office that it is most needful that we should bear in mind—viz., the principle of Authority.

We have seen that Church worship is, always and in every place, the worship of the whole Church. Every Eucharist is the offering, not of this or that particular congregation, but of the whole Church— that is to say, of Jesus Christ and the members of His Body. So, too, the Divine Office, wherever it is recited, is the voice of the whole Church—that is to say, of Jesus Christ and the members of His Body.

And this fact emphasizes the necessity of being in a state of grace; for if any individual is, at any moment, out of a state of grace, he can have neither part nor lot in the voice of Jesus Christ and the members of His Body. "Unto the ungodly, said God, why dost thou preach My laws *and takest My Covenant* in thy mouth "?

But beyond this, the principle of Authority bids us be very careful as to how the Divine Office is recited. For what makes the Divine Office the voice of the whole Church—" the voice of the Bridegroom and the voice of the Bride"—is that it is recited according to the form set forth by Authority in any given part of the Church.

We English Churchmen do not recite the Office in the Prayer-Book form because we consider it better or more beautiful than the form in the Roman Breviary, but because it is the form imposed upon us by the Authority of the Church. And we cannot help seeing how this great fact is forgotten or overlooked amongst us. Let us give two or three examples of this failure to grasp the principle of Authority.

We sometimes find clergy, who are under the obligation of the Divine Office, speaking slightingly and contemptuously of the English Offices. They say them, but they do not seem to regard them as the Divine Office. Now, surely, a very little thought ought to show us that what makes the Office the voice of the whole Church is that it bears the stamp of authority. Suppose a Roman Priest were to say that he preferred to say the Office after the Eastern form, or that a Russian Priest were to prefer to say his Office after the Roman form, in either case it would lack the one thing needful—viz., the authority of the Church. The Eastern form in the East, the Roman form in the dioceses under the Roman obedience, and the English form in the English provinces, is, in each of those parts of the Church, the authoritative form, and therefore the voice of the whole Church. It is only

Psalms, Lessons, and Canticles

quite recently that the Roman Breviary has become the authoritative form throughout the Roman Communion, and even now it is not the authoritative form in the Diocese of Milan. It does not matter what particular form the Office takes. What does matter is that it should be the authorized form.

Take, again, that tampering with the Prayer-Book Office that is, alas! not uncommon amongst us. Clergy seem to think that they may pick and choose Psalms and Lessons for themselves. Now, what is the result of this? The result is that it is not the Divine Office at all. It has become merely the family prayer of a particular congregation. When Priests allow themselves to tamper with the Office in this way, they are robbing the Church of the Divine Office. If they had any adequate idea of what the Office is, they could not act in this way.

And what shall we say about clergy who will not say the Athanasian Creed when it is ordered by Authority?

Well, we will not go into their reasons, but we will merely say that on those days they have not said the Divine Office; they have not commemorated the Hours of the Passion of our Lord. They may have said a more or less edifying family prayer for a congregation, but it was not " the Voice of the Bridegroom and the Voice of the Bride."

Why should Priests play tricks of their own with the Divine Office? It is far too serious a thing to be trifled with. The authority of the Church is what makes the Divine Office the Voice of the Bridegroom and the Voice of the Bride. How sad if, by tampering with that authority to please ourselves, we should rob it of that universal character and make it merely the family prayers of a little congregation!

Prayer-Book Ideals

In laying down these three great broad principles, we have said enough to show that the recitation of the Divine Office is a very serious matter indeed, and lays us open to very grave responsibilities. If a man thinks that he will be all right for Matins or Evensong while he shrinks from the responsibilities of the Eucharist and Sacramental Communion, it only shows that he has no adequate conception at all of what the Divine Office is, and of what the reciting of it implies.

And now, with this sense of the seriousness of the Divine Office well before us, we will take some of the salient points of the Office, and set before ourselves one or two considerations about them from the devotional point of view.

The Psalter.—The Psalter, or Book of Psalms, is the main part of the Divine Office. We may roughly divide the Psalms into three classes: (1) Psalms of Penitence; (2) Psalms of Imprecation; (3) Psalms of Praise. We do not mean that they are rigidly blocked off under these three divisions, but that this is their threefold spirit.

Think a moment of Psalms of Penitence. We are struck, of course, at once by the recurrence of the words " I " and " my," " my sins," " my soul," etc. Now, at once we must ask ourselves who is this person who is speaking in the Psalms of Penitence. Whose sins ? Whose soul ? etc. When you say these Psalms whom are you thinking about ?

Let us go into a fashionable London church on a Sunday morning that happens, we will say, to be the eighth day of the month. It is past eleven. The congregation have had a good breakfast at a not too early hour, and are comfortable and at ease in their best

clothes. The organ is playing, and the choir and congregation are singing. Let us hear what they are
saying. Listen : " Put me not to rebuke, O Lord,
in Thine anger, neither chasten me in Thy heavy displeasure." " My sins have taken such hold upon me
that I am not able to look up; yea, they are more in
number than the hairs of my head, and my heart hath
failed me." " Thine arrows stick fast in me, and Thy
hand presseth me sore." " There is no health in my
body because of Thy displeasure; neither is there any
rest in my bones by reason of my sin." " My wounds
stink and are corrupt through my foolishness," etc.
So the singing goes on. What does it all mean ?
Whose sins ? Whose body ? Whose bones ? Who
has God's arrows stuck fast in him ? These well-
dressed people who sing these words so calmly, these
well-dressed people who have managed to get to church
by eleven or half-past eleven do not seem to represent
all this !

Let us ask one of them what they mean when they
sing this Psalm, and what will they say ? Probably
they do not know in the least what they mean. Perhaps
they have never been to Communion, and do not
intend to go. They have " come to Church " because
they did not think it mattered much. It is just
" Choral Matins," and they suppose it is all right.

But we know whose voice this is that is speaking
in this anguish of soul. It is the Voice of the Bridegroom, the Voice of Jesus Christ. He has so " borne
our griefs and carried our sorrows " that He has made
them His own. It is His dear Bones in which there is
no rest, by reason of the sin that He deigns to call
His own. It is He in whom the arrows of God's
justice " stick fast." It is His Voice from Gethsemane

bowed down in His Agony and Bloody Sweat; His
Voice from where He has fallen beneath the weight of
our sins, on the ground that He made. It is the Voice
of the Bridegroom. And inasmuch as Christ and His
Church are one, it is the Voice of the Bride. These
words can only be ours because we are one with Him.
So throughout the Psalms of Penitence we have the
Voice of the Bridegroom and the Voice of the Bride.
What a wonderful and solemn thing it is to recite the
Matins of the eighth day, or the Evensong of the fourth
day !

Then, think a moment of the Psalms of Imprecation.
People allow themselves to say dreadful things about
the Psalms of Imprecation. Your average Englishman thinks it is not quite nice to say such things about
enemies. It does not seem to occur to him that it is
a terrible thing for him to sit in judgment on the words
of God !

We will go into our London church on a Sunday
that happens to be the twenty-second day of the month.
It is Evensong, and the choir and congregation are
singing again. What are they singing now ? Listen :
" When sentence is given upon him let him be condemned; and let his prayer be turned into sin." " His
delight was in cursing, and it shall happen unto him;
he loved not blessing, therefore shall it be far from
him." " Let it thus happen from the Lord unto
mine enemies; and to those that speak evil against
my soul." What are these people talking about ?
What do they mean ? They thought it quite a simple
and easy thing to go to Matins or Evensong; it did
not seem to mean anything much. And yet, how deep
we must get into the counsels of God to understand at
all His hatred of evil ! Who is it that is speaking in

this Psalm? About whose enemies is the Psalm speaking? Who is crying for the vengeance of God? Whose voice is it? It is the Voice of the Bridegroom. The enemies are the enemies of God and of the Lamb; those enemies of whom it is said that they shall all be put under the feet of our Lord. Those who finally and persistently oppose themselves to God are the enemies of God. Evil cannot be permanent if God is God. To think that evil can permanently set up its throne against the throne of God is to deny the very existence of God. " O ye that love the Lord, see that ye hate the thing that is evil." It is the Voice of the Bridegroom speaking out of the ruling Passion of His Sacred Heart, the Passion for the Glory of God, that speaks in these Psalms.

And it is the Voice of the Bride. Just in proportion as the children of the Church are in union with Jesus Christ will the Glory of God, and therefore the hatred of evil, be the ruling passion of their life. The Church never condemns an individual. She never says of any given soul that it is lost. That is left to the infallible judgment of our Lord. But the hatred of evil, the hatred of the enemies of God, is the reverse side of the love of God; and the sentiment of comparative indifference to evil, which is so characteristic of our time, is the sure sign of want of love of God. And therefore we ask ourselves whether our London congregation who are chanting this Psalm really know what they are about. Can it be in them the passionate expression of the love of God that it is in the Voice of the Bridegroom and the Voice of the Bride? And yet it is thought a perfectly simple and easy thing to do to go to Matins and Evensong—a thing that need commit us to nothing very particular !

One word as to the Psalms of Praise. Again, they are the Voice of the Bridegroom and the Voice of the Bride. Praise from the creature to the Creator can only come through the Mediation of the Sacred Humanity. "No man cometh unto the Father but by Me." Praise is impossible for any creature that is not at the moment in living relation to Jesus Christ. Cain may bring his offering, but the Lord does not "have respect" to it; and we are told that the sacrifice of the wicked is abomination in the sight of God. A sacrifice it may be, but a sacrifice that is a mockery of God, and therefore an increase of damnation. Go again to our London church on the thirtieth day of the month. Again the well-dressed congregation are singing with the choir. What are they saying now? "O sing unto the Lord a new song: let the congregation of saints praise Him. Let Israel rejoice in Him that made him: and let the children of Sion be joyful in their King." Here, again, is the Voice of the Bridegroom and the Voice of the Bride; the Voice of Jesus Christ and the Voice of His Church. Have all these people considered whether they have a right to such words? "Children of Sion!" Are they children of Sion? "Their King!" Is Jesus Christ their King? They need the Mediator that day for their praise quite as much as they will need Him in the hour of death and in the Day of Judgment. How *can* men think that anyone is fit to "go to Church," and that if it is only Matins or Evensong, it commits them to nothing?

Now for a thought about the Lessons. The Bible is all about the Incarnation of our Lord, and nothing else at all in the world. The Lessons in the Divine Office are always the proclamation of the truth that the Seed of the Woman bruises the head of the serpent; the truth that salvation is in Christ, and in Him alone; the truth is that nothing but our fellowship in Christ stands between any one of us and the eternal damnation of hell. Of every one of us it is true that we are either saved by our fellowship in Christ, or are lost. Let us go back to our London congregation at Choral Matins. The Psalms are over, and they are seated for the Lesson. It may be the Lesson about Esau and Jacob; it may be the Lesson about Hagar and Ishmael; it may be the Lesson about David and Saul. What does it mean to them? It is the Voice of Christ and His Church. But are they in that vital union with the Church of Christ that makes that Lesson the echo of the profound conviction of their own soul that their one and only hope, their one and only plea before God, is that they are, through grace, at that moment, one with Christ in the fellowship of His Mystical Body? We cannot think it. Too many of them have come to Matins as a substitute for the Eucharist, because they thought it meant nothing much, and committed them to nothing in particular. What can the history of the Covenant be to a man who is at that moment outside of that Covenant?

The Canticles.—The Office culminates, as we have seen, in the glorious Gospel songs of the Incarnation. These blessed songs are pre-eminently the Voice of Jesus Christ and of His Church. They gather up, and focus at one point, all that we have striven to express in the rest of the Office. They are the irrepressible cry of redeemed Creation. They are the daily expression of our conviction that we are saved by the grace of our Lord Jesus Christ. What can it possibly be to me that God has visited and redeemed His people, if I am not myself in a state of grace? What can it possibly be to me that God has delivered His people out of the hands of the enemy, if I myself am, at that moment, in the bondage of unforgiven sin?

To the average Englishman, Matins may represent a sort of family prayer from the creature to the Supreme Providence Who has created him. To the true Christian it is the glad song of those who know that they are redeemed by the Precious Blood.

If we will but lay these things to our heart, we shall see that, so far from Matins and Evensong being the Outer Court of the Temple, they represent the very inmost shrine, the Holy of Holies of God. If any " profane man " dare to recite the Office in a state of sin, how terrible is that sin! It is the breaking of the Third Commandment, pure and simple. How *can* people think that they are fit to " go to church " if they are not fit to go to Communion?

Let us, in conclusion, sum up the whole matter quite shortly.

1. " There is one God, and one Mediator between God and men, the Man Christ Jesus."

" Everlasting salvation is offered to men through Christ, Who is the One Mediator between God and men, being both God and Man."

This is the sum and substance of the Christian religion. Nothing short of this can be called Christian in any sense of the word.

2. God delivers His people out of darkness that He may bring them into light. He brings His people out of Egypt, that He may bring them into Canaan. In

the pregnant sentence of the Holy Bible, " He brought them out that He might bring them in." We are delivered from our enemies that we may serve Him. The bringing out of Egypt, the deliverance from our enemies, is but a preliminary, a means to an end. The positive side of it, the *raison d'être* of the deliverance, is that we may dwell in His Church and serve Him.

3. The Catholic Faith is this, that we worship. Without true worship there is no religion. We have tried to think out the philosophy of worship, and we bring it down to a point in the Prayer-Book worship which is the authoritative worship for an English Christian; the true worship of Eucharist and Divine Office, not of Divine Office as a substitute for the Eucharist. This can never be. The Eucharist is, as we have seen, *the* Divine Service instituted by our Lord Himself; the Divine Office is the expression of the instinct of the Catholic Church as the supplement to, not a substitute for, Divine Service. The worship of God is the exclusive prerogative of the children of God. It is not a means that may ultimately bring us to forgiveness; it presupposes that forgiveness, without which it is impossible. It is only because we have been brought out of Egypt that we can dwell in Canaan. We cannot sing the Lord's song in a strange land; it is only just in so far as, and because, we are children of Sion that we can sing the songs of Sion and rejoice in our King. Oh, that we would understand and lay hold of this great truth ! Then would the words of the Church's great song be the daily expression of daily experience: " Blessed be the Lord God of Israel; for He hath visited and redeemed His people; and hath raised up a mighty salvation for us in

the house of His servant David; as He spake by the mouth of His holy prophets, which have been since the world began, that we, being delivered out of the hands of our enemies, might serve Him without fear, in holiness and righteousness before Him all the days of our life."

PART II

IDEALS OF LIFE

CHAPTER XIII

THE PRAYER-BOOK MAN

UP to this point we have been considering the Prayer-Book ideals of worship. We now turn to think of the Prayer-Book ideals of life.

But in making this division for the purpose of clearness, let us be quite sure that this is a division in thought only, for convenience' sake. There is no real distinction between worship and life. For worship is life summed up in a point; and life is worship consistently carried out. Do let us, in the face of modern English thought and practice, get our feet firm down on the bed-rock of a great principle; and let us express this great unvarying principle in two terms:

1. There can be no true life without true worship.
2. There can be no true worship without true life.

And having safeguarded ourselves by the reassertion of this great fact, we may now betake ourselves to the Prayer-Book ideal of life, as distinguishable (though in thought only) from the Prayer-Book ideal of worship at which we have already glanced.

And here let us once more remind ourselves that inasmuch as Catholicity is the test of truth in Faith, Worship, and Morals, and inasmuch as the " Church of England " is that integral portion of the Catholic Church planted among English-speaking people, therefore it follows that the Prayer-Book ideal is the Catholic ideal. So that the " Prayer-Book man " is man as God intends him to be.

Let us, then, in this Chapter, try and see the broad, general outline of that great phonemenon, the Prayer-Book man. And we speak advisedly of the " phenomenon " of the Prayer-Book man. The life of the Catholic Christian is *the* phenomenon of the world in all places and at all times.

When Père Lacordaire began his famous Conference at Nôtre Dame to try to win back the men of France to the Faith that so many of them had lost, he did not start from abstract ideas at all. He did not begin by a disquisition on right and wrong, for that would have been for them debatable ground. He did not begin with the thought of God, for numbers of them did not believe in God. He started from a solid patent fact that the sturdiest unbelievers could not attempt to deny. Men may fence with abstract ideas, but " facts are stubborn things." So he began by appealing to a solid fact patent before their eyes : and that fact was the phenomenon of the Catholic Church. Whether they liked it or whether they did not; whether they thought it right or whether they thought it wrong, there it was before their eyes a Society of men quite apart from all other men, with different thoughts, different aims, and different ideals from all other men.

" Now," practically says Père Lacordaire, " you must account for this phenomenon, for there can be no effect without a cause."

So in considering the standard of life set before us Englishmen in the Prayer-Book, we have to account for the appearance amongst us of such a phenomenon as the Prayer-Book man. Here is a life that is clean contrary to the ordinary life of the children of this world. How comes it that it exists at all.?

In attempting to answer this initial question we lay our finger upon the point that the life of the Prayer-Book man is *professedly supernatural*. It does not for a moment pretend to be anything else. The Prayer-Book never professes to teach men how to be Christians. Of the Prayer-Book Man—*i.e.*, the Catholic Christian—we say, as is said of a poet : " Nascitur non fit." He must be born to it; you cannot make him into it.

It is of the extremest importance that we should recognize this unfaltering claim made by the Prayer-Book Man. He exhibits a standard of life which is altogether different from the standard of all other Englishmen (and, as we shall see, is immeasurably higher and more noble than the standard of other Englishmen), and he proclaims from the first that he is only able to raise his life to this standard by a power that is wholly supernatural. The Prayer-Book Man lives emphatically " by faith."

He starts with the assumption that he has been born again. He never professes for a moment to base his life upon any other foundation. He claims a supernatural origin for his wonderful life. His Baptism is confessedly the beginning and the cause of everything that follows. He is able to receive the seven gifts of the Spirit in Confirmation because, and only because, he is a child of God. His spiritual life is nourished and sustained by Sacramental Communion because Communion is " the Children's Bread," and he can claim to be one of the children whose Bread it is.

If he falls into sin and wanders away from his Father's Home, he is able, at any moment that he " comes to himself," to return to that Home because he has rights there as being his Father's child: and Sacramental Absolution is the receiving back into the Home of a child of God who has strayed away from his natural place.

His Marriage, again, is based upon his Baptism. Because he has been born again, and in that new birth has been made a child of God, he is able to enter upon the awful sanctity of that " great mystery." The key to, and the secret of, his married life is that " God has consecrated the holy estate of matrimony to such an excellent mystery that in it is signified and represented the spiritual marriage and unity that is between Christ and His Church."

His attitude towards sickness and death, as towards all the afflictions of life, is again based entirely upon his baptism. Because he is a member of Christ, it is mere common sense to him that " there should be no greater joy to a Christian man than to be made like unto Christ." That the Head should go one way and the members another would be sheer nonsense to him.

And as with sickness so with death. Death is no surprise to the Prayer-Book Man, because the very essence and meaning of his life is that he was baptized into Christ's Death that so, and so only, he might be partaker of His Resurrection. And so, in death as in life, he says, " I look for the Resurrection of the dead and the Life of the world to come " : and the Prayer-Book Man, being professedly only the child of God, and the member of Christ, is laid in his grave " in sure and certain hope of the Resurrection to Eternal Life through our Lord Jesus Christ." The whole *raison d'être* of the life of the Prayer-Book Man is that he believes himself to be endowed with a new and supernatural life. Unbelievers may say that they think he is mistaken in his belief. They may, as they do, scorn the whole estimate of the Prayer-Book as to faith, worship, and morals. But one thing they cannot do. With the Prayer-Book as with the Bible, they cannot eliminate the supernatural without tearing the whole thing to tatters: and with the Prayer-Book as with the Bible, their attempts to do so are as ridiculous as they are dishonest, and that makes them very, very ridiculous indeed.

Now let us pass to another bird's-eye view of the Prayer-Book Man.

He claims not only that by virtue of his Baptism he has a different nature from other men, but that by virtue of his Baptism he has entered upon a definite and distinct covenant with God; and that all his duties, moral and religious (if we like to make such a division), spring directly out of that definite covenant.

His education is based upon this fact. Education! that thorny subject that attracts so much attention at the present moment!

The Prayer-Book Man has quite clear and definite ideas about education. He knows how it is to begin. He knows what is the first thing that a child of God is to be taught, " so soon as it be able to learn "—whether it goes to a Board School or not, it is to learn, *first of all*, the obligation of being under a definite and distinct covenant. Madame Swetchine has a very pithy saying: " Je veux bien qu'on soit Saint, mais surtout qu'on soit honnête homme." It is a fine thing to be a Saint, but one must begin by being honest, and the Prayer-Book Man's education begins by his being taught that it is *not* honest to enter into a solemn covenant, and to turn round and repudiate it directly he thinks it convenient to do so ! And so the first thing he is taught is the obligation of his covenant, that he may, at least, be an honest man.

And as the education begins, so it goes on. Anyone who takes but a cursory glance at the Catechism, must see that it is entirely based upon the fact of Baptism and the Baptismal Covenant. Unbelievers and half-hearted Christians may not, and do not, like this; but they cannot eliminate the Baptismal Covenant from the Catechism without tearing the whole thing to pieces. And as his education is, so will the man be. The Prayer-Book Man stands firm on the rock of his definite covenant. He has learnt, at least, to be an honest man. And so he knows, and rejoices to know, that for him the door of unlimited speculation on theological and moral questions is definitely and finally closed by the terms of his covenant. He is an honest man, and so will honestly abide by the terms of his covenant.

Of course the unbelievers will make merry over this. They will say that it is such a slavish and miserable thing to be in any way limited in thought or action. Of course they will; and of course we know where this comes from. They are the followers of him who said : " I will exalt my throne above the stars of God. . . . I will ascend above the heights of the clouds; I will be like the Most High." They are the lineal descendants of the men who said: " Let us make us a tower whose top may reach to Heaven." They make themselves the supreme arbiters of all things in Heaven and earth and under the earth.

But the Prayer-Book Man knows quite well how to answer their taunts. Licence is not liberty. You would not call it an exercise of liberty if a man were

The Prayer-Book Man

to put out his eyes in order that he might be able to say that he could not see that there is a sun in the heavens. Nor is moral licence liberty. We should hardly call it an exercise of liberty that a man should ruin his health and his reason by plunging into unrestricted debauchery.

But this is a merely negative answer to the taunt. The Prayer-Book Man has a positive answer to give which is more weighty still. He does not speculate, *because he knows*. He leaves it to those who do not know to air their ridiculous speculations. He knows that as the fear of the Lord is perfect wisdom, so the service of God is perfect freedom. It is the old story of the fox who, having lost his tail in the trap, tried to persuade the other foxes that it was much better, and much more dignified, to be without a tail. So the unbelievers, being in the outer darkness of ignorance themselves as to God and His Creation, being in the outer darkness as to theological and moral truth, want to persuade the Prayer-Book Man that it is a splendid thing to be ignorant. But his answer will be, " No, thank you ! You may speculate if you like; but I happen to know." He is not going to come down from the liberty and heights of knowledge, to grope and grovel with them in the dark. The Prayer-Book Man, then, in spite of the sneers of unbelievers, considers that he is bound by the terms of his solemn covenant. The way of the covenant is the way of life. It is the " state of salvation " of which the Catechism speaks. Sin is the transgression of the covenant. Forgiveness of sin restores him to the status of the covenant. It is all very definite. He knows perfectly well whether he has or has not " a quiet conscience." You cannot read the Prayer-Book and not see how, at every turn of the road of life, the Prayer-Book Man is driven back upon the covenant.

His education, as we have seen, is based upon it. When he comes to receive Confirmation he makes a solemn renewal of the covenant before the Bishop. In his preparation for Communion, it is along the lines of the covenant (" by the rule of God's commandments ") that he is to make his self-examination.

And at the close of his life, the Church, in the Visitation of the Sick, bids him remember the solemn covenant of his Baptism, and judge his life by the terms of that covenant.

There, then, we have the strong outline of the portrait of the Prayer-Book Man. He claims to have and to live a supernatural life; and he lives that life under the terms of a definite and distinct covenant. This is the phenomenon that the Prayer-Book Man presents to the English world. In an age that refuses to believe anything that it cannot see or that transcends in any way the mere natural reason of man, he is frankly supernatural. In an age when men are impatient of any restraint, and set up a purely personal and individual standard of faith and morals, he exhibits the disciplined life of obedience to a definite covenant.

Is not this a phenomenon indeed ? Men must account for this phenomenon, for here it is, and facts are stubborn things.

Did this phenomenon suddenly start up in the year 1662 ? Was it the new invention of the First Prayer-Book of 1549 ? Certainly not. There is nothing new about it at all.

Nor is it exclusively English. North, South, East, and West, we find the same characteristics in the children of the Catholic Church. The life of Catholic Christendom is professedly supernatural, and it is lived in obedience to the terms of a definite covenant. The Prayer-Book Man is not a new phenomenon. The type of life set forth in the Prayer-Book is the type that is universal in Catholic Christendom. It expresses the mind of the One Spirit who indwells the One Body. The Prayer-Book Man is the Abel, the Noah, the Abraham, the Moses of his day. He carries on here in England the tradition of the Apostles, the Martyrs, the Confessors, the Doctors, the Saints of Catholic Christendom. He brings those traditions down to our own doors, in our own day—and will hand them on to the generations of Englishmen that are "yet for to come." He is the stuff out of which Saints are made.

And now, having taken this comprehensive glance at the Prayer-Book Man, it may be useful if we try and see how his leading characteristics will work, how he will be found to act under given circumstances.

The inveterate hatred of the prince of this world for Jesus Christ produces the ceaseless conflict of the world against the Church. If the conflict seems to wane for a moment, it is but for a moment. If one method of attack seems to be failing, the enemy will soon be upon us again from another quarter; and so we find ourselves perpetually face to face with something or other that is called " a burning question," or " a crisis."

What is the attitude of the Prayer-Book Man toward a burning question or a crisis?

His consciousness of supernatural power will keep him from being " fussed " or " upset ": while the steady remembrance of his covenant will ensure that he will not be carried away with any wind of doctrine, theological or moral. Let us take an example of such burning questions (1) in the region of Faith, and (2) in the region of Morals.

1. We have lived to see, in our own day, a question raised by unbelievers outside the camp, and, what is worse, by traitors within the camp, as to the Virginity of the Mother of God. That such a question should be raised at all marks a degree of insolence in impiety that is shocking. It is the reproduction, in our day, of the fetching of the Ark of the Covenant out of the Holy of Holies, and parading it in the battle-field. Specious and shallow appeals to the text of Scripture, under the disintegrating force of what is called Higher Criticism, are brought to bear upon this awful and fundamental truth; and the weak-kneed Christian is cowed and frightened and " upset." But the Prayer-Book Man knows that the Virginity of the Mother of God does not rest upon the interpretation of a text, and does not hang upon a debatable meaning of a Hebrew word. It is an essential part of that body of truth that he has sworn to believe, as part of the terms of his covenant. He is an honest man, and therefore it is simply impossible that an Article of Faith should be, to him, open to question. If he be a man of leisure and culture, who has had time and opportunity to have read Church History, he will know, of course, that there is nothing new in this blasphemous suggestion. It is a mere *réchauffée* of the abomination of Nestorianism, which the Church had to face in the fourth century. He will know that to deny the " Virgin Birth " is to deny the Divinity of Christ—and that, *take it at its best*, such denial lands him in naked Nestorianism.

But the men of leisure and culture are in the minority

—most Christians have neither the time nor the opportunity to study the heresies of the fourth century. But all are partakers of grace, and all Prayer-Book Men have learnt to be honest men; and so, whether learned or simple, they just take their stand upon the terms of the covenant, and their answer to such blasphemous questionings will be : " I believe in Jesus Christ—who was incarnate by the Holy Ghost of the Virgin Mary, and was made man." He will not be timid or anxious; he will be sorrowful and indignant that the honour of God and His Blessed Virgin Mother should thus be trailed in the mud; but he will not be " upset," nor bate one jot of his faith or his honesty— he simply holds to the terms of his covenant.

2. Let us consider how the Prayer-Book Man will act when face to face with the " burning question " of the so-called marriage with a deceased wife's sister.

He will not be shaken or " upset " by foolish arguments from this or that text of Scripture. Even the enemies of Catholic Morality admit that the Church forbids such so-called marriage.

If the Prayer-Book Man is one who has leisure and opportunity to study the question, he will know that the Church's table of forbidden degrees is based upon the principle of the " great mystery " of Holy Matrimony. He will know that that great mystery is connected with the creation of Eve; and he will know how our Lord and His Apostles used the argument of that great mystery, and how it is connected with the mystery of the Oneness of Christ and His Church. He will know also how such marriage is regarded in undivided Christendom.

But if he is not a man of leisure, and has not had opportunity to study the question, he has at any rate learnt to be an honest man; and, having professed to believe in the Holy Catholic Church, and knowing that the Holy Catholic Church has forbidden such marriage, he will simply take his stand upon the terms of his covenant.

The steady conviction, then, that he lives by a supernatural power, and the steady adherence to the terms of a supernatural covenant are the main characteristics of the Prayer-Book Man, because they are the main characteristics of the Children of God in all times and in all places.

And it is just this perseveringly supernatural attitude that is, in all ages and always, the strength of the Church. Church history throughout bears testimony to this fact.

Let us, in conclusion, take one instance out of thousands of the victorious supremacy of this quiet steadfastness. The First Book of Samuel opens with a most depressing picture of religious and moral decadence in the Church. These were dark days in our history. The age of heroes seemed past. The Philistines were still there, the Anti-Christ of the moment, but no Gideon or Samson arose. What central political power there was had drifted into the feeble hands of Eli, while the Tabernacle at Shiloh was become a byword and a proverb through the greed and the gross immorality of Hophni and Phinehas, and one must suppose, of the Priesthood generally. But side by side with all this decadence and corruption, we have the beautiful picture of Elkanah quietly going his way along the lines of the covenant. Everything seemed going by the board; religion had sunk to a frightful depth of degradation. But neither the gloominess of the political outlook nor the awful scenes at Shiloh could upset or move this

The Prayer-Book Man

" Prayer-Book Man." The Priesthood might have made itself vile, so that weak-kneed children of God " abhorred the offering of the Lord." But Elkanah will be true to his covenant in spite of all. In spite of it all we read that Elkanah went up to Shiloh year by year to offer the yearly sacrifice. He did not " give it all up," as people say, because things were in a bad way; nor did he rush into the street to wave the flag of reform. He quietly stood himself on the fixed and unchanging ground of his own covenant. And it was out of this quiet steadfastness that, humanly speaking, Samuel sprang.

So, if our lot is cast, as it is, in most evil and corrupt days, when religion is at a very low ebb, and lawlessness and disobedience flourish, let our part be that of righteous Elkanah. We are not to wring our hands in despair, and, as people so often say, think we must " give it all up "; nor are we to rush into some crude and shallow scheme of reforms, based upon that silly idea that we " must do *something*." We are to revert to our true type, study the Prayer-Book Man, and go tranquilly on in the assurance of supernatural life and strength, and, like honest men, determine at all costs to keep the definite terms of that definite covenant by which we rejoice to find ourselves bound.

CHAPTER XIV

HOLY BAPTISM

WE may now begin to examine in detail the wonderful phenomenon of the Prayer-Book Man. And, of course, we begin with his Baptism.

No one can possibly read the Prayer-Book and not see that, whether it is right or whether it is wrong, the Prayer-Book does, as a simple matter of fact, connect Regeneration with Baptism. Protestant Sectarians may try to explain away our Lord's plain words. They may say, as some do, that " Water " does not mean real water; they may try to argue that Baptism with water is one thing, and that Baptism with the Spirit is quite another; they may scornfully, in their superior wisdom, despise the Church's plain definition of a Sacrament which links together, in one solid whole, the outward visible sign and the inward spiritual grace in an inseparable connection. But we need not waste time over them and their " vain conceits," for our business is with the Prayer-Book, to which, as honest Churchmen, we are bound.

And so we need only just refer to one or two passages (out of many) in support of our statement that the Prayer-Book with no faltering voice does distinctly connect regeneration with the Sacrament of Baptism.

" Forasmuch as . . . our Saviour Christ saith none

can enter into the Kingdom of Heaven, except he be regenerate and born anew of water and of the Holy Ghost; I beseech you to call upon God the Father, through our Lord Jesus Christ, that of His bounteous mercy He will grant to this child that thing which by nature he cannot have; that he may be baptized with Water and the Holy Ghost, and received into Christ's Holy Church, and be made a lively member of the same." And again, immediately after Baptism: " Seeing now, dearly beloved, that this child is re-generate and grafted into the Body of Christ's Church." And in the reception of a child who has been already privately baptized the Church adds the emphatic words to the above statement, and says: " Seeing now, dearly beloved brethren, that this child is *by Baptism* regenerate," etc. And again, at the Baptism of adults, these words occur in one of the prayers: " That they, coming to Thy Holy Baptism, may receive remission of their sins by spiritual regeneration "— words which effectually close the door, as far as the Prayer-Book is concerned, to the Anabaptist perver-sion of the truth—viz., that the regeneration lies in the goodwill of the adult, and that the Baptism is a mere sign of something that has already been done. One might multiply instances *ad infinitum*, but these few specimens will show the mind of the Prayer-Book in the matter; while a steady perusal of that wonderful book will convince any honest reader that to eliminate the truth of Baptismal Regeneration from the Prayer-Book is to tear the whole book to pieces.

It being so, then, that the mind of the Prayer-Book is perfectly clear as to the connection between Regeneration and Baptism, we ask why the Prayer-Book is so emphatic as to this connection. And the answer comes at once: "*Because Baptism is a Sacrament.*" And so we will turn our attention for a moment to the exceedingly accurate, pithy, and pregnant definition of a Sacrament that is given in the Prayer-Book—viz., that it is "an outward visible sign of an inward spiritual grace given unto us, ordained by Christ Himself as a means whereby we receive the same, and a pledge to assure us thereof."

1. We observe that a Sacrament is *one* thing that consists of two parts, the two parts being inseparably linked together and forming together the one whole.

Baptism is a Sacrament. Consequently it consists of an outward visible sign—viz., water—and an inward spiritual grace—viz., Regeneration. Neither the water without the Regeneration, nor the regeneration without the water, would be a Sacrament.

2. We observe that these two parts are connected as cause and effect. The outward visible sign is the means whereby we receive spiritual grace, and it is also the pledge to assure us that we do receive that inward spiritual grace.

If Baptism is reduced, as the Baptists would tell us, to a mere sign of a regeneration that has taken place in some other way, it would occur to us at once that if we are already in possession of the regeneration, it cannot matter much whether we have the outward sign or not; and, as a matter of fact, this is the sensible and logical conclusion that Protestants have mostly come to draw from their premiss. Already even the Wesleyans have come to doubt *officially* whether it is necessary for a man to be baptized in order to be a Wesleyan! But that is not our immediate contention. What we Prayer-Book Christians have to say is that if Baptism be merely an outward visible sign, it cannot be a Sacrament. For it is of the essence of a Sacrament that it consist of an inward spiritual grace, as well as an outward visible sign. If it were possible to eliminate either of these *two* parts, Baptism could not be a Sacrament. The outward visible sign must convey the inward spiritual grace, otherwise it is not a Sacrament.

Men may dislike and disbelieve in the Sacramental system, but with the Prayer-Book definition staring us in the face we shall not allow them to use the word " Sacrament " in a non-natural sense.

The Athanasian Creed gives us the definition of human nature when it tells us that man is " of a reasonable soul and human flesh subsisting." It also tells us that " the reasonable soul and the flesh is one man." Neither the body without the soul, nor the soul without the body, is man. So we say of a Sacrament. Neither the outward visible sign without the inward spiritual grace, nor the inward spiritual grace without the outward visible sign, can possibly be a Sacrament.

But we go much deeper than mere analogy. It is said of the Sacraments that they are the " extension of the Incarnation." Consequently it is more than an accidental analogy that exists between the Sacraments and the Incarnation. The truth about the Incarnation is that there are in our Blessed Lord two whole and perfect natures, yet but One Personality. And it is this fact that accounts for the nature and essence of the Sacraments. The decay of faith in the Sacramental system of the Church is the direct outcome of the decay in the faith in the Incarnation. Protestantism in its attempt to put asunder that which God hath joined together, in its attempt to effect a divorce between the outward visible sign and the inward spiritual grace, is just reproducing in our day the abomination of Nestorius, who attempted to divide the Personality of our Lord.

Baptism is a Sacrament. Therefore the water is the outward visible sign of the inward spiritual grace. It, the water, is the means whereby we receive the inward spiritual grace of regeneration—and the water is the pledge to assure us that we receive the regeneration. If words have any meaning at all, the Sacramental system is embedded in the Prayer-Book. It could not, of course, be otherwise, for the Church of England is merely an integral part of the whole Body of Christ, and cannot set up a new religion of its own. And the unfaltering words of the Prayer-Book are the words of the One Spirit who indwells the One Body.

We must now see something of (1) the outward visible sign of Baptism, and (2) its inward spiritual grace.

The outward visible sign of Baptism is water; but not merely water. It is water wherein the person is baptized in the Name of the Father and of the Son and of the Holy Ghost.

There are, then, three things which together make up the outward visible sign of Baptism:

1. There must be water.

2. The person must be baptized in, or with, the water.

3. The person must be baptized with the water in the Name of the Father and of the Son and of the Holy Ghost. If any of these things are not done, then there is no Sacrament, for the outward visible sign will be lacking.

" Water, wherein the person is baptized." You will

Holy Baptism

see by your Prayer-Book that Baptism by immersion—
i.e., by dipping the person to be baptized into the water
—is the rule of the Church, but that Baptism by
affusion, or pouring water, is permitted and is
expressly said to be sufficient. It is much to be
regretted that throughout the West Baptism by affusion should have come to be the almost universal
practice, Baptism by immersion being quite exceptional. In the East Baptism is administered by
immersion.

A good deal of dust has been thrown in people's eyes
as regards the controversy between the Church and
the Baptists on this very subject of immersion.
Ignorant people are apt to think that the difference
between the Church and the Baptists is that the Baptists baptize by immersion, and the Church by affusion.
But we have no quarrel with the Baptists as regards
immersion. They are perfectly right to baptize by
immersion. Of course, they show their ignorance and
conceit in scornfully disregarding the rest of Western
Christendom, which declares that affusion is sufficient;
still, there is no harm, but quite the reverse, in baptizing
by immersion. But the real difference between the
Church and the Baptists is that the Church believes
Baptism to be a Sacrament, whereas the Baptist, for
all his parade about immersion, regards it merely as
an outward sign of something that has already taken
place. Do not let us confuse the issues as if it were a
question between immersion and affusion. Immersion,
then, is the Church's rule, but affusion suffices. The
water must touch the person to be baptized, otherwise there is no Sacrament. If there is any doubt
in any particular case on either of the three essential
parts of the outward visible sign of Baptism, then the

person is to be conditionally or hypothetically baptized according to the Form given in the Prayer-Book.

We next come to the question as to who is to baptize. Unquestionably, the ordinary minister of Baptism is the Bishop or the Priest. But this is for the safeguarding of the dignity of the Sacrament. We are told in the Prayer-Book that " in the absence of the Priest " the Deacon may baptize. This, of itself, would show that there is nothing exclusively sacerdotal about the administration of Baptism, for no Deacon " in the absence of the Priest " could celebrate the Holy Eucharist, or absolve, or bless. Not only the Deacon but, in case of grave necessity, any layman or any woman may administer Baptism. All that is necessary for the valid administration of Baptism is that someone should pour water on the person to be baptized, in the Name of the Father and of the Son and of the Holy Ghost, and such Baptism, by whomsoever administered, is a valid Sacrament. But Baptism should ordinarily be administered by a Priest, and lay Baptism must only be resorted to in the gravest emergency.

This last sentence leads us to the kindred consideration of the place for the administration of Holy Baptism. Normally, of course, the place is the Church. In heathen countries, when, by the efforts of missionaries, a number of adults have been converted, it often happens that Holy Baptism is most impressively administered in a river, as we sometimes read in the history, for example, of Missions in India. But in the Prayer-Book we find Baptism in the Church contrasted with Baptism in private houses. And the clergy are directed to warn the faithful that they are not to seek for the private Baptism for their children except in case of urgent need.

Two instances of disregard of this injunction are all too common among us to-day.

It will be found that it is a common practice in our workhouses to administer private Baptism to children who are in no danger of death. When children are born in the workhouse, it is a common rule that the child shall be baptized before the mother leaves the workhouse. The intention, no doubt, is good, but the result is that Baptism is administered contrary to the injunction of the Church.

Another instance of disregard of the Church's rule is to be found in the case of parents who " do not object to having their children baptized," but strenuously object to the Church's rule about sponsors. They think they will, so to speak, " get round " the Church by having their children privately baptized.

Now, these and kindred instances of disregard of the plain injunctions of the Church arise out of ignorance of, or disregard of, the great principle that underlies those injunctions.

That principle is that, inasmuch as Baptism is the solemn entering upon a solemn and definite covenant, and inasmuch as both parties to the covenant must take their part in the making of such covenant, the Church *never* administers Baptism indiscriminately or unconditionally. In the case of the Baptism of infants, the infant pledges itself to the terms of the covenant by its godparents or sponsors. If a child is privately baptized in a case of grave illness, it is only on the understanding that, if it lives, it is to be brought by its sponsors to the Church, that it may publicly testify its adhesion to the terms of its covenant.

If parents who " object to sponsors " ask for private Baptism for their child on that ground, *it would be refused*. The Church knows nothing of unconditional Baptism. It may be, and unfortunately is, that the system of sponsors has largely become an unreality; but nevertheless there it is, testifying to the great truth that Holy Baptism is never administered unconditionally. In heathen countries missionaries are not allowed to baptize the children of heathen parents unless the child is wholly given over to the Mission to be brought up. And everywhere the Church insists upon a guarantee of the faith and repentance of the person about to be baptized, whether infant or adult.

The Church, then, is most careful to safeguard the great truth of Holy Baptism as the solemn entrance upon a covenant. Well indeed it would be for us if we were more attentive to this great principle of Church life ! A good many of our misfortunes may be traced to the indiscriminate administration of Holy Baptism. The Church has thrown the door very wide open. She will not debar infants from Holy Baptism in grave illness by insisting upon sponsors at the moment. She allows the Deacon or any lay person to administer Baptism in case of grave necessity. But it seems to me that this mercifulness on the part of the Church is being often greatly abused.

One constantly comes across the expression among eager and zealous Church workers, " The great thing is to get the children baptized." Is that really the " great thing " in the mind of the Church ? Surely not. It is not considered the " great thing " to baptize the children of heathen parents in the Mission-field. The "great thing," surely, is that due regard should be paid to the awful solemnity and responsibility of the Holy Sacrament of Baptism. Is there this due regard when, *e.g.*, an enthusiastic district visitor comes to tell us that she has got Mr. So-and-so, a Baptist, to "have his children baptized," without apparently having thought what was going to happen then? Is there that due regard when a mother brings her child without any sponsors at all, and the father cannot even interest himself enough in the matter to trouble himself to come round to the church? Is it quite in accordance with the dignity of the Sacrament when a Sister is told off to go down to the Church on a Sunday afternoon and "stand" to any child that may be brought? Does not all this look as if the Sacrament of Baptism were regarded somewhat as a charm? Surely we need to lay seriously to heart the great truth that the Church never administers Holy Baptism unconditionally; and if, in any of the ways that we have enumerated, men seem to be making light of the covenant aspect of Holy Baptism, they are doing so in the teeth of the Church's regulations.

We sum up, then, our consideration as to the outward visible sign or form of Baptism. It is of the essence of Baptism—

1. That it should be administered with water.

2. That the water should touch the person to be baptized.

3. That the Baptism should be administered in the Name of the Father and of the Son and of the Holy Ghost.

These three things are of *absolute necessity*. Failure

in either of these three respects destroys the Sacrament and renders the whole thing invalid.

It is right for the dignity of the Sacrament of Baptism—

1. That it should be administered by a Bishop or a Priest except in case of urgent necessity.

2. That it should be administered in the Church except in the case of urgent need.

3. That it never be administered unconditionally.

When we come to consider the inward spiritual grace of the Sacrament of Baptism, one point especially calls for our serious attention—viz., that the first inward spiritual grace of this Sacrament is a *death*. We are so familiar with the words " a death unto sin, and a new birth unto righteousness," that they too often leave but a very blurred and indistinct impression on our minds. Many of us, if we were asked to explain these words, would say that " a death unto sin " means to forsake sin, and " a new birth unto righteousness " means trying to be good. Others would recognize the fact that the " new birth " was the gift of God, and gave us grace to enable us to live a new life.

But a large proportion of Christians would be found to think that the " death unto sin " lay in our willingness to forsake sin, even if they believed that the " new birth unto righteousness " implied a supernatural gift of grace.

This idea is inadequate and wrong. The Church teaches us that the " death unto sin " is quite as much the gift of God by grace as is the new birth unto righteousness.

In our Baptism we receive a death unto sin. We receive the power of being as dead to sin as the dead

Holy Baptism

in their graves are to the things of this world. And
it is to this gift of death in Baptism that the Apostles
are always appealing. Let us bring St. Paul or St. John
before a Christian congregation, and tell them these
people have all received Holy Baptism. We know
what they would say to such people. St. Paul would
say: " Ye are dead, and your life is hid with Christ in
God." He would cry to that congregation: " Know
ye not that so many of us as were baptized into Jesus
Christ were baptized into His Death ? Therefore we
are buried with Him by Baptism *unto death :* that,
like as Christ was raised *from the dead* by the glory of
the Father, *even so* we also should walk in newness of
life."

And St. Peter would remind a Christian congrega-
tion of the same truth. He would say to them :
" Baptism doth now save us by the Resurrection of
Jesus Christ."

And St. John would break out in burning words to
such a congregation. He would say of them: " They
cannot sin, because they are born of God." For he
that is " born of God " can only sin by going clean
contrary to his nature. In so far as we are born of God,
we cannot sin. If we baptized people fall away
into sin, it can only be by repudiating our true
nature.

Oh, how wonderful is the vision of the Prayer-Book
Man ! He is dead and buried with Christ. He has
received the " death unto sin," and so has received
the " new birth unto righteousness." For his new
life is a resurrection life, springing out of death.
" Like as Christ was raised from the dead, even so we
. . . walk in newness of life."

" Even so !" The daily life of the Prayer-Book

Man is the Resurrection life of Jesus Christ. Let us think of the awful solemnity of this great truth. We shall then see what a wonderful and holy thing is a baptized child, and that will place us in the right frame of mind to consider, as we shall in our next chapter, the momentous subject of the care and education of such a supernatural being.

CHAPTER XV

CHRISTIAN EDUCATION

WE have tried to see something of the exceeding mystery of the origin of the Prayer-Book Man. We have seen how, by Baptism, he has been supernaturally " born to God," so that (1) he has received the grace of being " dead indeed unto sin," and therefore (2) he lives his wonderful supernatural life by the power of the Resurrection of our Lord, and that thus (3) he has entered into a definite and solemn covenant with God, in which covenant he is saved, and by the terms of which covenant he is judged, so that his eternal salvation or eternal damnation is bound up in his obedience or disobedience to the definite and express terms of the covenant. Such is the condition of every baptized child. It is under these wonderful conditions that he faces life in the world. Can anything be more important than the care and training, the " education " or bringing up of such a child ?

We will, then, try and think in this chapter, in a simple, homely way, about Christian education, and we will divide our thoughts on this momentous subject under three heads—viz. :

1. What is the end and object of the education of the Prayer-Book Man ?

2. Who is to educate him ?

3. How is he to be educated ?

Prayer-Book Ideals

1. *The end and object of the education of the Prayer-Book Man* is the formation of the Christian character, and when we speak of the Christian character we mean, of course, the reproduction in the individual Christian of the characteristics of the life of Jesus Christ; in other words, he is to be taught how to develop the supernatural life which has been born in him, or into which he has been born.

We cannot insist too strongly that the end and object of education is the formation of character.

" In Christ Jesus neither circumcision availeth anything, nor uncircumcision, but *a new creature*." We may sometimes ask ourselves why we are certain that if we get to Heaven we shall never again fall away. It will not, of course, be that our will has ceased to be free; it will be because the character of Jesus Christ will have been perfectly formed in us, so that it will have become morally impossible for us to sin.

But this moral impossibility of sin, which is the only guarantee of the eternity of our life in Heaven, is the completion and full growth of the life into which we have been born in Holy Baptism. The capacity of the heavenly character is born in us in our Baptism, and all education has for its end and object the full development of this character—the " forming," as the Holy Bible says, " of Christ " in us.

The Prayer-Book Man is the lineal descendant of the Saints, and he has to learn habitually, like them, to " live by faith." His education is to be such that life, death, and resurrection will lead, naturally, one into the other. As in a technical school a man has to be fitted for the peculiar craft that he is going to carry on, and the course of education is to be just that that will be fit for him, so the education of the Prayer-Book

Man is to fit him for the heavenly life that he is expecting and looking for—to fit him for the perfect vision and perfect knowledge of God, which is eternal life, and which can only be attained by perfect conformity to the Sacred Humanity of Jesus, the Son of Mary. What a tremendous ideal! And yet it is the merely logical and common-sense outcome of the fact of the new birth in Holy Baptism. What is the good of the gift of life if it is not to be able to grow and develop? To have been born is not an end in itself. It is a means to an end, and the only reason why we should have been born is that we may live; so, unless our Holy Baptism can eventuate in the perfect vision and perfect knowledge of God, it were better not to have been born with that new and heavenly birth. Shall we not now begin to see something of the fallacy of the idea that " the great thing is to get the children baptized ?" Shall we not see something of the danger of overlooking the covenant aspect of Holy Baptism ?

We reach, then, the tremendous conclusion that the natural end that lies before any and every baptized child is the Beatific Vision, that perfect vision and perfect knowledge of God that is eternal life, and that his education is to lead him up to that end and to fit him for it.

2. *Who is to educate him ?*—Who are the wonderful people to whom is to be entrusted the bringing up of a child of God ? We answer at once, " The godfathers and godmothers."

It would seem that the mind of the Church is more or less averse to the parents themselves standing as sponsors. In the Eastern Church it is absolutely forbidden, and, to mark the newness of spiritual relations into which a child enters at his Baptism, it is the custom that at a certain point in the Baptismal Office the parents withdraw, leaving the child in the charge of the sponsors, and a very strong light is thrown upon the reality and gravity of the office of sponsor when we find, as we do to this day in the East, that marriage may not be contracted between persons who have stood as godfather and godmother to the same child. Normally, then, the sponsors should be others than the parents of the child, and the fact that, at the present time, we are thankful if we can even get the father and mother to stand sponsors for their own children shows how far we have fallen from the Prayer-Book ideal, inasmuch as it reveals the " nakedness of the land " in showing how few there are who will undertake the " charitable work " of bringing an infant to Holy Baptism.

There are to be three sponsors to every child: For a boy, two godfathers and one godmother; for a girl, two godmothers and one godfather. And here again we mark the decline from the Prayer-Book standard. Our experience is that it is quite the exception to find the adequate number of sponsors. If, on coming to the Baptistery to baptize a boy, we find two godfathers and a godmother, we feel almost as the Holy Bible says a man feels if borrowed money is returned —we feel it is " something found."

We pass to the qualifications of godfathers and godmothers. We have seen that Baptism cannot be administered to the children of heathen parents unless the parents hand over the child unreservedly to its sponsors. It is obvious that a man who is not himself a Christian cannot bring an infant to Holy Baptism, pronounce his vows for him, and undertake to see that he is brought up as a Christian; therefore it need

Christian Education

hardly be said that a person who is not himself baptized cannot possibly stand as a sponsor. Equally we see at a glance that it would be merely indecent that people who have themselves neglected Confirmation should be allowed to stand as sponsors, to undertake, that is to say, to instruct the child for Confirmation, and to present the said child to the Bishop to be confirmed as soon as they have so instructed him.

These things are so obvious that we need not waste more time over them. Even in these degenerate days the sentiment, to a certain extent, remains that godparents should be persons who have themselves received Confirmation; but even this common-sense conclusion is beginning to grow dim.

But when we come to think about it we see that it is really just as indecent that a person should act as sponsor who is himself (or herself) at the moment living in any wilful breach of any of the terms of the Christian covenant. You would hardly put Fagin the Jew to expound the Eighth Commandment, or knowingly place an adulterer in the professorial chair of moral philosophy. How, then, can it possibly be right for men or women to act as sponsors if they are not themselves at the moment in a state of salvation? It is absolutely indecent that a person who is living in any sin, whether that sin be a breach of the first or of the second Table of the Law, should venture to stand as sponsor to a child. It is, for instance, absolutely indecent that a person who has not even made his (or her) Easter Communion should act as sponsor; they are themselves living in the habitual breach of the Baptismal Covenant. How, then, can they dare to undertake to bring up a child in the terms of that Covenant?

It is, then, an essential qualification for godfathers and godmothers that they should themselves be actually in a state of salvation—*i.e.*, that they should themselves be zealous for the Baptismal Covenant.

We cannot altogether blame the present race of godfathers and godmothers; they are, to a large extent, what circumstances have made them, and there is a vast amount of ignorance that must, perforce, be winked at. But we lay our finger on the original cause of the awful decadence of the spiritual life among us when we find that those to whom the care and education of Christian children is committed are themselves habitually violating the Covenant in the terms of which they are to educate the child.

It is, then, upon godfathers and godmothers that the tremendous responsibility is laid of educating the Christian child for his eternal life. Such is the ideal held up before us in the Prayer-Book.

It may be said that the ideal is one that it is well-nigh impossible to see realized as things now are, so appalling is the contrast between the ideal and the actual.

Two courses, under these circumstances, seem to suggest themselves:

(1) There are those who argue that, because the ideal is impossible as things are, we must let the ideal go, and do our best with things as we find them. They point out that in the days when the Prayer-Book was written people ordinarily lived and remained in one place, that the godparents were pretty sure to be in contact with their godchild up to the time of Confirmation, whereas now, owing to the facility of locomotion, the chances are that either the godparents or the godchild move and lose touch with each other;

therefore, they argue, the Prayer-Book ideal is antiquated and out of date, and we must be content to have the parents only as sponsors, if we are to have sponsors at all.

Or, again, they argue that in the days when the Prayer-Book was written religion had much more real hold on the people than it has now; that now, in the face of the enormous increase of the population, and the rush and turmoil of life, we cannot expect that godparents can ever be what the Prayer-Book means them to be, and so we had better face facts, and get the children baptized anyhow.

But these arguments simply amount to this—viz., that if an ideal has become difficult of realization, we had better let it go; in other words, that we are to lower our ideal to the level of the actual, instead of trying to raise the actual to the level of the ideal.

(2) The other course open to us is to cling to the ideal at all hazards, and trust that, if we will but retain it as the ideal, it will in time become a reality.

This, of course, is God's method. The ideal is always, with God, the truly real. The message of the prophets to people who have fallen from their ideal standard is not to say " peace " when there is no peace, but to recall the people of God to the initial and fundamental facts that they had forgotten.

And to apply this principle to the matter in hand, it is not our business to try and improve upon the system of the Church according to our own fancy, but to hold to the form, at any rate, that in His own time God may breathe into it again the breath of life. The mere retention of the Church's rule as to godparents is something, even if, for the moment, it can presumedly be not much more than a form; it is the old story of the five barley loaves. They are infinitesimally small and valueless in themselves, but they are the raw material out of which our Lord works His miracle; so with forms that seem for the time being to have dropped into being forms and nothing else. Your common-sense Englishmen is impatient of them, and says, " Sweep them away "; but the Christian knows better. We remember how Tennyson's lovely " Palace of Art " ends:

"Yet pull not down my palace towers that are so lightly,
   beautifully built,
 Perchance I shall return with others there,
 When I have purged my guilt."

Instead of lowering your ideal to suit the irreligion of the time, cling to it through thick and thin. Instead of the shallow, hasty policy (from which we have suffered such untold things in England) of throwing away a form because it is a form merely, hold on to it till better days come, so that when it pleases God to breathe life into us again, He may find the material for His wondrous work all ready to His hand.

3. *How is the Prayer-Book Child to be educated by his godparents ?*—This is, of course, an enormous subject that I cannot enter into now. We are going, in the next two chapters, to make one or two suggestions on this head. We will merely, in concluding the present chapter, say one word as to preliminary requisites for the carrying out of the Prayer-Book Man's education —viz., (1) Atmosphere, and (2) example.

(1) *Atmosphere.*—We have heard a great deal lately, in the education controversy, about the importance of atmosphere. Every one of us, when we look back upon our own childhood, must know how early impressions came to us indirectly from our surroundings.

Christian Education

It was the prevailing atmosphere of our home that affected us much more than direct instruction that we received. If the Christian child is to be trained for the eternal life into which he was born at his Baptism, he must in his home be surrounded with the atmosphere of heavenly things. No amount of direct teaching can make up for an atmosphere that is uncongenial to that teaching. What he learns directly by the teaching, he will unlearn by the home atmosphere that runs counter to that teaching. Our own experience tells us that the indirect influence of the prevailing atmosphere of the home was more powerful than the direct teaching; and so we conclude that if the teaching goes one way and the home atmosphere another, it is the home atmosphere, in the long run, that will win the day, and that therefore, unless the direct teaching be backed up by the home atmosphere, it will have but little chance.

(2) *Example.*—It is a sort of copy-book truism that example is better than precept. If a parent or godparent has to teach a child to do things that he himself is obviously not doing, he is giving the lie to his own teaching. He is, almost in so many words, saying that his teaching is not to be believed.

To take an example which, alas! is the common one in English homes: If the parent teaches the child that it is right for him to go to church on a Sunday morning, while he himself lies in bed, or reads the newspaper, or goes fishing, etc., the obvious thing that the child learns is that he is to go to church till he grows up, and that then he may lie in bed, read the newspaper, or go fishing instead. And the English child, being brought up in precept that is contradicted by example, learns his lesson only too well, and looks forward to being emancipated from church-going when he grows up.

And here again our own experience will tell us that if precept goes one way and example the other, it is example that is the stronger of the two, and will invariably win in the long run.

The Church presupposes a Christian atmosphere and a Christian example in the home to which she entrusts the new-born Christian for his bringing up; and in all that need be said about direct and indirect methods of education, we take it for granted that there is to be no contradiction between the teaching and the atmosphere, between the precept and the example.

And having said thus much by way of preface, we shall proceed in the next chapter to consider the methods by which the Church enjoins the godparents to carry on the education of the Prayer-Book Child.

CHAPTER XVI

THE CATECHISM

BEFORE we pass on to consider the exact methods by which the parents and godparents are to carry on the education of the Christian child, let us emphasize the necessity of a truly Christian education.

It is obvious that a man must always be brought up with reference to the nature in which he was born, and the surroundings into which that nature will lead him. A man must be taught—*e.g.*, the broad lines of the laws of life and health. Nobody supposes for a moment that a child is to be left to his own unassisted experience to find out what is poisonous and what is not, whether food and sleep are necessary, or whether they are not, whether he requires clothing, or whether he does not, etc. Of course not! Few children, if any, would grow up to manhood if such were the case. It is not enough for a child to have been born, if he is then to be left to shift for himself.

And as with natural life, so with social life; a child must be brought up along the broad lines of the laws of social life. He is not left to his own unassisted experience to decide what is to be his attitude towards his fellow-men; he must be taught the ways and manners of civilized life. He must be taught to know something of the rights of other men. He cannot be left, *e.g.*, just to take what he wants, without inquiring whose those things are, etc.

So, too, with the life of citizenship. Nobody is left to his own unassisted experience to find out what are the laws of the country in which he lives. If he were to assert his "individualism" freely—*e.g.*, in this country—he would immediately find himself in the hands of the police. He is born with a certain nature and under certain social conditions; he must be trained to respect that nature and those conditions.

Now this is exactly what the Church claims for the children of God. They have received a new nature and been born, by their Baptism, into certain social conditions; they must therefore be trained to respect that nature and those conditions. Therefore, as we have seen, the Church, before she will administer the Sacrament of the New Birth, requires a guarantee that the child, when born again, will be taught to respect its new nature and its new social conditions.

The Church has a right to assume that those who bring a child to Holy Baptism do so because they believe in Holy Baptism. If they do not believe in it, why do they bring the child at all? The Church, that is to say, presupposes for the child a Christian home with a Christian atmosphere and a Christian example. To that Christian home and to the Christian educators in that home, she entrusts the new-born child of God to be brought up in accordance with the nature that it has received, and with reference to the society into which it has been incorporated. To suppose that the new-born child of God is to be left to itself to carve out its own way along the lines of individualism is so ridiculous that to state the proposition is to show its absurdity and impossibility. No child of God could grow to Christian manhood and the perfection of eternal life under such conditions; he had better not have been born at all. God's work in the preservation of life is as essential as His work in the giving of life; if life given cannot be preserved, it had better not be given. This is why the Church insists on guarantees from the godparents before she will administer the Sacrament of Baptism.

It being, then, clearly laid down (1) that the Christian child is to be brought up as a Christian, and (2) that it is the parents and godparents who are responsible for this bringing up, we turn to see how the parents and godparents of the Prayer-Book Man are to set about their tremendous task.

The Church begins by stating the principle on which the whole education is to be carried out: " It is your parts and duties to see that this child be taught, so soon as he shall be able to learn, what a solemn vow, promise, and profession, he hath here made by you." Then, having laid down the broad fundamental principle, the Church goes on to direct that the parents and godparents are to carry out this principle—(1) by direct methods; (2) by indirect methods.

Direct methods: " That he may know these things the better, ye shall call upon him to hear Sermons; and chiefly ye shall provide that he may learn the Creed, the Lord's Prayer, and the Ten Commandments in the vulgar tongue, and all other things which a Christian ought to know and believe to his soul's health."

Let us summarize this. The Christian child is (1) to hear Sermons, (2) to learn the Creed, the Lord's Prayer and the Ten Commandments in his own language; (3) to learn other things necessary for the Christian's life.

Let us think a little about each of these requirements.

1. "Ye shall call upon him to hear Sermons." On this head I would remark that if the Prayer-Book child is to hear Sermons, he must be *where* the Sermons are preached, *when* they are preached.

Now the Prayer-Book is quite explicit on these two heads. The place where Sermons are preached is the parish church. The time when Sermons are preached is at the Holy Eucharist, immediately after the Nicene Creed.

There is no hint in the Prayer-Book of the preaching of a Sermon at the Divine Office. A habit has grown up of late years of preaching a Sermon after Evensong on Sunday, and certain other days, but this is mere custom, and one of quite recent date.

But if a Sermon after Evensong be a comparatively modern custom, what shall we say of " Matins and Sermon " ? We have already dealt with this in our thoughts on the ideal of Worship, and will therefore content ourselves now with saying once more that whatever else it may be, it is *not* " Prayer-Book."

The Prayer-Book Child, then, is to be called upon to hear Sermons, and the Sermon is, according to the Prayer-Book, at the Holy Eucharist. Therefore the Prayer-Book Child is to be at the Holy Eucharist on Sundays, and I need hardly remind you that there is no provision in the Prayer-Book for the Prayer-Book Child leaving the church after the Sermon in the middle of the service, nor can there be the slightest excuse for his doing so, inasmuch as he is neither unbaptized nor excommunicate. And so the Prayer-Book Child becomes a " non-communicating attendant," whatever pompous platitudes people in high places may bring forward. For whatever may be said for taking children out of church on a Sunday morning after the Sermon, it is an absolutely " un-Prayer-Book " thing to do.

But now comes the question what the Prayer-Book supposes that the child will hear in the Sermon.

The Prayer-Book leaves us in no sort of doubt on this matter. The child is to hear Sermons in order that he may " know the better " what a solemn vow, promise, and profession he made, by his godparents, in his Baptism.

Oh, English parsons, think of that ! Think of the unfortunate Church of England child to-day, doomed, if his godparents have " called upon him to hear Sermons," to listen to some explaining away of the Christian belief in the name of " Higher Criticism," or to some brilliant aphorisms on some " topic of the hour," to amuse a fashionable congregation till it is time for church parade in the park !

Think of the grim humour of supposing that the ordinary average Sunday morning Sermon will teach a child what a solemn vow, promise, and profession he has made ! Run your eye down the gruesome list of " Preachers and teachers for to-morrow;" think of the " Sermons " that bore us to extinction by their dull platitudes; think of the " Sermons " that air Mr. So-and-so's peculiar fad or " ism "; and if it were not that one is too angry and sad, one could laugh, long and loud, at the bare idea of the poor child being brought there to learn the better what a solemn vow, promise, and profession he made in his Baptism.

But now let us think of the expression " call upon him " to hear Sermons.

This might be done in various ways. It might be that mother, slatternly and untidy, in curl-papers and slippers, might " call " from her back kitchen to poor little John that it is time for his Sermon, or that father, from between his sheets, at half-past ten in the morning, may " call " to little William that he is to be off at once to hear his Sermon; and one would picture the poor little waif, left to find his own way to the church with the dim thought at the back of his mind that when he is a man he will not have to go to church on a Sunday morning, but may look forward to staying at home, like father and mother. That is one way of " calling on " a child to hear Sermons, and a good many of our Christian children are not even called upon in this way, but are turned out to find any religion or Sunday School they may prefer. Yes! that is one way of " calling upon " a child to hear Sermons, but, needless to say, that is not what the Prayer-Book means.

The Prayer-Book surely contemplates that father and mother, or father at least, will take the child by the hand and bring him to the Holy Eucharist on the Sunday morning, when the Sermon is preached, if only on the common-sense principle that, if you want a thing done, you had better do it yourself. But more than that, another piece of common sense would suggest the question why, if they did not mean to bring the child up as a Christian, did they have him made a Christian at all.

The parents, then, are to bring the child to church on a Sunday morning. But it is the godparents who are to see that it is done; and so the Prayer-Book would

The Catechism

surely contemplate the probability of the godparents calling at the house to see if the child had been taken to church on a given Sunday, and that, if they found that the parents had neglected their duty in this respect they would warn them not to do so in future, or would come themselves to fetch the child, if they found no other way.

So much for the hearing of Sermons. Now think a moment of the other positive directions and the education of the Prayer-Book Child.

2. The godparents are to " provide " that the child learn the Creed, the Lord's Prayer, and the Ten Commandments in his own language.

Again one says: " If you want a thing done, do it yourself." Here are five people—viz., two parents and three godparents—to see that one child learns these three simple things. Surely among them they ought to be able to do just this much ! But if they really are so ignorant, or so lazy, that they cannot even do this, then they must take the child to some person, or send him to some school, where it will be done.

I pause on the word " provide." Is it " providing " for this learning to turn a child out to find a Sunday School for himself ? Is it no business of the parents or the godparents whether the child goes to church or to some chapel or salvation hall ? Is the question of where the child is to go to be decided by where he will get the biggest bun or the most attractive treat ?

How many parents who have " had their children baptized " are utterly indifferent as to what religion they follow ! And as for godparents, if the child has any, they too commonly neither know nor care anything about the matter.

But the Prayer-Book says that godparents are to
" provide " that the child learns the Creed, the Lord's
Prayer, and the Ten Commandments, in his own
language !

Sometimes one has even to be thankful if parents do
not actively hinder the baptized child from these things.
I heard of a parent the other day who, as far as I know,
never sets foot inside a church or receives a Sacrament;
yet she took her child away from the Sunday School
in the parish church because, as she said, the parish
church was Roman Catholic, and she was Church of
England ! Again one could laugh long and loud, if it
were not so sad !

But surely there ought to be no question of Sunday
School to learn the Creed, the Lord's Prayer, and the
Ten Commandments. Two parents and three godparents might surely be trusted to do this for themselves !

3. We pass to the consideration of " all other things
that a Christian ought to know and believe to his soul's
health."

The Prayer-Book Child, then, is to be taught the
Catechism because, and because only, he has been
baptized.

It having been clearly ascertained that the child
presented for instruction is one who is capable of
receiving that instruction—*i.e.*, that he has been baptized—the Catechism plunges him at once into the
subject of the definite and distinct covenant on which
he has entered, and the absolute obligation of the
terms of that covenant upon him. He is asked what
his godfathers and godmothers promised in his name,
and whether he considers himself bound by those
promises.

The Catechism

So the foundation is laid of all that follows.

And here, again, we would pause and ask whether Christian instruction in the Church of England of to-day is always based on the great fundamental truths of the Covenant and its obligations. The Catechism lays down, as we have said, the lines on which Christian instruction must go, and all more advanced instruction can be merely the amplification of that which we have in its elementary form in the Catechism.

Bishop Dupanloup forcibly says that all Christian instruction must " rouler sur le Catechisme," and Henry Martyn says that one must always take hold of a child by the handle of its Baptismal Covenant.

But what about the average Sermon that English Church-people of to-day are doomed to hear ? We put out of sight the studied insolence that uses the Church pulpits to decry and belittle the Christian religion. We need not for the moment do more than say that " Sermons " of this class are an outrage and an insult. But what of the moral essays that would be just as applicable to heathens as to Christians, those neat moral essays that so largely do duty for " Sermons " ? Or again, who, in listening to your average preacher, would suppose that he was addressing people whose only claim to a right to be there before him is that they *have* been born again, that they *have* been brought out of darkness into light, that they *have* been delivered from the bondage of corruption into the glorious liberty of the children of God. No one, surely, would gather this from the tone of the sermon.

The Apostles always speak to Christians as Christians. They speak to them as "the Saints," "the Elect," as those whose "sins are forgiven for His Name's sake." In other words, they base their instruction on the fact of Baptismal Regeneration. So does the Catechism. It instructs the Prayer-Book Child as St. Paul or St. John would have instructed him. But our latter-day Apostles and Prophets seem to know better than St. Paul or St. John. They will talk to Christians as if they were still in darkness and in the shadow of death, and their dreary morality would suit a heathen congregation pretty nearly as well as a Christian one.

If one of us were to get up in a twentieth-century London pulpit and just preach the first Epistle of St. John in modern colloquial English, we should be put down as lunatics, and be thought to be promulgating some strange and new doctrine !

All Christian instruction, then, is based upon the fact of Baptismal Regeneration, and the appeal to the Christian conscience is the appeal to the definite terms of the Christian Covenant.

To resume our examination of the Catechism. The terms of the Covenant and their binding force upon the Christian child having been clearly laid down, the Catechism proceeds to instruct upon the Articles of the Christian Faith that the child has promised to believe, and the Commandments he has promised to keep, the Creed and the Commandments being first recited, and then summarized—the Creed in the answer to the question, "What dost thou chiefly learn in these Articles of thy belief ?" and the Commandments in the answer to the questions, "What is thy duty towards God ?" and "What is thy duty towards thy neighbour ?"

The Catechism

Then follows the last division of the Catechism—viz., the instruction as to Prayer and the Sacraments, which is prefaced by the very remarkable address made, at this point, to the Prayer-Book Child : "My good child, know this, that thou art not able to do these things of thyself, nor to walk in the Commandments of God, and to serve Him without His special grace: which thou must learn at all times to call for by diligent prayer. Let me hear, therefore, if thou canst say the Lord's Prayer."

And the instruction on the Sacraments (which the Prayer-Book, at any rate, states to be generally necessary to salvation) brings the Catechism to a close.

So we sum up the subject-matter of the Catechism as follows: (1) The fact of the Covenant. (2) The terms of the Covenant. (3) The means whereby alone those terms can be kept.

Godparents and parents, then, are to "provide" that the child learns the Catechism. Again we would cry: "Do it yourselves." What a new atmosphere would come over the home where father and mother made a point of themselves teaching their children the Catechism ! So new, that we can hardly fancy its being done ! As we conjure up the vision, whether in Belgravia or Bethnal Green, of a father hearing his children say the Catechism, we seem to be thinking of some wild Utopian vision. The bare thought of it carries us back to the homes of a century ago rather than to those of to-day. And yet, how inconceivably simple it is ! It is quite within the reach of gentle and simple alike. It is only just to take a Prayer-Book and teach the little ones to say the answers to the questions.

And this very simple duty performed in our homes

would raise the whole tone of life in parents and children alike.

But if (and what a sigh we heave over that "if"! how sad to see the beautiful vision fade!)—if it is really impossible for children to be taught the Catechism at home, then resort must be had to some such clumsy makeshift as a Church Day School or Sunday School. But in that case the godparents must not only see that it *is* a Church School, but must take the trouble to ascertain that the Catechism is taught in that school. For many so-called Church Schools are wasting their time pottering round "Bible Stories," "History of Joseph," "Old Testament Types," etc., all excellent in their place, but too often tending to oust the Catechism, which is the one thing the Church Day or Sunday School has to look to first of all. Well would it be for Church Schools if parents would clamour about the Catechism. But this is hardly likely to happen, for of course if parents cared about the Catechism they would be teaching it themselves!

One word to those who teach the Catechism. Remember that the first thing the child has got to learn is *the Catechism itself*. Make them word perfect in the letter of the Catechism first of all. We are often so eager to "point the moral and adorn the tale," that we are constantly interrupting the words of the Catechism with our own, often senseless, chatter. Do see that the children have the actual words of the Catechism at their finger ends. Once thoroughly learnt in this way it will stick by a man for his life. Why do so few grown-up people in any walk of life know the Catechism nowadays? Because they were never made to learn it thoroughly. The neat little lessons on it out of the neat little books struck in with their twaddle, and

The Catechism

obscured the main things. No one, of course, remembers the neat little books or what they said; but they would have remembered the words of the Catechism if they had been made severely to learn them by heart.

The Prayer-Book Child, then, must learn the words of the Church Catechism, and he must learn them in their entirety. There are not wanting those who approve of the Catechism up to a certain point, but shy at it in its entirety. Such persons will perhaps teach the earlier portion of the Catechism, but will be inclined to slur over or omit the concluding portion of it. We say, then, to those who are going to teach the Catechism: " Teach the words, and teach the whole Catechism."

The Prayer-Book Child, it is assumed, will know by heart the Creed, the Lord's Prayer, and the Ten Commandments, and be able to answer the questions asked in the Catechism.

But the " further instruction in the Church Catechism," of course, implies more than the mere knowledge of the words, indispensable as this may be as a foundation. The teaching of the Catechism has got to be practically applied, and all practical application of the Catechism must result from an appreciation on the part of the teacher of what it is that (to use a homely expression) the Catechism is driving at. The Catechism is bent on showing the child that he starts life under a solemn and definite obligation to believe and to act in a certain definite way; that he has laid down for him a rule of faith, a rule of prayer, and a rule of life, that is imposed upon him by the authority of God, and the godparents are to see that he knows what he is to believe, how he is to pray, and how he is to live.

Prayer-Book Ideals

To the child who is familiar with the words of the Catechism, it ought not to be difficult to apply, in everyday life, the teaching of the Catechism; to appeal to that teaching, and to use it practically as a moral lever.

But this rather leads us to the indirect methods by which the Prayer-Book Child is to be educated, methods which we will consider in our next chapter.

CHAPTER XVII

A GODLY AND CHRISTIAN LIFE

WE have now to consider what, for want of a better expression, we may call the indirect methods by which the education of the Prayer-Book Man is to be carried on.

We have seen that the direct methods of education enjoined upon parents and godparents are—

1. To call upon the child to hear Sermons.

2. To provide that he learn the Creed, the Lord's Prayer, and the Ten Commandments.

3. To provide that he learn the Catechism.

And the end and object at which these direct methods aim is that the child, by these means, may better know what a solemn vow, promise, and profession he made by his godparents in his Baptism.

But the education of the Prayer-Book Child is not to stop here. A further object is set before the godparents that they are to aim at fulfilling; and we will now proceed to consider that object and the methods by which it is to be attained.

The Prayer-Book, having spoken of the Baptismal vow and the means whereby its obligations are to be brought home to the child, goes on to say that the godparents are to provide that the child may be virtuously brought up to lead a godly and a Christian life. Let us try and think a little what this means, and we shall then be better able to consider how it may be done.

Our attention is arrested by those two words " godly " and " Christian." Simple as the words sound, they carry us very deep indeed.

A " godly " life ! Not, you will observe, a " good " life, but a " godly " or " God-like " life.

Two thoughts seem to suggest themselves here :

1. If a man is to live a " godly " life, he must, surely, look at all created things, his own life included, from the point of view of God. He must see things as God sees them. God looks upon His Creation as something that is emphatically His Own. All created things are the outcome of His Eternal Wisdom, that Eternal Word by Whom all things were made, and without Whom was not anything made that was made.

Again, God sees all things as upheld by the Word of His Power. He sees all things as simply contingent upon, and relative to, Himself. A creation, or a created life, that could in any way exist independently of God is simply unthinkable.

So the " godly " or " God-like " man will look upon all created things, himself included. He will, to use the forcible expression of the Holy Bible, " see Him Who is Invisible." God, and the things of God, and the relation in which he stands to God, will be to him the obvious things. He will know that the beginning of pride is when one departeth from his Maker; and he will shrink in horror from the spectacle of a will that in any way sets itself against the Will of God. The absolute sovereignty and supremacy of God will be to him, moment by moment, the obvious thing.

2. If a man is to be " godly "—*i.e.*, like God—his life must have the same end before it as the Life of God.

A Godly and Christian Life

If we try to go back in thought to what we must, in our stupid, bungling way, call the Eternity before Creation, we see that the Life of God is absolutely complete and perfect in itself. There was no necessity for a creation at all. Creation adds nothing to the essential Glory of God; His Own infinite and absolute perfections are all-sufficient. So we dimly see in our blindness what a vision opens before us as our Lord says so simply to the Eternal Father: " The glory which I had with Thee before the world was ;" or, again, when He says: " Thou lovedst Me before the foundation of the world." To find the end of one's being in anything but God is to be quite unlike God, whose end is in Himself.

How wonderful to remember, as the Prayer-Book in these simple words bids us remember, that the only reason why we are alive to-day is that we may eventually see God face to face, and know God even as also we are known. There can be no other reason for our creation and for our preservation at all.

So St. Ignatius sums up for us these two thoughts about godliness when, at the outset of his Spiritual Exercises, he reminds us (1) that God is the End of our being: and (2) that all created things, as far as we individually are concerned, exist for one purpose only— viz., to bring us to our End, which is God.

So far as this our very common sense would take us. But our third thought about godliness will carry us into the region of God; Revelation of Himself.

3. It has pleased God to reveal Himself to His Creatures in the Incarnation of the Eternal Son.

We are not left to abstract speculation about God. St. John, speaking of the Incarnation of our Lord Jesus Christ, tells us that " the Life was manifested, and we have seen it, and bear witness, and show unto you that

Eternal Life that was with the Father and was manifested unto us." The " godly " or God-like life is the life that follows the example, and obeys the precepts, of Jesus Christ, Who, being Perfect Man as well as Perfect God, manifests to us the Life of God Himself. If your life, or mine, is like the Life of Jesus the Son of Mary, it is " godly ": if not, it is not " godly," whatever else may be said for it.

And so we reach the tremendous conclusion that all moral systems that do not spring out of faith in the Incarnation are merely so many forms of idolatry; and in the face of the modern attempt to discard faith and take refuge in moral philosophy—to build up, that is to say, a system of morals while the Incarnation is regarded as an open question—in the face, I say, of this modern revolt from God, we surely need especially to take to heart the last warning of St. John: " Little children, keep yourselves from idols."

Here, then, we have some fragmentary suggestions as to what is meant by a " godly life," and bearing these suggestions in mind, we remind ourselves that godparents are to provide that their godchildren are brought up to lead a " godly life."

We pass now to ask what is meant by a " Christian " life. And we remark, in passing, how the term " Christian " is abused amongst us English people at the present time. Men pick out certain virtues that commend themselves to their taste and dub those who possess such virtues " Christians." Or we have the straitest sects of Pharisaic Protestantism, who have certain shibboleths of their own, and, according as a man can, or cannot, subscribe to those shibboleths he will, or will not, be styled " a Christian."

Then we have the unbelievers who indulge in the

silly pastime of making Christians of their own imagination. They make their "man of straw" kind of Christian, and then plume themselves upon being able to knock him down. And worse almost than these are the lofty and superior patronizers of, and apologizers for, Christianity. They build up a fictitious "Christian" hero out of some shreds and patches of morality, and hold him up for the admiration of the world: and a gruesome spectacle it is!

Now, the fault of all these people is one and the same. They are like the proverbial writer on natural history, who sits in his study to write upon the camel. He describes the camel as he thinks it ought to be; whereas, of course, the true student of natural history will carefully observe what, as a matter of fact, the camel is and does. So these foolish people, in their various ways, sit making Christians, and either knocking down their dummies when they have made them, or patting them on the back and calling men to admire them; whereas the Christian life is a simple historical fact that is always capable of observation. The question is not what Mr. So-and-so thinks a Christian ought to be, but what have always been the characteristics of the Christian life from the beginning.

As a matter of historical fact, we have the Christian life (the life, that is to say, that is the outcome of faith in Jesus Christ), exhibited before us in the lives of the Saints of the Old and New Covenants; and we cannot fail to notice two characteristics of Christian life that stand out prominently all along the line of human history.

The first of these characteristics is their firm and persistent faith in a Personal Saviour. From the earliest dawn of history the Christian life is the life of those whose whole hope was set upon the promise that the Seed of the woman should bruise the head of the serpent. In the eleventh chapter of the Epistle to the Hebrews, we have the names of some of the prominent leaders of the Christian life; and the faith of the Saints of the Old Covenant is appealed to as the pattern for the Saints of the New Covenant.

The history of Christianity does not begin, as some people seem to think, with the birth of our Lord. Christianity is not a startling phenomenon suddenly and unexpectedly sprung upon the world. The history of Christianity begins at the least when the Lord planted a garden eastward in Eden; and it may more properly be said to have begun when the Lord divided the light from the darkness.

If the Prayer-Book Man is to live a " Christian " life, he must have the same rooted belief in the Seed of the woman as righteous Abel had. His faith in a Personal Saviour must uphold him as it upheld Noah in the 120 years of the building of the Ark. His faith in Jesus Christ must be stronger than his natural affections, as Abram's was when he came out of the Chaldees. His belief in Jesus Christ must be to him a ruling passion as it was to Moses on that day when he refused to be called the son of Pharaoh's daughter, and cast in his lot with the down-trodden slaves, because he esteemed the reproach of Christ greater riches than the treasures in Egypt. Jesus Christ must be more obvious to him than life itself, as it was to the Martyrs and Confessors. It is a tremendous thing to be called to live a Christian life, for it means being called into the company of all the Saints of God from the foundation of the world!

Think of this, and then suddenly think of the " Chris-

A Godly and Christian Life

tian " of modern thought; the well-behaved, decent, benevolent people who are called " Christians " in modern parlance; the " Christians " of Pharisaic Protestantism; the " Christians " whom the unbelievers have made and set up as dummies at which they may amuse themselves by throwing stones; and the insufferable " Christians " who are held up to our admiration by the conceited writers of a certain class of modern fiction !

" The Christian " is, all along the line of human history, the man whose life is based upon the belief in the Seed of the woman Who bruised the head of the serpent. He may have been called Christian first in Antioch; but there he was from the very beginning, in the Old Testament as in the New, for (to quote once more the words of the Article) " both in the Old Testament and in the New, Christ is set forth as the One Mediator between God and men, being both God and man."

But if faith in a Personal Saviour is the first unvarying characteristic of the Christian in all ages, the second unvarying characteristic is hostility to the world.

The Christian can never be at home in the world which is the place wherein Christ was crucified, and therefore he is always more or less in tribulation.

Never mind what Mr. Somebody Something thinks a Christian ought to be; never mind the dummy Christians that are stuck up all about us; never mind the idols. Turn your face from them and go and look for yourselves at Christian life as history shows it to us, and you will find that they are indeed the enemies of the world.

Look a moment ! There is righteous Abel stretched

bleeding and dead on the ground. There is Noah bent with the toil of his hard labour. There is Abraham living as an exile and a stranger in the land of promise. There is Jacob lying on the hard ground at Luz with a stone for his pillow. There is Stephen stoned to death outside Jerusalem. There are the Apostles, beaten, imprisoned, made " the filth of the world and the offscouring of all things," and finally killed; St. Peter crucified, St. Paul beheaded, St. James beaten to death, St. Bartholomew flayed alive, etc. Think of Rome in the days of the ten persecutions; think of the long line of noble confessors in all ages in their afflicted, self-denying lives. Think of all these and the great multitude which no man can number, who have all come out of great tribulation. Think, I say, of all these historical personages, and you must see that tribulation in this life is to be the mark of a Christian life.

Now let us sum up these few thoughts about " a godly and Christian life."

It means—

1. That a man looks upon Creation as God looks upon it.

2. That he has the same end of being as the End of the Being of God.

3. That he is like Jesus Christ.

4. That he is with all Saints of God in his faith in a Personal Saviour.

5. That he counts all things but loss for the excellency of the knowledge of Jesus Christ.

And godparents are to provide that the Prayer-Book Child be brought up to lead " a godly and a Christian life !"

How tremendous is the task that is laid upon the

A Godly and Christian Life

godparents of the Prayer-Book Child, and what sanctity and watchfulness does it presuppose !

And now, having seen just a glimpse of what is meant by a godly and Christian life, the question arises as to how godparents are to set about this great task, and again one sees at a glance that it must be the parents that are to carry on this daily task in the home; but the godparents are to see, so far as they may, that it is done.

It is quite out of the question to attempt, in half a chapter, to say how a child is to be brought up " to lead a godly and Christian life." Let us just remember that it must be by surrounding him with a " godly and Christian " atmosphere, and by setting before him a " godly and Christian " example. Let us just briefly consider three things that will help towards the end we have in view:

1. If the child is to be godly it must learn to look upon itself as belonging simply to God; it must be taught that the mere following of its own free-will and inclination is walking in the steps of the devil in his refusal to submit himself to the Will of God; therefore it must be trained in the habit of strict, instant, and implicit obedience. Where there is not obedience there can be no godliness. The larger part of the earthly life of God Incarnate is summed up in a sentence when we are told that He went down to Nazareth, and was subject to His parents. Where there is not strict and ready obedience there is no likeness to God.

Now obedience is conspicuous, in this ungodly age, by its absence. To get strict obedience requires great self-restraint and patience on the part of the parents. The average English parent fails in both these respects.

His want of self-restraint is shown in giving impossible orders to the child that he never really means obeyed; that constant pecking and nagging about things that really do not matter; that chafe the child and " provoke it to wrath "; or that, by their hasty minuteness, are well-nigh impossible for the child to carry out. Again, the want of self-restraint is often shown in awful threats shouted out in a tremendous voice— threats that the child knows perfectly well cannot and will not be put into practice—the child, of course, continuing to do what it wants to do, and caring no more for the threat than the wind that blows.

It is a golden rule in dealing with children, whether at home or in school, that the parent, master, or mistress speak quietly. If they shout, it implies that the children are not expected to listen. Speak quietly, and insist on being heard and attended to.

If a child is to be godly, parents must practise self-control in four directions. They must—

(1) Not give unnecessary orders.

(2) Speak quietly.

(3) Take the trouble to see that their order is instantly obeyed, and punish if it is not.

(4) Not threaten, but act.

2. If the child is to be godly and Christian, his education must be modelled on the example of our Lord and His Saints.

Therefore children must be familiar with the life of our Lord and with the lives of His Saints.

We English lose so much by our scorn of external help, such as pictures or images of our Lord and His Saints.

To the child of the Church in other countries our Lord, His Blessed Mother, and His Saints are, if I may so say, familiar friends. The false spirituality of Protestantism, which springs from a feeble grasp (to say the least) on the truth of the Incarnation, has brought it about that our Lord, His Blessed Mother, and His Saints, are shadowy abstractions rather than living realities.

Let us think how images and pictures are practically used in countries where Christianity is more practical than, alas ! it is in England.

Many years ago a mother was carrying her baby through the gateway of the Béguinage at Bruges. In the side of the gateway is a crucifix. The mother stopped, showed the child the crucifix, curtsied, and kissed her hand. Again she pointed to the crucifix, again she curtsied, and made the little one kiss its hand.

In the Church of San Giovanni in Bragora, at Venice, a gondolier came in with his little child on his shoulder. Near the door was placed a Pieta—*i.e.*, an image of the dead Christ in His Mother's arms. The gondolier goes up with his child to kiss the five Sacred Wounds of the dead Christ.

In the parish church of Mentone, one Friday in Lent, little children were running in and out of the altar rails. Being a Friday in Lent, a crucifix was laid on the altar steps, with a lamp burning before it. The little ones were busy there kissing the Sacred Wounds.

Give an Italian child a picture of our Lord, the Madonna, or a Saint, and he will at once kiss it. Watch Italians at their devotions. If they have a book of prayers, the places will be marked by little pious pictures. Every time they come upon one of these pictures they cover it with kisses.

Some little ragamuffins came round an English

Priest at Chioggia. He gave them his Office Book to look at, the places being marked with little pious pictures. Every picture they came to they took up and kissed.

At every festival in Italy you will find people at the door selling little halfpenny pictures of our Lord, His Blessed Mother, or the Saints. Thus children are familiarized with the living realities of the lives of our Lord and His Saints, on whose lives they are to model their own.

Now contrast with this our English habits. A Priest in a village spoke to the children in the school about the advantages of having a crucifix where they said their prayers, and offered to give a crucifix picture to any child that liked to ask him for one. Imagine his delight when, on going into a cottage, he found two of these pictures exactly alike set up over the chimney-piece in the kitchen !

A Priest in a country town had just bought two little statuettes of Our Lady and St. Joseph, each with the Holy Child. The housekeeper coming in, said: " Oh, what a pretty little babby !"

If the life is to be Christian, the child must be familiarized with the Christian life. Our Lord, His Blessed Mother, and His Saints must be living realities to him, not abstract ideas. Godparents and parents must use every means in their power to make the child familiar with the life of our Lord, His Blessed Mother, and His Saints. The appeal must be made to the status of the child as being a member of Christ, fellow-citizen with the Saints, and of the Household of God. Our Lord, His Blessed Mother, and the Saints must be as real to the child as the people among whom he lives, and, as I have said, every means must be resorted to

A Godly and Christian Life

And for want of devotion to the Will of God how many lives are being frittered away! If they would listen they would hear the Will of God, but they do not listen, and therefore, of course, they do not hear. It has been so beautifully said: " God speaks very gently, and we must listen if we want to hear what He says." It is sad to think how many vocations are missed in this way.

Priests are needed, monks and nuns are needed, Sisters of Charity are needed. We know they are needed, and we suppose that some people will come forward as Priests, or Missionaries, or Religious. It has been well said: " If there is anything that has got to be done, show some very good reason why you should not be the person who has got to do it." We say: " I should think some people ought to go out as Missionaries; I should think some people ought to be Monks, or Nuns, or Sisters of Charity—these things are so badly needed." But it never occurs to us to ask whether, perhaps, God meant us to do any of these things. So countless lives are frittered away. They do not hear God call, because they are not listening for it; they do not listen for it, because they have not been taught in any practical way the supremacy of the Will of God.

A priest was one day at the Convent of a Community of Sisters of Charity. Applications were pouring in on all sides for Sisters to work in various parishes. They had to be refused because they have not nearly Sisters enough. The Reverend Mother said to him: " Cannot you send me some of those idle girls who are always playing golf?" Oh, that one could! Golf and tennis have become to many the supreme business of life simply because they have never asked themselves why they are alive, and what God wants them to do. If He wants them to play golf and tennis for most of their lives, well and good. They are following their vocation. But have they ever stopped to ask themselves what He does want?

We cannot suppose that they have. And the reason why so obvious a question has never been asked by them is because they were not " virtuously brought up to lead a godly and Christian life."

Oh, that English Churchmen would turn their eyes to the ideal of Christian education set before us in the Prayer-Book!

CHAPTER XVIII

CONFIRMATION

WE now have to consider the Prayer-Book Man as regards his Confirmation.

The whole subject of Confirmation is so overlaid with cartloads of rubbish that we must attempt to clear away some of it.

We find—(1) Wrong ideas as to what Confirmation is; (2) wrong ideas in respect of preparation for Confirmation; (3) a great deal of rubbish overlaying the simplicity of the Confirmation Service itself. So we will begin, as we have done on former occasions, by ruling certain things out of our conception of Confirmation, so that we may, having got rid of the accumulated rubbish, get down to the truth as to Confirmation.

1. *Wrong Ideas about Confirmation.*—If your average Englishman were asked what Confirmation is, he would be pretty sure to descant upon the renewal of Baptismal vows, which is merely an incident preparatory to Confirmation. If you look at the pious literature of some fifty years ago you will invariably find that the whole point of Confirmation is supposed to reside in the answer " I do " that the children make to the question put to them by the Bishop, and out of this mistake of looking upon a preparatory incident as though

it constituted the essence of Confirmation arise other absurd and disastrous notions. The lowest and most ridiculous of such ideas is that up to the time of Confirmation the godparents are responsible for the child's misdeeds, but that when he is confirmed he takes this responsibility on himself.

The obvious answer to this is that, if this were so, a person would be a great fool to be confirmed at all. If our godparents can bear our responsibilities we had better let them do so.

But short of such amazing folly as this people have an idea that Confirmation increases our responsibility, and that if they continue unconfirmed they will not take responsibilities upon themselves! And this quite ridiculous idea keeps people back from Confirmation.

What is the matter with these people? Why, this: They have forgotten that they cannot be more committed to the Christian life in all its fulness than they are already by the vows of their Baptism. Whether they renew their vows or whether they do not, they have made them, and it is by the keeping or breaking of their vows that they stand or fall, and that they will ultimately be judged. Strange that people should so wholly forget the vows of their Baptism! Yet they do. We constantly hear people say, " I do not profess anything," so that one is tempted to answer, " Don't tell lies. You have professed, and you are, and will be, held responsible for that solemn profession."

But there is a lurking idea at the back of people's minds that they individually had no voice in the matter, and that therefore they ought not to be held responsible until they have taken the vow upon themselves.

I would answer such people by asking whether they

Confirmation

were consulted as to their wishes before they were born into human life with all its responsibilities. Are they prepared to say: "I was not consulted before I was born, and therefore I am free from the responsibilities of human life"? Let them make such a claim, and see if human society will respect it! Or, again, can an Englishman object that he was not consulted as to whether he was to be born in England or in Japan, and that therefore he is free from the obligations of British citizenship? Let him advance such a claim, and see whether the tax-collector or the police will endorse it! It is by the mercy of God that a man is born into natural life; it is by the mercy of God that he is born in one country rather than another. He had no choice in the matter. So it is by the mercy of God that he is born into the spiritual life, and he will find that he can no more shirk his responsibilities in one case than he can in the other. A man may just as well say, "I was not asked whether I would be born an Englishman, therefore I still hold myself free to live the life of a Hottentot in the streets of London," as say, "I was not consulted before my Baptism, and therefore I shall hold myself free to live as a heathen in the Kingdom of God." No Israelite could claim exemption from keeping the covenant on the ground that he was only eight days old when he was circumcised, and no Christian can claim exemption from his covenant on the ground that he was brought into it before he could speak for himself. We rule, then, out of our conception of Confirmation all idea of increased responsibility. There still remains the curious idea that the purpose of Confirmation is the renewal of Baptismal vows, and a strange and curious notion it is.

But people may say: "The Bishop says, in the Confirmation service, that the children are openly to ratify and ' confirm ' the promises made by their godparents." I answer: " That is perfectly true, but you seem to forget that the godparents were told to bring the child to the Bishop to *be* confirmed by him." If children come to Confirmation to confirm, where does the Bishop come in ? Is it worth the Bishop's while to take time and trouble to hear the children confirm themselves ? They renew their Baptismal vows every time they say the Catechism. To say " I will " before the Bishop is no more than to say " By God's help so I will " before the godparents or the Parish Priest.

The Bishop does not come to hear the children confirm themselves; he comes to confirm them. It would not be in the least worth his while to take all the trouble merely to hear the children say what they have been saying already all their lives in the Catechism; it *is* worth his while to come there to administer Confirmation to the children by the laying on of his hands.

If once we can get into our heads that Confirmation adds no new responsibility; that children are brought to the Bishop, not to confirm but to be confirmed; not to do something, but to receive something—then we shall have carted away a lot of the rubbish that obscures, in the English mind, the truth about Confirmation.

Let us now take the rubbish-cart round to see what wrong ideas there are to be found as regards preparation for Confirmation, and when we get there, with our rubbish-cart ready, we say: " Oh dear, what a mess there is here !"

We will set to work upon this department of Confirmation, and see if we cannot clean it up a little.

Let us consider the ordinary course of events at the approach of a Confirmation. The time for the Con-

Confirmation

firmation being fixed, the clergy or their district visitors beat round the parish to find out who wish (or to put it perhaps more truly, who are willing) to be confirmed. Parents generally are ready to put spokes in the wheel. This child is too young; this one will not understand; that one will not live up to it. Some more obliging parents say that they have no objection; that the child may please him- (or her-) self. In the course of this weary peregrination the parson finds older people who have never been confirmed. They have an idea that Confirmation will increase their responsibilities, and they do not wish to increase them. At present, as they think, they do not " profess " anything, but if they did " profess " they would not be like So-and-so and So-and-so, but they would " live up to it "; but as they have no intention of " living up to it " they will not be confirmed, thank you. Or the unfortunate parson has to encounter the Protestant who does not believe in these outward ceremonies, and sees no good in Confirmation. " Religion is a thing of the heart," etc. So the poor man goes his weary round, and at last he has collected a certain number of children whose parents don't mind if they are confirmed, and a certain number of adults whom he has been able to persuade to come forward. Now, before we pursue the subject of preparation for Confirmation any farther we will pause at this point, and see what the Prayer-Book has to say about all this.

Would you be surprised to know that there is not a hint of all this in the Prayer-Book? Will it surprise you to hear that it is not the business of the parson or the district visitor to be hunting up Confirmation candidates? Yet this is a sober fact. It is high time that the parochial clergy should " turn," like the proverbial worm, and emphatically protest against the wholly erroneous idea that it is their business to " get " people to be confirmed. There is not a word in the Prayer-Book that even hints at the clergy having to do anything of the sort! All this weary business of the clergy beating round their parishes to hunt up Confirmation candidates is most emphatically not Prayer-Book religion. It is not the business of the clergy at all, and they never undertook to do it.

Whose business is it, then? I answer at once: " It is the business of the godparents, or of the parents." Before the newly baptized child is taken out of the church these words are addressed to the godparents: " Ye are to take care that this child be brought to the Bishop to be confirmed by him." When the time for Confirmation is announced, the Prayer-Book contemplates that the godparents will bring the children to the clergy, knowing the Creed, the Lord's Prayer, the Ten Commandments, and the Catechism. The clergy are the medium of communication between the godparents and the Bishops.

All that weary beating round the parish is foreign to the Prayer-Book religion. If the clergy do it, it means that they have to do the work of godparents and parents because these are too ignorant, or too careless, or too lazy to do it themselves.

Let us return to the dreary spectacle of the course of events before a Confirmation.

The candidates having been got together, are sorted out into those dreadful things that are called Confirmation classes. " Confirmation class for boys such a time," " Confirmation class for girls such a time," and into the " class " they go. Some are grown up. They must not be put with the children, and the un-

Confirmation

fortunate parson is supposed to leave his ordinary work and drudge away at the " Confirmation classes " ; and a nice task it is ! Some know the Catechism, some do not; some can say the Lord's Prayer and perhaps the Creed, but do not know the Ten Commandments. Some have been so well instructed that they know why they wish to be confirmed. Some know nothing about it at all ; but the magical " class " is to put all straight and work wonders. Wonders, indeed ! For it is supposed to do in six weeks or two months the work of ten years or so. Perhaps the parson has an elaborate scheme of instruction mapped out which seems designed to make theologians of the poor children. Perhaps he has a beautiful series of addresses for his " class." Anyhow, the " class " goes on. Possibly just before the Confirmation he finds accidentally that So-and-so has never been baptized. Perhaps he does not find it out till after they have been confirmed. If he is a wise man, knowing his English world, he will find out about the Baptism of his candidate at the outset, but all parsons are not wise men, and so these little contretemps occur from time to time.

Occasionally the monotony of the proceedings is varied by a message from a fond parent to the effect that he or she does not object to Tommy being confirmed, but he, or she, will not allow him to " take the Sacrament " ; or the fond parent sends a wrathful message to say that he, or she, will not allow the child to be taught anything about Confession.

So the " class " pursues its dreary way, and we ask: " Is this what the Prayer-Book contemplates ? " We answer: " Certainly not." Search your Prayer-Book through and through, and you will not find a hint about Confirmation classes. We contemplate that the two parents and three godparents will among them teach the child the Creed, the Lord's Prayer, and the Ten Commandments, and that they will at any rate have " provided " that he be further instructed in the Church Catechism. This " further instruction " in the Catechism is provided for in the Prayer-Book by the direction for public catechizing in the church by the Parish Priest.

If all this had been going on for ten years or so of the child's life he surely ought to be fit for Confirmation at the end of it. But as a practical matter of fact, time has been frittered away in the Sunday School over some of those neat little courses of lessons published by various Societies, and the Sunday School has not been looked upon or used as a preparation for Confirmation. We have drifted into a system of teaching children in Sunday School about all and sundry, and then at the end of it the child is suddenly asked if he will be confirmed, and drafted into a " Confirmation class." From this admirable system the child will learn that the neat little lessons on parables and miracles, or on Old Testament types, constitute the essence of religion, while Confirmation comes in, in a sort of accidental way, for those who happen to think they would like to be confirmed, much like violin playing or water-colour drawing, or any other " extra " in a school curriculum.

But even if Sunday Schools are carried out on a sensible principle, they are not contemplated in the Prayer-Book system. There we have home instruction supplemented by public catechizing by the Parish Priest.

So much for " Confirmation classes."

Now for the next piece of rubbish that we find

cumbering the ground, about the preparation for Confirmation. I mean the age limit.

A pernicious custom has been allowed to arise that the Bishop should fix an age for Confirmation.

With the Prayer-Book in one's hand one wonders by what right, or by what authority, Bishops have come to do this. There is no limit of age in the Prayer-Book at all.

In the Confirmation Service, it is true, the words are used, " Having come to years of discretion "; but the Prayer-Book has defined for us what it means by " years of discretion." " Ye are to take care that this child be brought to the Bishop to be confirmed by him so soon as he can say the Creed, the Lord's Prayer, and the Ten Commandments in the vulgar tongue, and be further instructed in the Church Catechism set forth for that purpose." So that presumably the words, " And having learnt what their godfather and godmothers promised for them in Baptism," are to be taken as synonymous with, and explanatory of, " having come to years of discretion."

But even supposing that this were not so, and that coming to years of discretion is something beside and beyond the knowledge of these things, how absurd it is to suppose that children come to years of discretion at a jump at one and the same moment in their various lives ! Fifty years ago sixteen was supposed to be the age. Now fourteen is put out as the magical moment.

The late Archbishop Temple is reported to have said very pithily: " You might just as well judge of them by weight." But still the silly superstition continues to a very large extent, and so it comes to pass that after the unfortunate parson has had to contend with parents and guardians, and has had to battle with the

" Confirmation class," a new lion starts up in the path, and he has to contend with the Bishop about the age limit. He is at this stage of the proceedings confronted with the " official list " on which has to be entered names *and ages* of those who are to be confirmed. And as we gaze at the paper with its column of ages, Archbishop Temple's words come to one's mind, " You might as well judge them by weight !" and a delightful and tempting vision arises before one's mind's eye of a Confirmation list arranged in this way:

John Jones, 15. Mary Smith, 8 stone 6.
Thomas Wilkins, 4 feet 2 inches.

May not the age limit be tipped into the rubbish-cart ?

But, seriously, this arbitrary age limit is a great infringement on our Christian liberty, and often does great injustice to children, their parents, and their godparents.

Now for rubbish that has accumulated on the Confirmation Service itself.

When we take the Prayer-Book and look at the Confirmation Service we cannot help noticing how short it is. But when we have to experience the twentieth-century Confirmation, we have a weariful sense of its inordinate length !

What makes this vast difference between the Prayer-Book Confirmation and Confirmations as we know them ?

The length of our Confirmation Service is to be laid at the door of two things: (1) " Charges," or sermons; (2) hymns.

The custom has grown up that the Bishop should give two " charges," one before and one after the

Confirmation

administration of Confirmation. That is to say, the children and those who bring them have to undergo *two* sermons.

One sermon at a Confirmation is bad enough, and does not seem to be contemplated by the Prayer-Book; but two ! What are our feelings when, having sat through one sermon of twenty-five minutes or so, the continuity of the Office is broken in upon by a hymn, after which we sink in despair into our seats as we find we have got to undergo a second sermon !

Now a few fatherly words of welcome and encouragement to the children would be natural and well placed; but we venture, with all respect, to suggest that too often it seems as if Bishops had not stopped to consider what is to be the end and object of the " charge."

Sometimes the charges take the form of prolonged instruction upon Confirmation and Communion. What is the good of that ? If the children have been presented for Confirmation they must have received such instruction, in which case it is superfluous and uncalled for to give it to them again. But if they have not already been instructed, it can hardly be supposed that the Bishop will supply the deficiency in twenty-five minutes ; therefore instruction at that moment would seem out of the question.

But it often happens that the charges are *nihil ad rem* to the matter in hand, and merely suggest the thought that the Bishop considered that he must say something, and either had nothing he particularly wanted to say, or was using the Confirmation charge as an opportunity for airing what happened to be uppermost in his mind.

Oh, that unfortunate idea that the Bishop must say something ! The Prayer-Book certainly lays no such necessity upon him, and though some people might think it odd to have a Confirmation without a " charge," many would hail with delight such a return to simple Prayer-Book ways.

Now we do not want to seem in any way lacking in respect for the Bishop. A few well-chosen words from the Bishop will carry great weight, and probably be remembered in after-years. But two long sermons overshoot the mark altogether, and are apt to produce nothing but a dejected sense of weariness, whatever may be their subject-matter; while two sermons that are *nihil ad rem* add a sense of injury to the weariness.

Let us give concrete instances of the inappropriateness of some Confirmation " charges."

One has heard of a Bishop who was apt to " charge " on the subject that happened to be uppermost in his mind at the time. On one occasion this happened to be the sin of so-called marriage with a deceased wife's sister. So the children were " charged " with respect to this sin ! Most wholesome doctrine ! But was this the time or the place to inculcate it ? It is said that after this Confirmation a father asked his child what the Bishop had said, to which the child answered perfectly correctly: " He said you must not marry Aunt Eliza !" One has heard of another Bishop who said that he was only going to give one charge, to which the vicar *is said to have* replied: " Oh, thank God for that !" But the good Vicar's thanksgiving was a little premature, for the said charge lasted fifty-six minutes. The subject of the charge was the desirability of studying the First Lesson for the day. Now nothing is more needful at the present time than that people should know how to read the Old Testament. But you will not teach this in fifty-six minutes, even supposing it to

Confirmation

be *the* thing that you want to say to people at their Confirmation.

When the same Bishop came to the same church the following year, the clergy (like the elders of Bethlehem in the Book of Samuel) " trembled at his coming." This time the charge only lasted thirty-five minutes, but the good Bishop began by saying: " You are come here to profess your belief in the Church of England." But the poor children, and those who had brought them there, thought they had come to be confirmed !

One has heard of another Bishop who used the opportunity of the Confirmation charge to air his views about the Intermediate State, so those who were there on that occasion had to listen to two sermons on the Intermediate State, one immediately before, and one immediately after, the laying on of hands !

Is there not here a lamentable want of a sense of the fitness of things, or of a want of a sense of humour, which is much the same thing ?

These wearisome vagaries arise out of our being in bondage to the idea that it is necessary that a Bishop should give a " charge " or two every time that he administers Confirmation. If we could get back to the simplicity of the Prayer-Book ideal, it would be, I venture to think, a great relief to Bishops as well as to others.

Then the beautiful simplicity of the order for Confirmation as set forth in the English Prayer-Book is marred and broken in upon by that pernicious habit of interlarding everything with hymns.

Notably in this case with those wretched hymns that are scattered all over the Confirmation Service as if they had been shaken out of a flour-dredger. Just when we want to be quiet, and are impressed with the solemnity of the whole thing, a stentorian voice roars out, " Hymn 567," " Hymn 234," and probably the first line of the said hymn. We inwardly say, " Oh, bother the hymns!" and struggle to our feet. Yes, there they are, scattered about all over the simple grandeur and continuity of the Prayer-Book " Order " —hymn to start, hymn before laying on of hands, hymn before second sermon, hymn after second sermon—and scarcely can the beautiful service run a few sentences but that awful voice bellows, " Hymn 123," " Hymn 456," till we wish the hymns and the stentorian voice at the bottom of the sea. It is such bathos, such vulgar prose.

Let *Veni Creator* be sung during the laying on of hands. This is a widespread custom, and how beautiful and touching it is anyone who has heard it will know. And this will put an end to the last item I shall notice— viz., the direction occasionally given that " the choir shall sing ' Amen ' after each laying on of hands." What a terrible idea! A long A-men on G repeated one hundred and fifty or two hundred times! And why are the choir to have anything to do with the matter? The Amen at the laying on of hands is printed in the same type as the rest of the words, which throughout the book indicates that it is said by the person who uses the words. Clearly the Prayer-Book knows nothing about the choir singing " Amen " at each laying on of hands. This may be tipped straight into the rubbish-cart!

Just see now what we have ruled out of the idea of Confirmation:

1. The idea of new responsibility.

2. The idea that the essence of Confirmation lies in the renewal of vows.

Confirmation

3. The idea that it is the parson's business to get people to be confirmed.

4. The idea that they are to be prepared in a six weeks' or two months' Confirmation class instead of a lifelong home instruction supplemented by public catechizing.

5. The age limit.

Then how simple and edifying will the actual Confirmation be if we can exclude—

1. Long and irrelevant sermons.

2. Perpetual interruption of hymns.

3. Amens on G.

But we must not expect to see all this rubbish disappear at once.

Victor Hugo, in " Les Misérables," has a wonderful passage about what he calls " mining with ideas." We get the true idea (or ideal, which comes to much the same thing) under all the accumulated rubbish; we keep on working away with the true ideal, keep on pegging away at the truth, and some day the mine will explode and scatter the rubbish, and men will wake up to say: " How could we have been such fools ?"

Let us hold on to our ideal through thick and thin, and keep it before ourselves and the world, and wait patiently for it to work.

And now, having tried to show what are the false ideas that are so prevalent as regards Confirmation, we shall in the next chapter proceed to consider the truth about Confirmation.

CHAPTER XIX

CONFIRMATION (*continued*)

IN the last chapter we cleared the ground for the consideration of the subject of the Prayer-Book Man's Confirmation by ruling out a whole accumulation of wrong ideas, which in one way and another have been allowed to grow up round Confirmation. We now take up the positive side of Confirmation and the place which it holds in the life of the Prayer-Book Man. We will again divide our subject under three heads:

1. What is Confirmation ?
2. What is the preparation for Confirmation ?
3. How should Confirmation be administered ?

1. *What is Confirmation ?*—We answer at once: " It is a Sacrament." " But," someone will say, " in the Church of England there are only two Sacraments." Softly, my friend, not so fast ! The Prayer-Book speaks of two " Sacraments of the Gospel," and five " commonly called Sacraments." And in the Catechism the Prayer-Book defines for us, in most careful and accurate language, in what sense it uses the word " Sacrament," when it confines it to the two " Sacraments of the Gospel." It does not say nakedly that there are only two Sacraments. What it does say is,

that there are only two as *generally necessary to salvation*.

Again, it marks off these two from the others by saying that the outward visible sign of the inward spiritual grace in each of these two Sacraments is ordained by Christ Himself. So it is quite clear that the Prayer-Book is using the word " Sacrament " in a most restricted sense, in which sense it can only apply to the two " Sacraments of the Gospel," the intention no doubt being not to diminish the glory of the other Sacraments, but to exalt the two " Sacraments of the Gospel."

But when we turn to the Article on the Sacraments we find the distinction sharply drawn between the two " Sacraments of the Gospel " and the five " commonly called Sacraments," and we are told that these are " such as have grown, partly of the corrupt following of the Apostles ; partly, are states of life allowed in the Scriptures." Now here it is quite clear that we have not an exhaustive division, inasmuch as Confirmation cannot fall under either of these heads. It is clearly not a corrupt following of the Apostles, inasmuch as it is especially enjoined in the Prayer-Book. Equally certainly it is not " a state of life allowed in the Scriptures." Therefore we are driven back upon the restricted sense in which the Prayer-Book uses the word " Sacrament "—viz., that it only applies the word to those two Sacraments which have an outward visible sign ordained by Christ Himself. Confirmation, then, is not a Sacrament *in this sense*, but, then, no one ever supposed that it was. When the Prayer-Book uses the word " Sacrament," it is most careful to define for us exactly the sense in which it uses the word.

But there is another sense in which the word " Sacrament " is used in undivided Christendom—viz., merely as an outward means of conveying an inward grace—and it is in this sense that Confirmation is called in undivided Christendom a " Sacrament." Therefore let no one run away with the idea that there is anything disloyal in calling Confirmation a Sacrament. All that we mean when we do so is that an inward grace is conveyed by the laying on of the Bishop's hands, and that the outward visible sign and the inward spiritual grace are inseparably connected together as cause and effect.

Now when we use the word " Sacrament " in this broad sense, we come to the division of Sacraments into—

(1) Sacraments of the dead; and
(2) Sacraments of the living.

This means that there are certain Sacraments which either give life to those that have never had it, or restore life to those who have lost it, and such Sacraments are called " Sacraments of the dead "; while, on the other hand, there are Sacraments which convey special gifts to those who are already in a state of grace, and these are called " Sacraments of the living." In other words, Sacraments of the dead are to make bad men good, while Sacraments of the living are to make good men better.

The " Sacraments of the dead " are Baptism and Penance, whereas Confirmation, Communion, Marriage, Orders, and Unction are " Sacraments of the living."

So we arrive at our first point—viz., that Confirmation is a Sacrament—inasmuch as it conveys a spiritual grace by an outward means, and that it is a " Sacra-

Confirmation

ment of the living," inasmuch as it is intended for those only who are already in a state of grace.

We note next that Confirmation is a Sacrament that *conveys character*, and can therefore only be administered once. This fact might be made a great lever in the preparation for Confirmation. What can only be done once must surely be done well.

If a person makes a careless or bad preparation for Confirmation, they cannot say " I will do better next time," for there is no " next time." So we urge that as it is the only time in their life that they are going to receive Confirmation, people may surely give themselves wholly for the time being to the great work of preparation.

The special gift received in Confirmation is the fulness of the Holy GHOST.

St. Thomas Aquinas says that the fulness of the Holy GHOST is received in Confirmation, for strength. Hence, of course, the name " Confirmation "—the Sacrament by which we are " confirmed " or strengthened.

The Holy GHOST bestows in Confirmation His fulness in the seven gifts of the Spirit. These gifts are enumerated in the solemn invocation of the Holy GHOST in the order of Confirmation—viz.:

> The Spirit of Wisdom and Understanding.
> The Spirit of Counsel and Ghostly Strength.
> The Spirit of Knowledge and True Godliness.
> The Spirit of God's Holy Fear.

Immediately after the descent of the Holy GHOST we find Confirmation in the Acts of the Holy Apostles. Thus, when the Samaritans had been converted and baptized by the ministry of St. Philip the Deacon, we find the Apostles at once sending down St. Peter and St. John, who proceeded to administer Confirmation to the newly "baptized." Note the words of the Holy Bible, for we shall find them exactly reproduced in the Confirmation of the Prayer-Book Man to-day. They (the two Apostles) "prayed for them that they might receive the Holy Ghost. . . . Then laid they their hands on them, and they received the Holy Ghost."

In the English Prayer-Book to-day, the Bishop first prays for them that they may receive the Holy Ghost in the solemn Invocation Prayer, and then lays his hands upon them, "that they may receive the Holy Ghost." And that there may be no mistake about the matter the Bishop is directed to say, in the prayer after Confirmation: "Upon whom, after the example of the Holy Apostles, we have now laid our hands," etc.

It will be remembered that when St. Paul found certain believers at Ephesus, he said to them, "Have ye received the Holy Ghost since ye believed?" which, put in modern English, would be, "Have you been confirmed?" and this question elicited the fact that they had not been baptized. Thereupon they were baptized, and St. Paul confirmed them.

We ought to note throughout the Epistles the stress that is laid upon this plenitude of the Holy Ghost that is bestowed in Confirmation. Sometimes it is spoken of as the "Seal," sometimes it is spoken of as the "Anointing," as, *e.g.*, when St. John says, "Ye have an Unction from the Holy One," etc.; sometimes it is spoken of in its effects, as, *e.g.*, when St. John says: "I write unto you young men because ye are strong." We notice here the intense reality of the gifts of the Holy Ghost in the minds of the Apostles. The Con-

Confirmation

firmation of the newly baptized is what the Apostles are primarily considering as concerning them, and therefore we find the Apostles constantly appealing to the reality of the Gift that was given to the baptized in their Confirmation. And in the face of this fact, that is so very patent in the New Testament, we may well consider how feeble is our grasp at this present time upon this great truth, and we ourselves may well make this same practical appeal to the reality of the Confirmation Gift, and try more than we do to stir up the Gift that is in us.

But now, before we leave the subject of what Confirmation really is, we must just notice a line of thought that comes to the fore at the present moment.

In the reaction from the utterly unworthy, mean, and inadequate conception of Confirmation above noticed (conceptions that, alas! still so largely prevail) men have been inclined to swing the pendulum too far in the opposite direction, and in their desire to vindicate the majesty of Confirmation they seem to be a little in danger of depreciating to a certain extent the Sacrament of Baptism.

Certain writers of to-day are so impressed with the magnificence of the gift of the Holy Ghost in Confirmation that they seem to suggest that Baptism is incomplete in itself, and requires Confirmation to make it a complete act. In other words, they seem to imply that Baptism and Confirmation are not two separate things, but two parts of one and the same thing. Now this view seems open to various objections. In the first place, this would practically reduce the number of the Sacraments to six, Baptism and Confirmation practically being reckoned as one. This runs counter to the conscience of undivided Christendom, which speaks of seven Sacraments. Again, this view seems faulty in respect of the analogy between natural and spiritual life.

In the natural life birth is one thing and full growth is another. Two children are born into the world—one dies in infancy, the other grows up to manhood. Are we prepared to say that the birth of the former was incomplete? Certainly not! The birth in each case was a complete act; so in the spiritual life Baptism is the Sacrament of Birth, Confirmation the Sacrament of full growth. The transition from not being (in things spiritual) to being is complete in Baptism. Then we pass from darkness to light and from the power of Satan to God; then we are made dead, indeed, unto sin, and alive unto God through Jesus Christ our Lord. Baptism is a "Sacrament of the dead." It gives the initial gift of life. Confirmation is a "Sacrament of the living." It confers the gift of the Spirit to those who are now capable of receiving it, because they are completely alive. But (and this is what especially concerns us at present) whatever there may be to be said for this view it is not "Prayer-Book." The English Prayer-Book, following the use of Western Christendom, interposes a delay of some years between Baptism and Confirmation. This cannot be justified if Baptism is, as it were, held in suspense all that time.

The Prayer-Book clearly looks upon Confirmation as something distinct from, and consequent upon, Baptism. Again, we must remember the Rubric at the end of the Order of Public Baptism, which says that it is certain by God's Word that children who are baptized, and who die before they commit actual sin, are undoubtedly saved. There can be no incompleteness about Baptism if this is so.

Confirmation

Once more, if Baptism is, as the Prayer-Book says it is, " generally necessary to Salvation," and if Confirmation is necessary for complete Baptism, it is difficult to escape from the conclusion that Confirmation is " generally necessary to salvation." But it is not! There are two Sacraments only that are generally necessary to Salvation—viz., Baptism and the Supper of the Lord. Therefore we conclude that any view of Confirmation that tends to consider Baptism as incomplete without it is contrary to fact, is against the analogy of natural life, and is certainly " un-Prayer-Book." But while we maintain this, we lay down most emphatically that Christianity knows nothing of people choosing, after their Baptism, whether they will be confirmed or not. When we think of grown-up Christians who have neglected, or despised or refused Confirmation, we do not know where to place them, or what to think about them; they are bad and lapsed Christians, and we can only hope and pray that they may be brought to repentance. Neither the Bible nor the Prayer-Book knows anything of such people at all.

We sum up our consideration as to what Confirmation really is :

(1) It is a Sacrament.

(2) It is a Sacrament of the living.

(3) It is a Sacrament that confers character.

(4) Its special gift is the fulness of the Holy Ghost, for strength.

(5) It is a Sacrament for the baptized only, but is distinct from the Sacrament of Baptism.

2. We now pass in the light of these great truths to consider how the Prayer-Book Man is to be prepared for Confirmation. We see at a glance that the great

preparation for Confirmation is that a person be actually at the moment of receiving Confirmation in a state of grace.

If you turn to the Exhortation at the beginning of the Confirmation Office, you will see that it is there stated that the Church—*i.e.*, this portion of the Church following, as it does, the use of Western Christendom —has thought fit to ordain that Confirmation should be deferred until the person to be confirmed have learnt certain things; but the Prayer-Book is careful to say that this is done for the more edification of those who are to receive Confirmation, and that this order is " convenient to be observed." It does not for a moment say that these things are necessary for the reception of Confirmation. Of course not ! The Prayer-Book could not say this in the face of the fact that to this day in the Holy Eastern Church Confirmation is administered to infants immediately after their Baptism.

All that the Prayer-Book says is, that it is " more edifying " and " convenient " that the custom of Western Christendom should be followed.

But it is *absolutely necessary* that the person who is to receive Confirmation should be in a state of salvation.

Now, when we have two things, one of which is necessary, while the other is merely " edifying and convenient," it is clear that the necessary comes first and the " convenient " quite second. Hence we see that in the preparation for Confirmation the being in a state of grace is the first point to be aimed at, whereas the instruction is a secondary matter.

But it is much to be feared that in the ordinary curriculum of " the Confirmation class " it is the secondary matter that holds the first place, while the main thing recedes into the background.

So essential is it that those who are to receive Confirmation should be in a state of grace, that if by any accident it should happen that Confirmation should have been given to an unbaptized person *it counts for nothing*, and the person would have to be confirmed after his Baptism.

You will find (if you look at the solemn Prayer of Invocation by which the Bishop, after the example of the Holy Apostles, " prays for them that they may receive the Holy Ghost ") that the Church distinctly excludes all who are not in a state of grace, for the Prayer-Book bids the Bishop say in that Prayer : " Almighty and everliving God, Who hast vouchsafed to regenerate these Thy servants by Water and the Holy Ghost, and hast given unto them forgiveness of all their sins," etc.

By these words the Church clearly intimates that the Bishop takes it for granted that those he has before him are in a fit state to receive Confirmation; consequently the main effort of those who are preparing candidates for Confirmation must be directed to this necessary thing. The whole thing will be based upon the fact of their Baptism, and if they have committed any mortal sin since their Baptism they must be certified of the forgiveness of GOD upon their true repentance.

About this we shall have more to say when we come to speak of the Prayer-Book Man receiving Absolution. We therefore merely state the fact now and leave it.

What has been said is sufficient to show how, too often, a wrong or inadequate conception of what Confirmation is produces evil fruit in the preparation, and how what is of secondary importance is too often made the primary thing, while what is of absolute necessity is made a secondary matter.

And, of course, the consideration of what is absolutely necessary for Confirmation throws a lurid light on the wholly unauthorized " age limit," for the " age limit " has reference to the intellectual and moral attainments which the Prayer-Book merely speaks of as " edifying " and " convenient," whereas the necessary qualification is possessed by children from the moment of their Baptism, and the fault of the age limit is that it exceeds even what Western Christendom considers " convenient," and substitutes an arbitrary and wholly unauthorized qualification for what the Prayer-Book distinctly lays down merely as " edifying."

The sole qualification for Confirmation which can be said to be *necessary* is that the person, having been baptized, should be at the moment actually in a state of salvation.

Would that this were remembered always in the preparation for Confirmation !

3. Let us now consider the actual administration of Confirmation.

We have seen that Confirmation has no outward visible sign or form ordained by Christ Himself. We find throughout Christendom that it is the Bishop who is the Minister of Confirmation; we have seen in the case of the Samaritans that two of the Apostles were sent down from Jerusalem to administer Confirmation to them.

In the East, Confirmation is actually administered by the Priest immediately after Baptism, but it is administered with Chrism that has been especially blessed by the Bishop for that specific purpose, so that it is the

Confirmation

Bishop ultimately who is the Minister of Confirmation, and the Bishop only. Should the Priest in the Eastern Church attempt to administer Confirmation with any other oil than that blessed by the Bishop for the purpose, it would not be Confirmation at all.

There are three ways in which Confirmation may be administered in the Catholic Church, all equally valid:

(1) By laying on of hands only, as with ourselves.

(2) By anointing only, as in the East.

(3) By anointing and laying on of hands, as in the Churches of the Roman Communion.

Whichever of these ways is used the Intention of the Church is to convey thereby the fulness of the Holy Ghost in the sevenfold Gifts of the Spirit.

As we have seen, the Bishops, after the example of the Holy Apostles, first pray for them that they " may receive the Holy Ghost," and then " lay their hands " on them (or anoint them, as in the East), that they " may receive the Holy Ghost."

This solemn Invocation and laying on of hands (or anointing) are of the essence of Confirmation. All else in the Order of Confirmation is secondary and subsidiary.

The question and answer on which such undue stress has been laid amongst us " English " are merely preparatory to the administration of Confirmation. They are placed there that the Bishop may, so far as in him lies, ensure that those to whom he is about to administer Confirmation are fit persons to receive it— *i.e.*, that they are in a state of grace. If a person who has been baptized is willing solemnly to renew the vows of his Baptism, he must be taken as meaning what he says, in which case he is in a state of grace, for no wilfully impenitent person could renew the vows of his Baptism. But we see that this is merely preparatory to the great Invocation and laying on of hands.

Look at the Order for Confirmation in the Prayer-Book, and you see how it all fits together. There is the ascertaining about the state of grace, there is the solemn Invocation, there is the laying on of hands, there is the prayer for the newly confirmed, and there is the Episcopal blessing—so plain and so simple! Then think of the two weariful sermons interpolated into it, and the pert hymns scattered about all over it. How the whole thing is vulgarized and obscured. Sermons about all and sundry, and hymns about all and sundry, breaking in upon the dignified simplicity of Confirmation, as the Prayer-Book Man knows it.

Let us hope that a more due appreciation of what Confirmation is will lead to a sweeping out of all this rubbish, and a return to the simplicity of the Prayer-Book ideal.

A delightful story is told of a Bishop who wanted to put down Ritualistic practices, and sent a message to a Vicar that the Confirmation was to be strictly in accordance with the Prayer-Book. The Bishop arrived on the given day, and began laying down the law as to the arrangements for the Confirmation Service.

" The hymns——" he began.

" No hymns, my lord."

" No hymns " ?

" No, my lord; you said the Service was to be strictly in accordance with the Prayer-Book. There are no hymns in the Prayer-Book, so there will be no hymns."

" Oh, very well, I shall give my address."

" No address, my lord."

Confirmation

" No address " ?

" No, my lord; you said the Service was to be strictly in accordance with the Prayer-Book. There will be no time for an address, for as you said the Service was to be strictly in accordance with the Prayer-Book, I have fixed Evensong for eight o'clock, so there can be no address."

So the crestfallen Bishop was hoist with his own petard, and *for once in his life* had to administer Confirmation as the Prayer-Book Man would always expect to find it administered.

CHAPTER XX

COMMUNION

WE now pass on to consider the Prayer-Book Man in connection with the Sacrament of Communion. Sacramental Communion may be considered in two ways: either from its liturgical point of view as the completion of the act of worship, or in relation to the spiritual life. The former of these two aspects has already been dealt with in Chapters VI. and VII. We now have to regard the Sacrament of Communion in relation to the spiritual life of the Prayer-Book Man. We do not mean, of course, that these two aspects are really separable, but only that we distinguish between them in thought for the purposes of our discussion.

Now, we must observe first that in speaking of the Sacrament of Communion the Catechism does not use precisely the same phraseology as it does in the case of the Sacrament of Baptism. The questions in respect of the Sacrament of Baptism are—(1) What is the outward visible sign or form in Baptism ? (2) What is the inward and spiritual grace ? Whereas, in respect of the Sacrament of Communion, the questions are— (1) What is the outward *part or sign* of the Lord's Supper ? (2) What is the inward *part or thing signified ?* And we learn by the answer that the outward part is

Communion

bread and wine, while the inward part is the Body and Blood of Christ.

It remains that we should see what is the effect of partaking of the Body and Blood of Christ—in other words, what is the special gift that such partaking bestows. The special gift imparted by Sacramental Communion is the gift of Eternal Life. Our Lord says: "Whoso eateth My Flesh and drinketh My Blood, hath Everlasting Life, and I will raise him up at the last day." And He teaches us the same truth negatively when He says: "Except ye eat the Flesh of the Son of Man, and drink His Blood, ye have no life in you."

Everlasting Life, then, is the Gift conveyed by Sacramental Communion. The Prayer-Book reminds us of this in more ways than one. Quoting our Lord's words, it says, enumerating the benefits of Sacramental Communion: "Then we dwell in Christ, and Christ in us; we are one with Christ, and Christ with us." But to dwell in Christ is to be a partaker of His Everlasting Life.

Again, in the words of administration, the Prayer-Book says: "The Body of our Lord Jesus Christ, which was given for thee, preserve thy body and soul unto Everlasting Life."

We need not multiply instances. These words of our Lord and of His Church are sufficient to show us that Sacramental Communion is God's appointed way for conveying to man the gift of Everlasting Life.

Now, the gift of Everlasting Life is something a great deal more than the mere recovery from the Fall. If we turn to see what is told us of man in his original righteousness, we find that not even then was Everlasting Life a part of his original equipment, if we may use such an expression. He was in a state of grace;

he had not fallen into sin; he did not need redemption; he did not require forgiveness. But still he had to attain Everlasting Life, and we read that when the Lord God planted a Garden eastward in Eden, the Tree of Life was there in the midst of the Garden, and we are told what it was there for. It was to convey to man Everlasting Life. "Lest he put forth his hand, and take also of the Tree of Life, and eat, and live for ever," etc. And it was to remove this possibility from him, after he had forfeited his right to it, that Adam was driven out of the Garden. "*Therefore* the Lord sent him forth from the Garden of Eden. And He placed at the east of the Garden of Eden Cherubim, and a flaming sword which turned every way, to keep the way of the Tree of Life."

In the Sacrament of Communion, then, we have something that goes behind the Fall. It does more than restore us to the grace that Adam lost; it gives us the Gift that we should still have needed if there had been no sin at all. And one cannot help observing what one may venture to call our Lord's choice of language in respect to the Sacrament of Communion. He speaks of Himself in Holy Communion as "the Bread of Life." Our attention is at once arrested by a familiar sound. "The Bread of Life!" "The Tree of Life!" It is the same expression: "Take of the Tree of Life, and eat, and live for ever." "I am the Bread of Life: if any man eat of this Bread, he shall live for ever." The two things are exactly parallel.

In a sense, then, the Sacrament of Communion goes back behind the Fall; but in another sense it is the remedy for the great result of the Fall. It is the sovereign antidote against death, and it is in this connection that we must think of it for a moment.

Communion

Everlasting Life is something quite beyond the mere immortality of the Soul. The belief in Everlasting Life presupposes the belief in the Resurrection of the body. The resurrection of the body is the great cardinal doctrine of Christianity. The resurrection of the body was the Gospel that the Apostles went out to preach. Even before the Day of Pentecost, St. Peter insisted that one must be ordained " to be a witness " with them " of the Resurrection." They went out to preach Jesus and the Resurrection. St. Paul at Athens urges repentance on the ground that the Resurrection was the proof that God had appointed the Risen Lord as Judge.

The whole atmosphere of the Acts and of the Epistles is charged with the resurrection of the body. When, for instance, St. Paul is standing before Agrippa, Festus tells the King that the question at issue was not at all what he had supposed, but that the Jews had certain questions against St. Paul of their own superstitions, and of one " Jesus, which was dead, whom Paul affirmed to be alive." The attempts to construct a Christianity in which the resurrection of the body should be left an open question is as ridiculous as it is impudent and dishonest. Either accept Christianity or reject it, but do not let people attempt, as many dishonest people do, to concoct a Christianity apart from belief in the resurrection of the body if they still wish to pass for sane and honest men.

" Everlasting Life," then, in the mouth of Christendom means the resurrection of the body. No mere acceptance of the fact of the immortality of the soul will pass muster with the Christian Creed. Triumphantly the symbol rings out: " I believe in the resurrection of the body, and the life everlasting. Amen."

T

When they hear this note of jubilant Faith, clever fools may still mock, as some did at Athens. They may look with pitying contempt upon those who can build upon such a faith as this, but no sane or honest man can say that the Christian Creed claims anything short of belief in the resurrection of the body.

Communion, then, being the Sacrament of Everlasting Life, implying the resurrection of the body, it would naturally follow that Communion should have to do with the resurrection of the body. But we are not left to draw this natural inference; our Lord expressly states it for us: " Whoso eateth My Flesh, and drinketh My Blood, hath Everlasting Life: and *I will raise him up at the last day*." And the Church is careful to keep this truth clearly before us, for the words of administration in the Prayer-Book runs thus: " The Body of our Lord Jesus Christ, which was given for thee, preserve *thy body* and soul unto Everlasting Life."

Resurrection is not, if I may use the expression, an external act; it is not that something or someone outside of ourselves comes and lifts us up; resurrection acts from within. St. Paul uses the analogy of seed and plant to make us understand the Christian doctrine of resurrection. The seed springs up because the life is there already inherent in it: " So is the resurrection of the dead."

Our bodies rise because the germ of resurrection life is already in them, and it is Sacramental Communion that gives this power of resurrection to our bodies as well as the power of eternal life to our souls. Dear Bishop King used to say: " We never shall know all that Communion has done for us till we rise from the dead."

The resurrection of the body, then, and the Life

Communion

Everlasting is the outcome of Sacramental Communion.

Now we can see why we are taught in the Prayer-Book that the Sacrament of Communion is generally necessary to Salvation, and now we are in a position to measure and estimate something of the horror and awfulness of those schemes and systems of so-called Christianity that make it possible for men to put the Sacrament of Communion in the background, and to treat it as a secondary or comparatively unimportant matter. This is the inevitable tendency of popular Protestantism, and as we meditate upon the Tree of Life, the Bread of Life, the Resurrection of the body, and the express words of our Lord and His Holy Church, our hatred of popular Protestantism and of the vile travesty of Christianity that it has engendered will be deepened and intensified. "Oh, ye that love the Lord, see that ye hate the thing that is evil.'

The hatred of heresy and error is the reverse side of the love of the Truth, and nothing can be more foreign to the spirit, let us say of St. John, than the system that cuts out of the Christian Creed or practice anything that any man or body of men may choose to deny, and whittles down the Revelation of God to suit the sin and unbelief of men—that system which flaunts itself now before us in England under the name of " Undenominationalism "! We will hate that with all our soul, for amongst many other abominations it dares to lay its impious hand on the Sacrament of Communion, and to trample under its vile feet the express words of our Lord and His Holy Church respecting that Holy and Divine Sacrament.

And it is when we realize the Sacrament of Com-

munion as something that stands in the Holy Catholic
Church, as the Tree of Life stood in the midst of the
Garden, as being Itself the Body and Blood of Christ,
as being God's divinely appointed means of conveying
to us the resurrection of the dead and the life of the
World to come—it is when we realize these things that
we begin to understand the awful warnings given us in
the Bible and in the Prayer-Book against any profanation of this Divine Sacrament by unworthy Communion. These awful warnings answer to the flaming
sword of the Cherubim that turned every way to keep
the way of the Tree of Life. Oh, that we realized this
more than we do!

The Holy Bible says: " He that eateth and drinketh
unworthily, eateth and drinketh damnation to himself,
not discerning the Lord's Body."

The Prayer-Book says: " So is the danger great if we
receive the same "—the Sacrament of Communion—
" unworthily; for then we are guilty of the Body and
Blood of CHRIST, our Saviour: we eat and drink our
own damnation, not considering the LORD's Body : we
kindle GOD's wrath against us : we provoke Him, to
plague us with divers diseases, and sundry kinds of
death." And again it says: " Repent you of your
sins, or else come not to that Holy Table: lest, after
the taking of that Holy Sacrament, the devil enter
into you, as he entered into Judas, and fill you full of
all iniquities, and bring you to destruction, both of
body and soul."

And note here the action of the Sacrament of Communion on the body as well as the soul. The Bible
says: " *For this cause*"—*i.e.*, for the cause of bad
Communion—" many are weak and sickly among you,
and many sleep."

Communion

The Prayer-Book warns us that unworthy Communions provoke GOD *to plague us with divers diseases and sundry kinds of death*, and that they will bring us to destruction of *body* as well as of Soul. If, as we have seen, the action of the Sacrament of Communion on the body is strong enough to counteract death, and to be within us the principle of resurrection to Eternal Life, we should naturally expect that the effect of a bad Communion would make itself felt on the body as well as on the soul, and we are positively told, both in the Bible and in the Prayer-Book, that this is actually the case.

The poison of Manicheism is continually making itself felt in the Church. Manicheism sets up a dualism of matter and spirit. Matter it conceives of as something evil in itself, while spirit alone is good. In passing, we note that this amounts to a denial of the Unity of GOD, inasmuch as it postulates an evil Creator who created matter, while Spirit is the work of the Good GOD. But the effect of this false conception on practical religion is that it regards the soul as imprisoned in the body, which is only, as it were, a temporary case to contain it for a while. The work of religion is, in the eyes of many people, to set the soul free from the body. There is no room in the Manichean theory for any belief in the resurrection of the body. Now, you get this Manichean theory in all its nakedness to-day in Swedenborgianism; but, short of naked Swedenborgianism, the pernicious influence of Manicheism makes itself felt among us at the present time in the false spirituality that so largely underlies popular Protestantism.

We see it in the common claptrap saying: " Religion is a thing of the heart and the mind." We see it in the scorn of Sacraments to which, sooner or later, Protestantism leads.

Protestantism has to a large extent lost sight of the body as an integral part of the man. The disposition of the mind and spirit are all that it takes cognizance of. Hence, while it does not discard Sacraments altogether, because of the positive enactments of our LORD, it cannot easily fit them into its philosophy.

The declarations of the Bible and the Prayer-Book as to the effect of Sacramental Communion, whether for good or for evil, upon the body, are a standing warning against the poison of Manicheism that is constantly cropping up in one form or another, against which the Church has always got to contend.

Our consideration as to what the Sacrament of Communion is in itself will lead us to three practical conclusions:

1. The fact that the Blessed Sacrament is the Body and Blood of CHRIST imposes upon us the duty of treating it as such.

The Human Nature of our LORD is inseparably united to His Divine Personality. St. Paul, you will remember, does not hesitate to speak of " the Blood of GOD." The Body of our Lord is the Body of GOD; the Blood of our LORD is the Blood of GOD. Therefore the Body and Blood of CHRIST are to be adored. If we refuse Adoration to the Blessed Sacrament, it can only be because we do not really believe that It is the Body and Blood of CHRIST, and so the adoration of the Blessed Sacrament is the touchstone of our belief in the Blessed Sacrament. If our LORD is very and Eternal GOD, He must be worshipped as such wherever He is to be found. The Act of Faith of the man who had been born blind was mere common sense. He said. " Lord, I believe; *and he worshipped Him.*" The Prayer-Book is careful to remind us that the Blessed Sacrament is a " Divine Thing "; therefore let us take care that we treat It as such.

It often falls to the lot of us Priests to carry the Blessed Sacrament through the streets of London to the sick and dying, and of all the wonderful things that we have to do, there is nothing more wonderful and beautiful than this—viz., when we are privileged to carry the Blessed Sacrament through the streets. We are lifted, as it were, into the very atmosphere of the Bible; we realize as we thread our way with our Precious Burden through the crowded streets that " He came unto His own, and His own received Him not."

Or, again, how this everyday experience of ours reproduces in twentieth-century London the mystery of the Visitation ! How like are these journeys of ours to that wonderful journey when Mary went from Galilee to the hill country of Judea bearing her GOD, as yet unborn, within her ! Those who met or passed her on the road had no suspicion that God was passing there. So like London to-day when the Blessed Sacrament is being quietly and hiddenly carried through its streets ! But sometimes the Blessed Sacrament, even in the streets of London, meets with the response of a simple faith. One Bank Holiday morning a Priest was carrying the Blessed Sacrament up Ladbroke Grove. A little lad all dressed in his best for his holiday outing was standing in the road. Seeing the Priest coming, and knowing from his attitude and bearing that he had the Blessed Sacrament with him, he at once fell on his knee in the *open street*. It was the simple faith of a simple child. He knew that the Blessed Sacrament is the Body of CHRIST, because our LORD has said that It is so, and therefore quite naturally and simply he treated It as such. "He said, Lord, I believe; and he worshipped Him." And in this connection, how our Lord's answer to the act of adoration comes home to us: "JESUS said, For judgment am I come into the world, that they which see not might see, and that they which see might be made blind."

The immediate consequence, then, of faith in the Blessed Sacrament is adoration. We sometimes hear people who fancy that they believe in the "Real Presence" say: "I do not adore the Sacrament; I adore Jesus present in the Sacrament." But this is merely reproducing in the sphere of the Blessed Sacrament the heresy of Nestorius. Nestorius would divide the Personality of our LORD. He would distinguish between the Eternal Son and JESUS, the Son of Mary; he would conceive of the Eternal Son as indwelling in some mysterious way JESUS the Son of Mary. Hence he would refuse Divine adoration to JESUS, the Son of Mary. Against this abominable and anti-Christian idea the Church in the Council of Ephesus maintained the Oneness of our LORD's Personality, and therefore decreed to the Blessed Virgin the title of Mother of GOD. The adoration of JESUS the Son of Mary is the touchstone of the truth as against the anti-Christ Nestorius.

So with the Blessed Sacrament. It is of the essence of a Sacrament that it is one thing consisting of two parts. To attempt to divide a Sacrament into two things is like the attempt of Nestorius to divide our LORD into two Persons. To attempt to distinguish between "the Sacrament" and "JESUS CHRIST present in the Sacrament" is merely a thinly veiled way

of denying that the Blessed Sacrament is the Body
and Blood of CHRIST. Either the Blessed Sacrament
is the Body of CHRIST or it is not. If It is, It must be
adored as such. So adoration is the touchstone of the
reality of one belief in the simple fact set before us by
our LORD and His Church—viz., that the Blessed
Sacrament " is " the Body and Blood of CHRIST.

2. Our second practical consideration will grow out
of the preceding one. It is just in proportion to the
reality of our faith in the truth of the Blessed Sacrament that we shall recognize the awfulness of the
neglect or misuse of It. In this, as in everything else,
Englishmen must face the alternative.

There is a large class of persons who are willing to
face facts up to a certain point, while they persistently
close their eyes to the inevitable consequences of the
admission of the fact. So as regards the Blessed
Sacrament, the man who habitually neglects It owns
that the reception of It is a duty imposed by the
positive command of our LORD, but he refuses to see
that the neglect of that duty must imperil his salvation. The careless Communicant makes his Communion because he recognizes it to be his duty to do
so, but he draws a veil over the inevitable consequence
of a bad Communion—viz., that he will thereby eat
and drink his own damnation. They accept the fact,
but reject the inevitable consequences of that fact;
they are willing to think that Communion may help
them toward their salvation, but they are not willing
to think that the neglect or misuse of it will work their
damnation.

Englishmen must be roused from this mental and
moral apathy. It is no fault of the Prayer-Book that
they have sunk into this state of mind. It thunders

out the warnings of GOD to them, but they will not heed them. If Communion is " necessary to salvation," then we cannot be saved without it. If a bad Communion conveys damnation, then we " eat and drink our own damnation." If we dare to approach Communion with one unforgiven mortal sin on our conscience, if the Blessed Sacrament is the Body of CHRIST, then to live without It is to live without CHRIST. If the Blessed Sacrament is the Body of Christ, then to profane It is to make ourselves " guilty of the Body and Blood of CHRIST." There is no middle course, and the Prayer-Book has not minced matters in any way. If the Englishman neglects or profanes the Blessed Sacrament, he cannot say that he was not warned.

3. Our third practical consideration grows out of the two former ones. We have before now noticed the absurd idea that the Prayer - Book represents a " moderate " or *via media* kind of religion that does not make any large demands upon the faith and practice of Englishmen. And here, in connection with the awful solemnity of Sacramental Communion, we would again draw attention to this supremely false idea that obtains such common currency amongst us. How can it be supposed that the Prayer-Book represents a " moderate " and easy-going religion in the face of the unfaltering boldness with which it proclaims the truth of the Blessed Sacrament ? It teaches us with no uncertain voice that the Blessed Sacrament is the Body of CHRIST; it shows us in plain and unmistakable language that Sacramental Communion either conveys eternal life or everlasting damnation. Can it take us higher than eternal life in GOD ? Can it take us any lower than eternal

Communion

damnation ? What, then, is the meaning of the idea that works at the back of the English mind—viz., that the perfection of the Saints is not to be expected in the Church of England ?

The Body and Blood of CHRIST must produce the same fruits in England as it does elsewhere, and surely there will be a rude awakening in store for us if we think that, because we are " Church of England " people, we may sit down at a comparatively low level of sanctity, and may have a religion that is more or less a compromise between the Church and the World. " To whom much is given, of him shall much be required." And to no one is more given than has been given in the mercy of GOD to the Prayer-Book Man.

CHAPTER XXI

COMMUNION (*continued*)

LET us recall some of the tremendous facts that we have considered respecting Sacramental Communion:

1. It is generally necessary to salvation.

2. It is a Sacrament of which the outward part is bread and wine, the inward part the Body and Blood of CHRIST.

3. The gift that it conveys is Eternal Life.

4. It therefore goes behind the Fall, and has its counterpart in the Tree of Life.

5. It is a Sacrament of the living, and is for those only who are actually in a state of grace.

6. Unworthy reception of Communion is fraught with such terrible danger that it is hedged about with special warnings and safeguards.

7. These warnings have their counterpart in the flaming sword of the Cherubim that turned every way to keep the way of the Tree of Life.

Bearing these tremendous facts in mind, we come to consider the Prayer-Book Man—

1. In his preparation for Communion.
2. In his reception of Communion.

1. *Preparation for Communion.* — The first thing that impresses us is, that the Prayer-Book looks upon

each Communion as a separate act, complete in itself. It knows nothing of a habit of life that is called by an extraordinary perversion of the English language " being a Communicant."

Let us once more remind ourselves that the word " Communicants " is never applied to a class of Christians, but signifies the people who are actually going to make their Communion at any given Service. Thus, in the Rubric we read: " At the time of the Celebration of the Communion, the Communicants being conveniently placed," etc. The " Communicants " are here distinguished from the rest of the congregation. Old-fashioned people used to be able to recall the custom in the days of their youth, of the Communicants moving forward into the Chancel at the beginning of the Exhortation. The word is strictly applied to those who are actually going to communicate at any particular Service. There is no hint of a certain class of people being called " Communicants," as opposed to a certain other class called " non-Communicants."

And the crass folly of this new-fangled way of talking shows itself when we come to inquire what constitutes a " Communicant " in what these silly people are pleased to call their " minds." When does a man cease to be a " Communicant "? Is he a Communicant if he once received " Communion "? If not, when did he cease to be a " Communicant " and become a " non-Communicant "? What is the meaning of the silly question so often asked the unfortunate clergy in those endless foolscap papers of statistics that for our sins we are supposed to waste our time in filling up ? " How many Communicants have you on your roll ?" What are Communicants, and what is a roll ?

Needless to say, the Church knows nothing of this rubbish. There is no class of people who are normally styled "Communicants," while as for those unhappy beings that modern Englishmen call non-Communicants, they are simply lapsed Christians who are living in mortal sin. But somehow or other we have got it into our stupid heads that "Communicants" are a sort of first-class Christians, while "non-Communicants" are not quite so good, but will get on all right.

Many years ago, in the country, a neighbouring Vicar, commending to the care of a Priest a woman who had moved into his parish, dropping his voice, said in awe-struck tones, "She is a Communicant, you know," very much as if he was telling him that she was an Obi woman or had a familiar spirit!

If anyone is ever silly enough to ask us if we are Communicants, do let us say, "Sometimes I am, and sometimes I'm not"; and that strictly truthful answer may make the questioner pause and think. But enough of this nonsense.

Remembering this extraordinary misuse of common English, let us beware of the great danger to which it has given rise. A man makes a good preparation, and makes his first Communion; then he is dubbed a "Communicant," and is regarded as having crossed a sort of Rubicon, and become a person who will always be ready to make his Communion. Communion becomes a habit of his life, and he takes it for granted that he is always fit for Communion because he has "become a Communicant." So it comes to be thought that the strict preparation which is acknowledged to be necessary for a non-Communicant is not necessary for him because he is a Communicant. One cannot but know that this is what many think at the present day.

A lady once came to speak to a Priest about Confession. She had made up her mind that she ought to go to Confession, but her difficulty was that she did not think she was sufficiently contrite to make a good Confession. He said to her: " Pray, are you in the habit of going to Communion?" And she promptly replied: " Oh yes; I go to Communion once a fortnight." So she went to Communion without any difficulty once a fortnight at the very time that she thought she was not sufficiently contrite to make a good Confession! How could she have got into such a tangle as this? Why, of course, she was brought up to consider that as she " was a Communicant" there was no more to be said or thought of, but to go to Communion as a matter of course. Think of the appalling muddle of this poor woman's ideas, and then think of the Cherubim and the flaming sword keeping the way of the Tree of Life!

Now, the Prayer-Book Man does not " become a Communicant." What he thinks of is the next Communion that he is going to make, and how he can make that next Communion worthily.

Another instance of the lamentable effect of this misuse of English is to be found in the people who flock to Confession at Christmas and Easter. There they come at all hours of the day or night, as if the skies would fall upon them if they did not go there and then. Ask them why, and they will say something about " My Christmas Communion" or " My Easter Communion." But what difference can there be between the Easter Communion and the Communion we make on any ordinary Monday morning?

Prayer-Book Ideals

These people seem to think something dreadful will happen to them if they cannot go to Confession before their Easter Communion, while at other times they will go to Communion quite happily without Confession.

Is it not too silly for words? The Prayer-Book Man knows nothing about such folly. All he thinks about is his next Communion, whether it be Easter or whether it be an ordinary weekday. His *next* Communion! There it stands, as a separate isolated fact. Is he, or is he not, in a fit state to make his *next* Communion? That is what he sets himself to work to find out.

Now, bearing in mind the Cherubim and the flaming sword, let us see how the Church guards the inestimable treasure of the Bread of Life. In the Rubric at the beginning of the Service, we see the mind of the Church in the exercise of that Godly discipline that we have practically lost for a while, and that year by year we say we want restored. We find there that those who intend to make their Communion are to send in their names to the Parish Priest at least some time in the week before. What is this for? Why, of course, that the Parish Priest may satisfy himself that he will be justified in giving them Communion; for we find in the same Rubric that he is to exercise the discipline of the Church by barring from the Holy Table notorious evil-livers and people who have quarrelled and have not made it up. These rules have fallen into abeyance, but there they stand as expressing the mind of the Church—that is to say, the mind of the Holy Ghost.

The Prayer-Book Man is bidden to begin his preparation for his next Communion by realizing what the Blessed Sacrament is : " It is our bounden duty to render most humble and hearty thanks to Almighty GOD for that He has given His Only Begotten Son *not only to die* for us, but also to be our Spiritual Food and Sustenance in that Holy Sacrament." Not only to die for us, but also to be our Spiritual Food and Sustenance in the Holy Sacrament ! What a vision of the truth of Christianity we have here ! The love of the Eternal Father shown in the Blessed Sacrament as really as in the Cross ! The Blessed Sacrament as much a part of the Divine plan as the Cross itself !

The Church knows nothing of the Cross apart from the Blessed Sacrament. God's plan, as revealed by the Holy Ghost, is that His CHRIST should die for our sins, and rise again for our justification. GOD's scheme for us is that, if when we were sinners we were reconciled to God by the death of His Son, by the death of His Son much more, being reconciled, we should be saved by His Life. He distinctly and deliberately gave His Only Begotten Son, not only to die for us, but also to be our Spiritual Food and Sustenance in the Holy Sacrament. The idea that lurks at the bottom of so many minds, that Christianity means the Cross, and that the Sacraments are secondary and comparatively unimportant matters, is wholly foreign to the Bible, and therefore to the Prayer-Book.

The Blessed Sacrament of Communion was instituted by CHRIST Himself. It is no after-thought, introduced at a later period to adorn and beautify the Christian System, but is an essential and integral part of Christianity. The same LORD who, in the beginning, planted a garden eastward in Eden, and in it put the man whom He had made; the same LORD who ordained that our first parents should partake of Eternal Life by eating the fruit of the Tree of Life—that same Lord, with Whom is no variableness nor shadow of turning, has given His Only Begotten Son, not only to die for us, but also to be our Spiritual Food and Sustenance in the Holy Sacrament of Communion.

No wonder that spiritual life is at such a low level in Protestant Christianity! No wonder that spiritual perceptions among Protestants are so dulled and blunted. They have laid hold of a half Gospel, and flourish it about as the whole. An old Wesleyan who had been converted to the truth in late life was being prepared for his first Communion by the Sisters of the Poor in Shoreditch. When they read to him the sixth chapter of St. John in the light of his newly awakened spiritual perceptions, he said, speaking of the Wesleyans among whom he had been brought up: "Why, they never taught me the best part!" Let these words of the Prayer-Book sink down into our hearts: "Not only to die for us, but also to be our Spiritual Food and Sustenance in that Holy Sacrament."

Thus the Prayer-Book Man is bidden to begin his preparation for Communion by humble thanksgiving to GOD for the gift of the Eternal Son in the Blessed Sacrament, and the Prayer-Book goes on to remind him that because the Blessed Sacrament is a "*Divine*" thing, therefore the blessing and comfort that it brings is inestimable; and that, for the same reason, the danger of unworthy Communion is appalling. The Cherubim and the flaming sword keep the way of the Tree of Life because it *is* the Tree of Life.

So the Prayer-Book Man, in thinking of his next Communion, is to be quite sure and certain that he is going to make a good Communion, and so he is told that "the way and means thereto is first to examine

Communion

your lives and conversations *by the rule of GOD's Commandments.*" He is reminded that it is not his individual conscience that is the measure of right and wrong, but that his conscience has to be conformed to a standard altogether independent of, and outside of, itself. We have already seen how terribly this truth is forgotten in modern English thought, and we need not go into it again. The Prayer-Book Man is distinctly told that he is to examine himself, not as to whether he has followed the dictates of his conscience, and done that which is right in his own eyes, but " by the rule of GOD's Commandments." This examination is to cover the ground of " will, word, and deed." Our LORD has given us in the Sermon on the Mount the authoritative and Divine interpretation of the Ten Commandments, and it is from that standpoint that the Prayer-Book Man is to regard them.

If he is conscious of sins against his neighbours, he is to reconcile himself to them, being ready to make restitution and satisfaction for all injuries or wrong done, and being ready to forgive others who have done him wrong; " for otherwise," says the Prayer-Book, " the receiving of the Holy Communion doth nothing else but increase your damnation." And what a light is thrown upon the " Rule of GOD's Commandments " when we find that malice and envy are classed with blasphemy and adultery as grievous crimes !

And the end and object of this strict self-examination, of course, is that the Prayer-Book Man may approach the Holy Table in a state of grace. Let me remind you once more that Communion is a Sacrament of the living. It is the Children's Bread that is not to be cast to dogs, and the only plea with which at any time we can draw near to the Holy Table is that we are at that moment living members of the Body of CHRIST.

Self-examination is the first step in repentance. It is to be followed by contrition, confession, and satisfaction—those three things that sum up all that we can bring towards the forgiveness of sins. The Prayer-Book Man is not to make his next Communion until he is sure that he has " a quiet conscience "—he is, that is to say, to bring to his next Communion the knowledge of sins forgiven. And therefore it is at this point, as we should expect that it would be, that we find mention of, and commandment in respect of, Sacramental Confession.

We shall have to deal with this matter at length in speaking of the Prayer-Book Man in his reception of the benefit of Absolution, and will not therefore go into it now. All that we will emphasize at this point is that the forgiveness of sins is GOD's act, not ours; and that therefore self-examination, contrition, confession, and satisfaction, being our acts, are but preparation for the forgiveness of sins. The quieting of the conscience, which nothing but GOD's forgiveness can give, is therefore GOD's act, not ours. If our self-examination shows us that we have not fallen out of a state of grace, our conscience is quiet, because of the Grace of our Baptism that was bestowed by GOD; but if our self-examination reveals to us that we have fallen out of a state of grace, then it is the " benefit of Absolution " that must quiet our conscience. In a word, it is not we that quiet our conscience, but GOD. The Cherubim and the flaming sword are placed by GOD to guard the way of the Tree of Life. We cannot remove them at our own will and pleasure, and if any force their way in they meet their doom. " He that eateth and drinketh unworthily, eateth and drinketh damnation to himself."

Here, then, are the tremendous issues that have to be faced in each Communion.

The Blessed Sacrament is a Divine Thing; none but the Children of GOD can approach it, therefore we have at each Communion to produce our credentials.

It has been well said that the preparation for Communion is the same as the preparation for death, because that when we die we go to GOD, and when we go to Communion GOD comes to us; so when we are face to face with our next Communion we must deal with that Communion as we should wish to do with our death. In some outlying districts of Russia people may be seen going to Communion in their grave clothes. This quaint custom comes of a true instinct; it bears testimony to the great truths that what will not do for death will not do for Communion ; and when we say " will not do for Communion " we mean " will not do for *our next Communion*."

Pause a moment here and let us ask ourselves how it can have come about that the Church of England is thought to represent " a moderate religion." To " be a Communicant " (as we so ridiculously call it) in the Church of England, seems such a simple and ordinary sort of thing. We have somehow thought it compatible with a comparatively low level of spiritual life; it did not seem to mean for us what we expected Communion to mean in other ages or in other parts of the Church. We have almost unconsciously drifted into a sort of idea that Church of England Communion is something that rather stands by itself; it is to bear the stamp of Church of

Englandism which is expressed in the favourite catch-words "sober" and "moderate." Our Communion is to be "moderate." It is not to take us too high nor bring us too low; it is to steer its judicious and moderate course between two extremes. But what becomes of these "moderate" ideas about Communion when we come to see what the Prayer-Book has to say to us about Communion ? If the Cross is "moderate" then Communion may be "moderate," for the Prayer-Book puts the Cross and the Blessed Sacrament on one footing. If the idea of GOD be a "moderate" one, then the Sacrament of Communion may be patient of a "moderate" view, for the Prayer-Book says it is a "Divine thing."

Away with this pernicious and most false notion that the Church of England represents a "sober," "moderate" middle-class *bourgeoise* sort of religion ! It is extreme of the extreme. At one extreme we have eternal life; at the other extreme we have damnation. There is nothing "moderate" about either of these great facts, nor is there any *via media* between the two. The Prayer-Book Man finds himself face to face with these two extremes in the very next Communion that he is going to make.

From these few thoughts about the preparation of the soul for the reception of Communion, we pass to the consideration so often, alas ! overlooked, of the needful preparation of the body. We speak, of course, of Fasting Communion.

Let us first dispose of the shocking innovation of Evening Communion. Let us here carry the war into the enemy's camp. No one pretends that Evening Communion is not an innovation on the practice of Universal Christendom. No one pretends that Even-

Communion

ing Communion was ever heard of in the Church of England before the middle of the nineteenth century. Well, then, in the case of an innovation the burden of proof lies with the innovators. It is not for us to prove that they are wrong; it is for them to prove to Universal Christendom that they are right, and that Universal Christendom is wrong.

We look in vain for any such proof. Sentiment there may be, arguments from opportunism there may be, *but proof there is none*. On our Catholic principle we say at once that Evening Communion is wrong, because it is against the practice of undivided Christendom. But Evening Communion is but the logical conclusion of any non-fasting Communion. If we may make our ordinary Communion when we are not fasting, it merely becomes a question of degree whether we communicate in the morning or in the evening. Have we ever, except in *articulo mortis*, the right to communicate otherwise than fasting ? If so, where did we get that right ?

Here, again, we are face to face with an innovation, and again the burden of proof lies with the innovators. It is for them to prove that they are right, and that undivided Christendom is wrong. Fasting Communion is the rule of the Eastern Church. It is the rule of the Roman Church—that is to say, that it was the rule of Undivided Christendom. If English people have a right to communicate when they are not fasting, where did they get it ? They may say that the Prayer-Book does not say that they are to fast; but I answer, " Of course it does not say so, any more than it says that you are to keep Sunday instead of keeping the Sabbath." Here is a rule of undivided Christendom about which the Prayer-Book says nothing. It has not abrogated the rule, therefore the rule stands. Again we must carry the war into the enemy's camp, and ask those who communicate when they are not fasting, *whether the Prayer-Book has given them leave to do so.*

In the case of an innovation, we want proof that the innovation is right. Have we any such proof? Many years ago an Archbishop, long since dead, fell foul of one of his clergy for teaching the duty of fasting Communion. The Priest in question, in replying to the Archbishop, quoted St. Chrysostom and St. Augustine as having said that fasting Communion was of Apostolic times. This elicited the following from the worthy Archbishop:

" To say that fasting Communion is of Apostolic times betrays an ignorance of ecclesiastical history *excusable perhaps in Chrysostom and Augustine,* but not in a well-informed English Churchman of the nineteenth century." This ought to be framed and glazed! It is exquisite in its impudence, but can it be called proof? The Prayer-Book Man, then, is to communicate fasting, *because the Prayer-Book has never given him leave to do otherwise.* And it is no use for people to come to the clergy for leave to communicate non-fasting, for the very simple reason that we have not got the leave to give. There are many good and holy people who are in the habit of communicating when they are not fasting because they cannot see that it is wrong; they are in all good faith, and all honour to them. But if they begin to have scruples, and come, as they sometimes do, to shift, as they think, the responsibility off their shoulders on to the clergy, by asking us to sanction their practice, they must be ruthlessly thrown back upon their own

Communion

responsibility. We cannot give a permission that is not entrusted to us to give.

There is a certain amount of confusion in men's minds about " dispensations." When a Bishop uses his dispensing power, he is using something that he has by the authority of the Church. He can " dispense " just so far as the Church authorizes him to do so, *and no farther*. We sometimes hear of Bishops giving a " dispensation " from fasting Communion. But where did they get the dispensation to give ? They cannot give what they have not got. Some years ago a Bishop who was anxious to get rid of the Reserved Sacrament, proposed to one of his clergy to give him a " dispensation " to celebrate for the sick without communicating himself !

What are we to think about such so-called " dispensations " as these ? Why, just this, that, like an idol, they are " nothing at all in the world," and are not worth the paper they are written on or the breath with which they are spoken. Even Bishops cannot give away what they have not got !

One word about the Prayer-Book Man in the actual reception of Communion. The Priest is bidden to deliver the Blessed Sacrament of the Body of CHRIST " into the hands " of the faithful. St. Cyril of Jerusalem tells us how the faithful are to place their hands for the reception of Communion. He tells us " to make our left hand a throne for our right, which is to receive the Lord of Glory." Let the Communicant kneel upright with his hands extended in this way, the left hand under the right, that the Blessed Sacrament may be placed in the palm of the right hand. Then let both hands be raised together to the mouth, and the Blessed Sacrament be swallowed whole. Let the Communicant look carefully into the palm of his right hand to see that no particle of the Blessed Sacrament remains there. Then as to the reception of the Chalice, how careful we must be ! Sometimes people come crouching to Communion, and fling themselves down, immediately after receiving, so that the Priest has absolutely to snatch away the Chalice to prevent some fearful accident.

Many people will not touch the Chalice with their hands through a mistaken idea of reverence. Is it quite reasonable to think that the hand which has just received the Precious Body is not good enough to touch the foot of the Chalice ? The best and safest way is for the Communicant to hold the foot of the Chalice (the Priest still holding it as before), and gently to guide it. If people wish to receive without touching the Chalice, they *must* throw their heads well back; otherwise there is great danger of accident, or it very likely happens that they do not receive at all. If ever we need sanctified common sense, it is in the reception of the Chalice. Need one utter a word of warning against the unspeakable horror of the ignorance that leads people to wipe their mouths after Communion ? A moment's reflection would show what an awful thing this is. One hopes that this warning is unnecessary, but, alas ! one has known such an awful thing done. And while we are thinking of the Chalice, does not one's whole soul revolt at the blasphemous and irreverent abomination of these latter days as to fear of infection ! How often is the Catholic heart horror-struck and plunged into an agony of grief at the sight of an ignorant and unbelieving Priest wiping the Chalice when giving Communion ! One does not dare think what becomes of

Communion

the linen thus stained with the Precious Blood. It is something to weep over, not to think about. Here we have sanitation run mad ! This abomination speaks to a dominion of the flesh over the spirit that is an appalling sign of the depths to which our Christianity has sunk.

One word in conclusion about thanksgiving after Communion. The common instinct of Christendom leads people to spend a little time after Communion in thanksgiving. And the instinct of Western Christendom has fastened upon the song of the Three Holy Children as the appropriate form that such thanksgiving should take; while the writings of Saints supply us with holy aspirations and prayers to help us in the great work of thanksgiving.

A good man has said that a devout thanksgiving for one Communion is the best preparation for the next; and, in the case of those who communicate once a week or once a month, he urges that the thankful remembrance of the past Communion should be with the Christian until he begins his preparation for his next Communion. And once more let us sweep out of mind for good and all the erroneous notion of " being a Communicant," and betake ourselves, with the Prayer-Book Man, to the thought of our *next* Communion.

CHAPTER XXII

ABSOLUTION

GOD " hath given power and commandment to His Ministers to declare and pronounce to His people, being penitent, the Absolution and Remission of their sins."

How hazy we English are about the forgiveness of sins! Talk to an Englishman about the forgiveness of sins, and he will tell you that he is sorry for his sins and wants to do better. He will think, as far as he knows how, about his own repentance. Ask him if his sins are forgiven, and he will tell you, perhaps, if he is a singularly honest man, that he does not know; or perhaps he will tell you that he hopes they may be; or perhaps he will even say that he believes that they are. But push him a little farther, and you will find that his belief that his sins are forgiven is based upon his repentance—*i.e.*, upon something that he has done. GOD's part in the matter seems to be overlooked. And yet what can be more fundamentally clear than that the forgiveness of sins is GOD's act, not ours? All that we can bring in the way of Repentance is but the preparation for receiving GOD's forgiveness. The imparting of Forgiveness is GOD's Act. Let us put it in another way. We find the average Englishman, perhaps, troubled at the thought of his sins. He will understand self-examination to a certain extent; but ask him what he means to do then, and he will say, " I must pray to GOD for forgiveness " ; or perhaps, " I have prayed to God for forgiveness " ; and there, at that excellent point, he seems inclined to leave the matter. But can it be left there ? Certainly not. If he says, " I will pray for forgiveness," we say, " Well, and how will God answer your prayer ?" If he says, " I have prayed for forgiveness," we will say, " Well, and has GOD answered your prayers ?" It is obvious that the first point lies here. Two people are concerned with sin—viz., the Sinner *and GOD*. The sinner has had his say in the matter in doing what he can in the direction of repentance. But GOD (with all reverence be it said) must have His say too. For, after all, it is GOD Who forgives, not the sinner. Now turn back in thought to the Sacrament of Baptism. " The One Baptism for the forgiveness of sins." Here we have the sinner bringing his part— viz., repentance and faith; but the repentance and faith are inoperative in themselves. It is the Sacrament of Baptism that is GOD'S answer to the faith and repentance of the sinner, and it is the Baptism, not the repentance, that conveys the forgiveness of sins. This is plain.

But now comes the question of sins committed after Baptism. What is to be done about them ? Is the merely subjective act of repentance to do in the second case what it obviously could not do in the first ? And if so, why ? So we should naturally expect to find an outward means for the conveying of the forgiveness of sins committed after Baptism. What is the outward means ? Certainly not Communion; for, as we have seen already, Communion can only be received

worthily by those whose sins have already been forgiven, and unworthy Communion conveys damnation.
The very nature of the case postulates some authoritative act on the part of GOD for conveying to the
penitent sinner the forgiveness of post-Baptismal sins;
and this authoritative Act is there in Sacramental
Absolution. Absolution has been ordained of GOD.
" God hath given power and commandment to His
Ministers to declare and pronounce to His people,
being penitent, the absolution and remission of their
sins." Absolution is GOD's answer to the repentance of the penitent Christian, just as Baptism is
GOD's answer to the faith and repentance of the
heathen.

Absolution, then, is, in the wide sense of the word, a
Sacrament. It authoritatively conveys to the penitent
by an outward act the inward spiritual grace of the
forgiveness of post-Baptismal sins. The forgiveness
of sins ! Here we must pause a moment, and think
what we mean by the forgiveness of sins. It seems to
us at first sight such a simple matter that GOD should
forgive sins, but it is not at all such a simple matter as
it seems.

Bishop Westcott has spoken of the forgiveness of
sins, and of the eternity of punishment. Eternal
punishment seems to shallow minds to be an in-
superable difficulty. But the great Bishop has pointed
out that it is not in the eternity of punishment that
the difficulty lies. The real difficulty, he tells us, is
as to how GOD, being what He is, can forgive sins
at all. Think a moment what it is that we mean
when we speak of forgiveness as between man and man.
A does a grievous wrong to B. He is sorry for it, and
asks B to forgive him. B says, " I forgive you."

Absolution

But what does this mean? It can only mean that B will change his mind with respect to A. He was angry with him; now he will be angry no more. He is willing to act as though the wrong had not been done. Forgiveness can mean no more than this between man and man. But can GOD forgive sins in this way? Certainly not. He cannot " change His mind," for " with Him is no variableness, neither shadow of turning." He cannot treat a sin as though it had not been done, for He is Perfect Justice and Perfect Truth ; and so, easy and simple as it seems to us that GOD should in a benevolent way forgive sins, He cannot forgive sins in this sort of way, just because He *is* GOD. And so we come to this great truth, that GOD forgives sin *by making the sinner righteous*. The forgiveness of sins is a creative act. " If any man be in CHRIST, *he is a new Creature.*" The cardinal error of Luther lay in his abominable doctrine of imputed righteousness. Luther's divergence from the Church lay where people do not commonly look for it. It was not the Papal Bull, nor the sale of indulgences, that made the hopeless cleavage between Lutheranism and the Church. Luther's error began when he denied that original righteousness was the Gift of Grace. He *would* think that man's original righteousness was a part of his nature. And what was the immediate consequence? Why, just this, that, according to Luther, man, in the Fall, lost a part of his nature, and the immediate consequence of this falsehood was that, according to Luther, man could never be wholly restored. His idea of Justification was that the sinner, remaining always a sinner, had some one else's righteousness " imputed " to him ; much as a man might hide his dirt and rags by having someone else's clean cloak thrown over him. The sinner remained a sinner as he was before, but by a sort of legal fiction he was to be considered as being righteous while really he was not so! So Luther seemed to think that GOD could stoop to a legal fiction: GOD, Who is Perfect Truth!

No! It is neither by changing His mind, nor by being willing to treat a sin as if it had not been done, nor by any sort of legal fiction that GOD can ever forgive a sin. It can only be by a creative act, whereby He makes the sinner righteous. The forgiveness of sin is the imparting of grace, and grace is nothing but our fellowship in the Sacred Humanity of JESUS, the Son of Mary. " If any man be in CHRIST, he is a new creature." Thus the original forgiveness of sins in Holy Baptism was by a new Birth.

" Except a man be born again of Water, and of the Spirit, he cannot enter into the Kingdom of GOD."

But we are concerned now with the sins of the baptized; here, too, the forgiveness of sins must be a creative act. Think of the distinction that there is between sins and sins in the baptized. St. John tells us that there is a sin unto death, and there is a sin not unto death. The Prayer-Book speaks of " deadly sins wilfully committed," and it also speaks of " infirmities." And the Church speaks of some sins as " mortal sins," while others are " venial sins." Let us think a moment about this distinction. We are taught by Our LORD and His Apostles that the Christian life is a life of vital union with CHRIST. Our LORD says, " I am the Vine, ye are the branches." And St. Paul teaches us the same truth, under the figure of the Body and the members. The life of any branch of the Vine is just that it is " abiding " in the

Absolution

Vine. The life of any member of the body is just that it is still in the body. Let a branch be broken off from the Vine, the Vine will go on living, but the branch will die. Why? Because, of course, the life of the Vine can no longer reach it. Let a hand, or an arm, be cut off from the body, the body will go on living, but the hand or the arm will die. Why? Because the life of the body can no longer reach it. Now this is just the effect of one mortal sin in the baptized. It separates the sinner from the fellowship of CHRIST. The separated life must die.

Now think of the branch broken off from the Vine, lying helpless on the ground. What can it do? Nothing at all, but just wither and die. But St. Paul reminds us that a branch broken off can *be grafted in* again. What does that mean? It means, of course, that it can be so reunited to the Vine that the life of the Vine can again flow into it; but this is not a work that the branch can do for itself, it must be done by the Gardener.

" I am the True Vine, and My Father is the Husbandman." So the forgiveness of post-Baptismal mortal sin is the authoritative act by which the sinner is reunited to the Body of CHRIST, and so made holy. By our Baptism we are placed in a state of Salvation, by mortal sin we fall out of a state of Salvation, by Absolution we are placed back in a state of Salvation.

Now let us put the matter in another way. The forgiveness of sins is a judicial act. It rests with the Judge to acquit or condemn. Our LORD teaches us that all judgment is committed to Him, because He is the Son of Man. Before His Ascension, He committed this judicial function to His Apostles.

Prayer-Book Ideals

" As My Father hath sent Me, even so send I you. Receive ye the Holy GHOST ; whose sins ye forgive, they are forgiven: and whose sins ye retain, they are retained."

Can we for a moment suppose that the judicial functions of CHRIST were to cease on the earth with the lives of the Apostles ? Certainly not; for what, then, would have become of His promise " Lo ! I am with you alway, even unto the end of the world "? As a matter of fact, throughout undivided Christendom the Bishops of the Church were regarded as having succeeded to the judicial functions committed by CHRIST to His Apostles; nor was this ever questioned for 1,500 years. The Prayer-Book is simply voicing the consensus of undivided Christendom when it tells us that GOD " hath given power and commandment to His Ministers to declare and pronounce to His people, being penitent, the Absolution and Remission of their sins." It is not for us to prove that the Protestants are wrong : it is for them, as the bringers in of a new teaching, to prove to undivided Christendom that they are right. But our business now is, not with the Protestants, but with the Prayer-Book Man; and for him, at any rate, there is no question about the matter ; for the Prayer-Book speaks on this subject with no faltering voice.

But let us look at the forgiveness of sins from yet another standpoint. The life of the Christian is the life of membership in the Body. We cannot insist too often or too loudly that there is no such thing as an isolated independent Christian life. This idea, which is the foundation of that hateful thing that calls itself " Individualism," is essentially anti-Christian. The Christian is a member of the Body of

Absolution

CHRIST. The unity of the Body of CHRIST is an organic unity.

"If one member suffer, all the members suffer with it." Sin is not a private matter between the individual soul and GOD. If a Christian sins, he sins against his fellow-Christians, as well as against GOD.

Consequently it would seem—*a priori*—to be reasonable and right that the Body should have something to say as to the forgiveness of sins, which, as we have seen, means nothing more nor less than the reception again into membership of one of the Body who had fallen out of its fellowship.

In a word, if sin is sin against the Body of which the sinner was a member, forgiveness must be an act of which the Body must take cognizance. Therefore the forgiveness of sins is a corporate act, and Sacramental Absolution is the means whereby the Body receives the lapsed member into its fellowship once more.

In this connection our attention is called to the words of the Rubric at the beginning of the Eucharistic Office. Speaking of "notorious evil livers," the Prayer-Book says that "the Curate" is to warn him off from Communion "until he hath *openly declared* himself to have truly repented," etc. And again, in respect of a man's sins against his neighbour, the same Rubric says that "the Curate" is not to "suffer" them to come to Communion until he "*knows*" them to be reconciled. So here we have, on the one hand, that the sinner is "openly to declare" his repentance ; and, on the other, that the Priest is to "know" that he is reconciled. And here one might record a witty answer made by a young man to a Protestant agitator. The man was abusing the Priests, and said, "Con-

fession! What can these Priests know about it?"
To which the young man promptly replied, "They
cannot know anything about it till we tell them."
The sinner is "openly to declare" his repentance, and
the Priest is to "know." Let us sum up as far as we
have gone.

1. Man cannot forgive himself : he must be forgiven
by GOD.

2. God forgives sin by recreating the sinner.

3. The forgiveness of sins is the incorporation of the
sinner into the Body of CHRIST.

4. The forgiveness of sins is a judicial act : it implies a
Judge, a judgment, and a formal acquittal.

5. The forgiveness of sins is a corporate act : it is
the reception again of the lapsed into the fellowship
of the Body.

On all these grounds the Ministry of Absolution is
required in the Church. It is along the lines of these
considerations that every Christian is to determine,
at any given moment in his life, whether he needs the
Ministry of Absolution or whether he does not—*i.e.*,
whether at *that given moment* he is in a state of Grace
or not. If he is in a state of Grace, Absolution is not
necessary for him, but if he is not in a state of Grace,
it is necessary.

Who is the Minister of Absolution? We at once
reply Jesus Christ. God has committed all judgment to Him, because He is the Son of Man. He is
the Judge : the man whom He acquits is acquitted, the
man whom He condemns is condemned, whatever
the man himself may think about it. It is Jesus the
Son of Mary who forgives sins, if they are forgiven
at all. And we remind ourselves once more that this
power of judgment—the power, that is to say, of

acquitting or condemning—is " committed " to Him, " because He is the Son of Man."

And it is when we bear this great fundamental fact in mind that we are able to see something of the meaning of the commission that He gave to His Church the night of His resurrection : " As My Father hath sent Me, *even so* send I you."

He had distinctly told us that the Father had committed all judgment to Him as being the Son of Man. It is, then, this judicial function, this commission to acquit or to condemn, that He solemnly committed before His Ascension to His Church ; the Bishops and Priests, in exercising the power of the Keys, are the official representatives of the power of judgment committed by our Lord to His Church. " GOD hath given power and commandment to His Ministers to declare and pronounce to His people, being penitent, the Absolution and Remission of their sins." The power by which they absolve or retain is the power committed to the Sacred Humanity of JESUS CHRIST. CHRIST and His Church are one. It is through the Church, which is His Body, that JESUS CHRIST exercises His judicial functions. Nor ought we to have any difficulty whatever in understanding this. " Quod facit per alium facit per se," is a maxim thoroughly understood and acted upon in civil society. All judicial functions reside in the Sovereign. If the Judge acquits, it is the Sovereign who acquits. If the Judge condemns, it is the condemnation of the Sovereign. From the Lord Chancellor down to the police who arrest, or the turnkey who locks up or opens the prison door, the whole authority comes from the Sovereign. No one is so silly as to suppose that the Sovereign must himself sit on the magistrate's bench or open the prison door. That the authority is his is perfectly recognized and understood. What would we say of the man who refused to accept the sentence of the Judge because the Judge is not the King? And what, then, shall we think of the man who refuses to submit to the tribunal of the Church, and says he will deal direct with GOD Himself? To act in this way is to ignore the Mediation of our LORD.

It is essentially anti-Christian. One really ought not to have to spend time in enlarging upon this matter. The doctrine of Absolution is written so large in the Prayer-Book that it is impossible for a man to deny or belittle it without running counter to the Prayer-Book. If people who call themselves Church of England people reject the doctrine of Absolution, the burden of proof lies with them. It is for them to prove that they are right and the Prayer-Book wrong. The Bishops and Priests of the Church, then, are the Ministers of Absolution, the channels through which the Sacred Humanity exercises its judicial functions.

Now one word as to the persons for whom Absolution is intended. The purpose of Absolution is to restore to the fellowship of CHRIST those who have separated themselves from the Body by mortal sin. Hence it is clear that Absolution is not a Sacrament that is generally necessary to salvation. The Church contemplates, as she has a right to contemplate, that those who have been born again into the fellowship of the Body of CHRIST will quietly live their life, and grow to their perfection in that fellowship. In the natural order we expect that those who are born into life will grow up to full manhood. Jairus's daughter and the widow's son at Nain had died in their youth. It pleased our

Absolution

LORD to restore them to life. But their case is not the normal; but the abnormal case. To speak of Absolution as generally necessary to salvation would be to assume that no Christian could abide in the fellowship of the Body of CHRIST. That a Christian should fall away from grace is not what GOD contemplates, as the normal thing in the spiritual life. Absolution, then, is ordained not for all Christians indiscriminately, but for a particular class of Christians—viz., for those who are in the unhappy condition of having fallen out of grace. Sacramental Confession is no doubt salutary for all. There are many Christians who go to Confession even when they are not conscious of mortal sin, and who will continue to make this the habit of their life. But we must be clear that the purpose for which GOD ordained Absolution was to restore to grace Christians who had fallen into mortal sin. Absolution, then, is a " Sacrament of the dead." It is ordained for the restoration of spiritual life to Christians who have lost it by mortal sin.

Lastly, I want to call your attention to the fact that GOD, who has given the power of the Keys to His Ministers, has given them Commandment to use that power. Thank GOD, our Priests are beginning to wake up to the fact that GOD has given them power and commandment to declare and pronounce to His people the Absolution and Remission of their sins. But what a terrible state of things it is that, in more than half of our parishes, if a Christian found that he needed Absolution, he would probably not be able to get it. There are still an appalling number of Priests who do not believe that they can absolve from sins. and there are an enormous proportion who, while they may theoretically believe that they have the power, have not the slightest idea of how they are to exercise it. It is a grievous scandal that if any Christian wish to receive Absolution, he cannot in nine parishes out of ten get what he has an indefeasible right to demand.

Yet so it is. Too often it happens that we cannot get our Confessions heard at all; while some of us know what it is to have come across Priests who do not hear Confessions, but are like the young lady in Gilbert's song, who "does not think she waltzes, but would rather like to try." Would you, if you had to undergo a surgical operation, care to trust yourself to a surgeon who had not been used to do such things but would "rather like to try"? Heaven save us when we require Absolution from the Priest who does not hear Confessions, but has no objection to trying! GOD has given commandment to His Ministers to give Absolution to His people if they are penitent, and it is therefore the bounden duty of the Minister to know how to deal with the penitent who may present himself at any moment. The Prayer-Book Man expects in his Parish Priest to find a man who is capable of dealing with the case that requires Absolution. It is clearly contemplated that the Priest will not be flustered or upset if he is called upon to hear a Confession. If Absolution be the Divinely appointed remedy for mortal sin, it ought to be a common experience in every parish; for mortal sin is, alas! too common an experience everywhere. Then do not let us tolerate a refusal to hear a Confession. A layman once said that he was sorry to say that there was such a thing as compulsory Confession in the Church of England, because he had had to compel a Priest to hear

Absolution

his Confession; but anyone who has had the misfortune to go to Confession to a Priest who does not know how to hear one, will know that this is a grievance to which no Christian ought to have to submit. There is nothing of this sort contemplated in the Prayer-Book. In whatever parish the Prayer-Book Man finds himself, he is supposed to be within reach of all the means of Grace. It is a truly terrible thing that in any given parish he must live and die without Absolution because the Vicar is Low Church. GOD has given commandment to His Ministers to " declare and pronounce " Absolution to the penitent. If they do not do so, what is their excuse ? It seems to me that we are much too lenient in our estimate of those Priests whose " views " do not agree with Confession and Absolution. It may be, and, alas ! is, that long disuse has built up a barrier of ignorance and prejudice that keeps English Christians from seeking for the benefit of Absolution; but who can tell how far this is due to the ignorance and incompetence of the Clergy ?

CHAPTER XXIII

ABSOLUTION (*continued*)

WE have now arrived at certain broad principles in respect of Absolution that may be summarized as follows:

1. Absolution is a Sacrament.

2. It is a Sacrament of the dead.

3. It conveys the remission of sins committed after Baptism, and therefore

4. It is applicable to the Baptized *only*.

5. The Minister of Absolution is the Priest.

6. He administers Absolution by the judicial authority of JESUS CHRIST, committed to him.

7. GOD, Who gives the Priest this authority, gives him the commandment to exercise it.

We have now to consider the practical application of these principles in everyday life.

The first question that arises is, " When does the Prayer-Book Man seek for Absolution ?"

The answer is clear, " When his conscience requires it." And so our first consideration will be as to what is meant by a " quiet conscience."

We find the mention of Absolution in a practical way in connection with the Prayer-Book Man's preparation for Communion. He is told that he is to seek for Absolution " if he cannot quiet his own conscience."

Absolution

Now, a moment's thought will show us that the quiet conscience must be an objective condition. Many a man can " quiet his own conscience " who has no right to quiet it. The conscience may be quiet because it is dead, or, as the Apostle says, " seared with a hot iron." A dead conscience, like a dead body, is a very " quiet " thing. Can anyone seriously think for a moment that this is what the Prayer-Book means by a quiet conscience ? Again, we meet with Absolution in a practical way in the Prayer-Book in the visitation of the sick. Here we find that the Prayer-Book Man is to seek for Absolution " if he feel his conscience troubled with any weighty matter," and at once we see that the whole point of the matter lies in what is meant by " a weighty matter "; and here, again, it is obvious that it points to an objective entity. The question, of course, is not whether the sick man has anything on his conscience that he thinks is weighty, but whether there is anything there that as an actual matter of fact *is* weighty.

Now your average Englishman looks at the " quiet conscience " and the " weighty matter " from a purely subjective point of view. He is, to all practical intents and purposes, a moral Sophist. He practically considers that there is no " matter " that is really " weighty " in itself; he (unconsciously perhaps, but none the less really) thinks that that is " weighty " which appears to any man to be weighty, and that that conscience is " quiet " that appears to any man to be quiet ! This is the very degradation of Moral thought, and this Sophism saps the very foundations of all morality. GOD the Father has committed all judgment to the Son, because He is the Son of Man; and the crucial question at any given moment is, not whether I think my conscience is quiet, but whether JESUS CHRIST sees that it has a right to be quiet ; not whether I think I have no weighty matter against me, but whether JESUS CHRIST sees that there is no weighty matter against me. This, of course, is simple common sense. But simple and common sense as it is, it is astounding to see how it is overlooked in England. It is that miserable Individualism cropping up again.

And this Sophistical temper of mind which is really subversive of all morality leads your average Englishman to look upon Sacramental Confession as merely the last resort for timid, weak, scrupulous souls. Surely the self-reliant, self-helpful Englishman ought to be able to quiet his own conscience, as he does everything else, for himself. But if there should be an Englishman who is such a poor creature that he really cannot do such a simple thing as that for himself, then let him seek for Absolution, as being the poor contemptible creature that he is. That is the John Bull aspect of the matter. No wonder that our neighbours laughingly say of us that we seem to think it open to question whether the Anglo-Saxon race did fall in Adam ! Again, this same spirit and temper of mind shows itself in the pompous twaddle that we hear too often talked in high places about Confession being a medicine, and that we must not take medicine too often. Of course it is a medicine ! But the question is, not how often we are to take medicine, but how often we are sufficiently ill to require it ! These pompous orators miss the whole point. If there is no objective right and wrong, and no objective Judge of right and wrong, then perhaps the most hardened conscience may fare the best; and then perhaps the wisest thing a man can do will be to harden his conscience like an athlete hardens his body. But if sin be an objective entity, and the Judge a Personal Reality, the question at once becomes, not whether I think my conscience is quiet, but whether *I am right in so thinking ;* not whether I think I have no weighty matter on my conscience, but whether, as a matter of fact, what I have on my conscience *is* weighty or not. The Prayer-Book Man, then, will seek for Absolution whenever he knows that he needs it—whenever, that is to say, he is conscious of being separated by mortal sin from the fellowship of JESUS CHRIST. Absolution, as we have seen, is a Sacrament of the dead. If a Christian is among " the dead," then Absolution is become a necessity for him.

We will suppose that the Prayer-Book Man has become conscious that he needs Absolution ; what will then be his *modus operandi ?* How is he to set about receiving it ?

Our immediate answer is that he must go to Confession if he needs Absolution, *because he cannot be absolved anyhow else.*

But here at once we hear people saying that Absolution is given at Matins and Evensong, and in the Eucharistic Office.

" How can you tell us," such people will say, " that we cannot be absolved anyhow else but in Confession ? What about the Absolution in public worship ?"

" Well," we will answer, " what about them ? Let us take a good look at them. We are not afraid of inquiring about them."

There is an idea abroad that, whereas Roman Catholics and Greek Catholics must go to Confession if they want Absolution, the Church of England has changed all this, and absolves people in a lump in the Public Services of the Church, so that no one but very foolish and scrupulous persons need ever " go to Confession " in the Church of England. Heaps of people have this strange idea. To such persons we should like to say, first, " What do you mean by the Church of England ?" secondly, " What makes you think that the Church of England has tried to introduce a new religion in respect of the reception of Absolution ?" and thirdly, " What makes you think that people can be absolved in this way at all ?"

We have dealt with this matter already in a former chapter, but the power of preconceived ideas is so great that we have to keep on repeating even elementary and simple truths, so we must just shortly restate the case.

1. What is the Church of England ? The Church of England is not a separate self-contained entity, but an integral part of the Catholic Church. Consequently, the Church of England follows in the matter of Absolution the law and practice of undivided Christendom. The Church of England cannot start new theories and invent new practices. If it could, it would cease to be an integral part of the whole Church. People never were absolved in a lump. Such a thing is absolutely unheard of in Christendom. Therefore the Church of England does not think of doing such a thing. The practice of the Church of England in this matter is, and can be nothing else than, the practice of undivided Christendom. If you cannot produce (as you cannot) any precedent for absolving people in a lump, then the Church of England cannot do such a thing, even if it wished to do it, which of course it does not.

2. What makes men think that the Church of

Absolution

England was making a change in the administration of Absolution ? People have an idea that this is so, because of the declaratory forms of Absolution at the Eucharist and in the Divine Office. But this flimsy theory falls to pieces, like a house of cards at a touch, and the touch that demolishes it is the very simple little question why these declaratory forms of Absolution are there at all. And directly we ask this simple question we find that those forms are there, because there always was such a declaratory form of Absolution in the administration of Communion. And as to the Morning and Evening Offices, nothing but ignorance of the old Service Books could possibly have made people build up a theory on the existence of those declaratory Absolutions in the English Prayer-Book. If the fact of those " Absolutions " standing in the Communion Office and at Morning and Evening Prayer had anything to do with the question of going to Confession or not, it would have quite as much to do with it for Roman Catholics as it would for English Churchmen; for there these Absolutions stand in the Roman Missal and in the Roman Breviary, so that nothing but crass ignorance or gross dishonesty can use the fact of these Absolutions as an argument that the " Church of England " contemplated a new departure as regards the administration of Absolution. They stand in the English Prayer-Book because in the old pre-Reformation Service Books there were corresponding forms of Absolution at Communion and at Morning and Evening Prayer. So any argument against Sacramental Confession and Absolution that is based upon their being there falls to the ground at once.

3. What makes people think that men could ever be absolved in a lump in this way ?

Here we fall back on our old contention that if an innovation is introduced, the burden of proof lies with the innovators.

If we ask whether Absolution was ever administered in this way, the answer is, "Certainly not." People sometimes tell us that there were public Absolutions in the primitive Church. Yes! but that was after public Confession. Penitents *who had publicly done penance* were publicly absolved. Public Confession gave rise to scandals, and was therefore abandoned in the Church; but never for a moment was it contemplated in undivided Christendom that a congregation should join in a general acknowledgment of sinfulness, and receive Absolution there and then. So it is only by breaking with undivided Christendom that we can imagine that people can receive Absolution in this sort of way. Nobody ever did receive Absolution in that way, and so nobody can receive it in that way. That is really the all-sufficient answer.

But when we look a little closer, we can see why this must be so; for the forgiveness of sins is, as we have seen, a judicial act. God, who gave the power to absolve, gave also the power to retain. The Church must have a chance of exercising a judgment in the matter, and his modern idea of " Church of Englandism " leaves no place for the exercise of a judgment. A man may say that he never needs Absolution, but he cannot say that if he needs it, he will get it in the public services of the Church. So we rule out once for all that absurd idea that in the Church of England you can get absolved at Communion, or in the Morning or Evening Office. We arrive, then, at this point—viz., that if the Prayer-Book Man needs Absolution, he must go to Confession before he can get it.

Absolution

We will suppose, then, that our Prayer-Book Man finds himself in a condition that necessitates his making his Confession. How is he to set about it? The Prayer-Book says that he is to go to the Parish Priest and " open his grief." It also says that the sick man is to be moved to " make a special Confession of his sins." But how is one to set about it? Where do we go to find our Priest, and how do we " open our grief " when we get there?

It is quite plain that if Englishmen in general were living, as they ought to be, by the rule of the Prayer-Book, the hearing of Confessions would take up a considerable time in the everyday life of every Parish Priest. It would not be left to haphazard for a stray penitent once or so in a year to knock at the door of the Priest's house, and have to ask if he may make his Confession; nor ought the penitent ever to be subjected to such an ordeal. There should be in every parish a fixed place where the Priest is known to hear Confessions, and fixed times when it will be known that he is there for the express purpose; in a word, the way would be made much smoother for the Prayer-Book Man if the hearing of Confessions was a regular recognized part of the parochial life. It is terrible to think how stumbling-blocks are placed in the way of CHRIST's people when Priests do not recognize the fact that the hearing of Confession is a primary part of their everyday duty.

A fixed place! Where should that fixed place be? We answer at once, " In the open Church." We older Catholics can recall gruesome days, when Confessions were heard in odd holes and corners, in studies or vestries. If it was in the Priest's study, one had to ring the bell and be shown in! If one had not made a previous appointment, one had to state one's business, perhaps, after a little preliminary conversation about the weather. Why should we be subject to this sort of thing? It is quite difficult enough for an Englishman to make his Confession under the most favourable circumstances. One can quite imagine that the absence of a proper place and a fixed time may just prove the last straw, and decide the man against attempting to receive the Absolution he so sorely needs. Let it once be understood that the Priest is in the regular place in the Church, vested in surplice and stole, at stated times, and an enormous difficulty in the way of receiving Absolution will have been removed.

It will be seen that Confession is an ordinary provision of the Church's everyday life, and sick and weary souls soon find their way to the rest and peace that they need.

Some years ago a Mission was held in a poor parish in London. The missionaries heard a great many first Confessions. They impressed it upon the Vicar that he ought to be accessible at stated times. Accordingly, the good Vicar installed himself in the vestry. But, alas! when the first timid penitent presented herself in the vestry, the force of habit in the slum parish was too much for the good man, so she was greeted with, "Well, and what do you want?"

No; there ought to be none of this ringing of the Vicarage bell or knocking at the vestry door. Let the Priest be in an appointed place at an appointed time, properly vested for the express purpose of hearing Confessions. Let this be the rule in every Parish Church in the kingdom, and then, and not till then, will the Prayer-Book Man have what he has a right to expect. Before we leave the subject of the appointed place for hearing Confessions, one cannot help calling attention to the perfectly childish fuss about Confessional " boxes." What a farce it was ! Clergy were solemnly asked if they had a Confessional " box." Bishops solemnly assured the Protestant world that there were no Confessional " boxes " in their Diocese. Of course, the point was, whether there was an appointed place for hearing Confessions. If there were, what could it matter whether it was a box or a basket ? Can anyone outside of Earlswood imagine for a moment that it was perfectly right if a Priest sat in a chair to hear Confessions, but that it became perfectly sinful if he had a lid over his head ? It was, indeed, a pitiful spectacle to see presumedly sane Englishmen working themselves into a fury over the magical and mysterious " box "; but it was an even more deplorable spectacle to see the Bishops eagerly disclaiming any knowledge of the " box." For this was so disingenuous, as well as so contemptible, for it was throwing dust in the poor Protestant eyes. If ever there was a time when a fool ought to have been answered according to his folly, here was the moment !

We will suppose, then, that we have landed our Church of England penitent in a Confessional (box or otherwise), where he finds himself confronted by a capable Priest, who is there for the purpose of hearing Confessions, and knows how to do it. Now he has only got to " open his grief." Yes ! " only." But there comes the rub ! How is he going to do it ? and what is he going to say ? Who is to speak first ? It is quite clear that the Priest need not ask him what he wants, for if he did not want to make a Confession, he would not be there. The custom of Western Christendom has provided us with a typical form in which to begin and end a Confession.

This is just as it should be. It puts matters on a businesslike footing, and takes away all awkwardness. Any one of the little Catholic books of devotions, of which there are now so many, will give the Form, which should just simply be read; then, if the penitent is wise, he will—at any rate, for the first few times of making Confessions—have written down all that he has to confess, which done, he will read the little Form of concluding a Confession. Is not this simple ? To " open one's grief " sounds rather formidable, but when we once know how to do it, it is simple and easy enough. In the Form of Confession ordinarily in use in Western Christendom the penitent makes Confession to Almighty GOD, to Blessed Mary, ever Virgin, Blessed Michael the Archangel, Blessed John the Baptist, the Holy Apostles Peter and Paul, and all the Saints, and to the Priest. If we come to think of it, we see how reasonable this instinct of the Church is. The Confession, of course, is made to GOD, against whom we have sinned; it is made to the Priest, who is the representative of the judicial functions of JESUS CHRIST; it is made to the Mother of GOD and the Saints as representing the perfection of the Body, out of whose fellowship we have fallen by our sins. The Form is, of course, not imperative; but the instinct of the Church has led to its falling into that shape that we can see is most complete. In all this the seeking for Absolution is put on what, with all reverence, we call a perfectly businesslike footing. The making of Confession and seeking Absolution must be as sharply as possible marked off from seeking advice, which may be done in the way of ordinary conversation. No doubt it will generally happen, as the Prayer-Book contemplates that it would, that spiritual counsel will be given in the Confessional; but this is a secondary and subsidiary matter. Advice can be got elsewhere and in other ways, but Absolution can only be obtained in Confession. It is strange how this is too often overlooked. We will suppose the case of an elderly and experienced Priest who goes to make his Confession. The presumption is that he does not need advice. Probably he is much more qualified to give advice to the Priest to whom he is making his Confession, yet it sometimes happens that such a Priest has to listen to some little sermonette in the Confessional, which is very likely singularly inappropriate, and all because the Priest who is hearing the Confession has got the idea that he must give some advice, whether it seems to be needed or not.

The time of making Confession may be used as a good opportunity for giving advice, or it may not. What the Prayer-Book Man goes to Confession for is Absolution. This is quite complete in itself, whether it is accompanied with " ghostly counsel and advice," or whether it is not. While I am speaking of spiritual counsel or advice, let me remind you that advice is " advice," and nothing more. There is, of course, a considerable amount of responsibility of making up one's own mind. But while this is true of advice, we must remember that it is far different with anything imposed as Penance. That is most distinctly of obligation. It is, perhaps, not too much to say that it is a condition of Absolution. If the Penance im-

posed is one that it is either impossible, or, at any
rate, very difficult, for the Penitent to perform, let
him at once say so, and ask if it may be commuted.
But the penance ultimately given in the Confessional
is of absolute obligation.

To sum up: The seeking for Absolution is, as it
must always be, a thing that must be definitely provided for in the Church. The need for Absolution
is co-extensive with mortal sin in the baptized. If
Christians lived as they can and ought to live, there
would not perhaps be the urgent need for Sacramental
Confession in every parish that there is. But as it is,
the remedy must be as widespread as the diseases.
Wherever the Prayer-Book Man finds himself, he has
an indefeasible right to expect that he will be able to
make his Confession if his conscience requires it. The
directions of the Prayer-Book as to Confession which
we find (as we should naturally expect to find them) in
reference to preparation for Communion and preparation for death presuppose that it is a recognized and
understood thing. The Prayer-Book presupposes that
the penitent knows how to make a Confession, and
that the Priest knows how to receive one. GOD has
given power to His Ministers to absolve His people,
and He has given them commandment to use that
power. That a Priest should not know how to deal
with a penitent is an intolerable scandal. So, too, it
is a scandalous thing that if a Christian finds himself
outside of a state of grace, he should not know how to
deal with such a state of things. Every Christian
ought to know how to set about seeking for Absolution when he requires it. The Church can never do
her work properly in the world, if through the carelessness or ignorance, or perversity of men she is to

Absolution

be robbed of the simple practical administration of the Sacrament of Penance.

Thank God, things are considerably better in this direction than they were, but an appalling amount of ignorance and carelessness has yet to be overcome before we find ourselves in practical everyday life at the level of the Prayer-Book Man.

CHAPTER XXIV

MARRIAGE—I

WE pass now to consider the Prayer-Book Man in respect of his marriage. And here, again, we will first consider Marriage in itself, and then the Prayer-Book Man in his Marriage.

Let us at the outset emphasize the fact that in the exceeding and awful mystery of Holy Marriage we are, indeed, upon holy ground, and we shall need all our faith and all our sanctity to support us in the rarefied atmosphere of that exceeding and stupendous mystery.

We have before this found it advisable to pause and see to what a height the Prayer-Book lifts us, and at what a height it bids us live. People have a sort of idea that the " Church of England " is a sort of *via media*, moderate, sober, and common-sense, if somewhat prosaic, kind of religion, that it neither lifts us very high nor lets us sink very low; that it does not lend itself to great enthusiasms, or make great demands upon our faith and practice; that therefore it is pre-eminently adapted to the practical, go-ahead temper of the British nation, and keeps its religion decently in the background, or exhibits it mainly on the side of practical, intelligible duties. We have seen before now that this common-sense,

Marriage

John Bull sort of view of the Prayer-Book implies strange ignorance of what the Prayer-Book says; that, so far from the Prayer-Book religion being a moderate *via media* kind of thing, it raises us to tremendous heights, and reveals to us awful depths. But nowhere is this more conspicuously shown than in the Prayer-Book teaching upon Holy Marriage. Marriage seems to us a sufficiently commonplace thing, an ordinary jog-trot part of ordinary, prosaic life. So we thought, and so to the child of the world no doubt it seems to be—an institution that can be easily dealt with by Acts of Parliament and courts of law. Marriage! Why, surely, that is a simple matter enough! And then the Prayer-Book takes us and plunges us into an atmosphere of such exceeding mystery that we catch our breath, as it were, and turn dizzy. If ever spiritual discernment of spiritual things were needed, we need it now, when we draw near to the awful mystery of Marriage. Here, in passing, let us note the working in respect of Holy Marriage of that great law, "Corruptio optimi pessima," which, put into colloquial English, we may paraphrase by saying that the higher and more noble a thing is in itself, the more awful is the depth of the degradation that will follow the failure to realize its height. And when we see Love and Marriage made the persiflage of idle chatter, and the theme of every frivolous and noxious novel; when we think of the way in which marriages are arranged— of matchmaking mothers selling their daughters to the highest bidder, and pursuing in the shameless way that they do "eligible parties"; when we hear of *mariages de convenance*, marriages for money, marriages for coronets, loveless marriages schemed for the most sordid motives, and all the diabolical

329

horrors of the marriage market—when we think of these things, and hundreds of suchlike abominations that time and perhaps decency forbid one to enter upon; when we think of these things in the pure, strong light of Marriage, as set before the Prayer-Book Man, we turn sick and faint. It is like the beautiful delicate petals of some fair flower stamped down in the mire and filth of the street: the fairest of all fair things ruined and blasted by the wanton wickedness of men. Oh, beware of the light word and the idle jest about Marriage! It is the first step down an incline, at the end of which is the bottomless pit of Hell. "Corruptio optimi pessima."

Let us, then, with these sobering thoughts in our mind, turn to see what the Prayer-Book has to say to the Prayer-Book Man about Marriage.

1. The Prayer-Book begins by telling us that Marriage "is an honourable estate instituted of GOD in the time of man's innocency, signifying unto us the spiritual marriage and unity that is betwixt CHRIST and His Church."

Here is a startling announcement!

"In the time of man's innocency, signifying the unity betwixt CHRIST and His Church"!

Have we been accustomed to think of CHRIST and His Church in connection with "the time of man's innocency"? Have we not rather been thinking that "CHRIST and His Church" were the result of man's fall? Here at the very outset the Prayer-Book lifts us up to the thought of the Eternal Counsels of GOD as regards the Incarnation. It is not forbidden to us to think that the Incarnation was in consequence of the Fall. But the more we think about it, the more we shall incline to the opposite opinion that so largely prevails in the Church—viz., that the Incarnation would have taken place *anyhow*, and that all that is due to the Fall is that the Incarnation has necessitated the Passion. And the thought set before us by the Prayer-Book that Marriage as signifying the unity betwixt CHRIST and His Church was instituted in the time of man's innocency, goes a long way towards convincing us that the Incarnation was not the result of the Fall, but is the result of Creation.

Bishop Westcott, in his essay on "The Gospel of Creation," which is appended to his commentary on the Epistles of St. John, sets out admirably for us the bearings of the question; and he shows us how the institution of Marriage becomes a great argument in the mouths of those who defend the Scotist position as regards the Incarnation. St. Bonaventura, for instance, states the argument in this way:

"If man had not fallen, the Sacrament of Marriage would have existed. If, therefore, man had remained unfallen, either the Sacrament of Marriage would have been a false sign, or the Son of God would have been incarnate. But the first supposition (*i.e.*, that Marriage could be a false sign) is impossible."

And another writer says that the relation of CHRIST to the Church as "the Head" cannot be supposed to be dependent on man's sin; and this, he thinks, was already shadowed forth in the record of Creation before the Fall.

And the Prayer-Book, to say the least of it, seems to point us in this direction when it emphatically tells us that Marriage was "instituted of GOD in the time of man's innocency, signifying to us the spiritual marriage and unity that is betwixt CHRIST and His Church."

2. When we turn to the Bible account of the institution of Marriage, we find it recorded both in the Old and the New Testaments; and each account begins with the same three words—viz., " For this cause."

In the Book of Genesis we read: " *For this cause* shall a man leave his father and mother, and be joined to his wife; and they two shall be one flesh." " For this cause !" For what cause ? We turn to the preceding verse to find what is the cause of the institution of Marriage, and we find it is because of the manner of the creation of Eve. " Adam said, This is now bone of my bone, and flesh of my flesh; she shall be called Woman because she was taken out of man. *For this cause* shall a man leave . . ." So that the institution of Marriage is the outcome of the fact that Eve was " taken out of " Adam. But the manner of the creation of Eve is in its turn the consequence of something that lies behind it; so in the Epistle to the Ephesians we again read: " For this cause shall a man leave his father and mother," etc.; and again we ask, " For what cause ?" And again we must look to the preceding verse for the answer to this question, and we find that it runs thus: " We are members of His Body, of His Flesh, and of His Bones. *For this cause* shall a man leave his father," etc. So here we find that the institution of Marriage springs out of the manner of the existence of the Holy Church.

So we sum up:

The institution of Marriage is in consequence of the manner of the creation of Eve.

The creation of Eve is in consequence of the manner of the existence of the Church.

" This is now bone of my bone, and flesh of my flesh ;

she shall be called Woman, because she was taken out of man. For this cause," etc.

" We are members of His Body, of His Flesh, and of His Bones. For this cause," etc.

We cannot grasp the mystery of Marriage unless we grasp the mystery of CHRIST and His Church. We cannot grasp the mystery of CHRIST and His Church unless we grasp the mystery of Marriage.

3. *The Mystery.*—One word, first, as to mysteries in general. The modern practical English mind is impatient of mysteries in general. It wants to see everything right through, and have it all cut-and-dried before it. Only the other day a lady who had had a great sorrow, and felt blinded and dazed by it, wanted to have it all explained to her. Her cry was: " It is so difficult." The answer to her was: " Why should it not be difficult ?" She said: " I cannot understand it." Again the answer was: " Why should it be necessary that you should understand it ?" Why are we to have this impatience of mystery ? It is of the essence of Divine mystery that it cannot be apprehended by the merely natural man. Mysteries require to be met by a peculiar faculty. " The natural man receiveth not the things of the Spirit of GOD. . . . They are foolishness unto him. . . . They are spiritually discerned." We no more expect a child of this world to grasp a mystery than we expect a man born blind to distinguish colours.

Now as to the mystery of Holy Marriage. St. Paul emphatically says: " This is a great mystery." What is the mystery of which he is speaking ? It is this— that a man and his wife are " no more two, but one *flesh*." Mark the words. He does not say that they must be of one *mind*. It is obvious that if a man and a woman are to live together for life, they must have a community of ideas and interests. But there is no " mystery " in this. It is mere obvious common sense. The " mystery " is that they are " *one flesh*." And note that when the Apostle speaks of the great mystery, it is difficult to say when he is speaking of CHRIST and His Church and when he is speaking of the man and his wife, the two things intertwine and run up one into the other. We may almost say that it is not so much two parallel mysteries as one mystery under two aspects. See how the argument runs. " We are members of His Body, of His Flesh, and of His Bones. For this cause shall a man leave his father and mother, and shall be joined unto his wife, and they two shall be one flesh. This is a great mystery; but I speak concerning CHRIST and His Church." We are always to take the two things together, and keep them together in our thoughts about Holy Marriage. No amount of " platonic affection," no amount of similarity of tastes and ideas, will constitute Marriage. Of course not, for no amount of admiration for, or reflection on, or agreement with, or approval of, JESUS CHRIST will make a man a Christian. Marriage is oneness of *flesh*, and Christianity is membership in the Body, the Flesh, and the Bones of JESUS CHRIST. Here, then, is the mystery—viz., that a man and his wife are one flesh, because CHRIST and His Church are not two, but one. Do we expect a heterogeneous Parliament of all religions and no religion to grasp the " mystery " of Marriage? Of course we do not, and therefore, if it were not so awfully sad, how unspeakably ludicrous would be the spectacle of the British Parliament discussing Divorce, or the Table of forbidden degrees!

Marriage

But, alas! to a great many people it seems quite reasonable that the British Parliament *should* discuss such things, because to the vast numbers of English people Marriage is no " mystery." St. Paul said most emphatically that it is; but the British public, in their superior knowledge, can afford to look down with pitying contempt upon St. Paul! But we are not dealing with the British public; we are thinking of the Prayer-Book Man, and as the Prayer-Book religion is the religion of JESUS CHRIST authoritatively brought before the English people, the Prayer-Book Man regards St. Paul as an Apostle of GOD, and accepts his teaching as stamped with Divine authority.

To attempt to deal with Holy Marriage as though the " mystery " were an open question is as ridiculous as it would be impious. To people who say that they can see no mystery about it the Christian can only answer: " Ye have neither part nor lot in this matter."

Let us once more summarize:

(*a*) Holy Marriage is a Divine institution.

(*b*) It goes back behind the Fall.

(*c*) It was instituted in the time of man's innocency, signifying unto the spiritual marriage and unity that there is betwixt CHRIST and His Church.

(*d*) Its institution rests on the manner of the creation of Eve.

(*e*) The creation of Eve was as it was because of the manner of the existence of the Holy Church.

(*f*) The mystery of Marriage is one with the mystery of CHRIST and His Church.

(*g*) The " mystery " of Marriage is that a man and his wife are no more two, but one flesh.

(*h*) The " mystery " of the Holy Church is that she is One with CHRIST. " We are members of His Body, of His Flesh, and of His Bones."

(*i*) This mystery cannot be discerned by the " natural man."

See to what heights the " moderate " common-sense Church of England religion takes us !

4. It is upon the " mystery " of oneness of flesh that all Christian Marriage rests. It is because of the " mystery " that the Marriage laws of Christendom are what they are; and it is out of the fact of the " mystery " that all the mutual duties of husband and wife spring.

So from the consideration of the " great mystery " we pass to the consideration of three consequences that immediately follow upon it :

(1) That Marriage cannot be dissolved.

(2) That Marriage is impossible within the forbidden degree.

(3) The practical duties of husbands to wives, and wives to husbands.

We will speak of the impossibility of divorce and of the table of forbidden degrees in the next chapter. Let us think a moment now of the mutual duties of husbands and wives that spring out of the fact of the " great mystery."

These are set before the Prayer-Book Man in the Exhortation at the end of the Marriage Office.

Because the man and his wife are one flesh, and that in consequence of the oneness of CHRIST and His Church, therefore the husband is to love his wife in a particular way—viz., " *as* CHRIST *did love His spouse the Church.*" And we are told of the nature and manner of this love. " Who gave Himself for it,

Marriage

nourishing and cherishing it even as His own Flesh." Such is to be the love of the husband to the wife, because of the " great mystery."

And, again, the husband is reminded that no man ever yet hated " *his own flesh*, but nourisheth and cherisheth it, *even as the* Lord, *the Church*." The " great mystery " is that the wife is the husband's own flesh, and he is to treat her as such. And as the duty of the husband to the wife, so the duty of the wife to the husband, springs directly out of the " great mystery." " For," we read, " the husband is the head of the wife, even as Christ is the Head of the Church: and He is the Saviour of the Body. *Therefore*, as the Church is subject to Christ, so let wives be to their own husbands in everything." From one point of view the wife is the equal of the husband, for they are no more two, but one flesh. From one point of view the Church is equal to Christ, because she is His Body, His Flesh, and His Bones; from another point of view the wife is to the husband as the body is to the head: as the Church is to Christ. " There can be no schism in the body," for the body and the head are one. Therefore the outcome of the " great mystery " is that the wife is to be to the husband as the body is to the head. " Therefore as the Church is subject to Christ, so let the wives be to their own husbands in everything. And again he says: Let the wife see that she reverence her husband."

That truly detestable creature, " the new woman," will laugh this to scorn. Of course she will ! because she has no grasp of the " great mystery." In her superior wisdom she has put mysteries under her feet; we cannot expect, and we do not expect, anything better from her. " Mysteries are revealed unto the meek," and her worst enemy could not accuse " the new woman " of any approach to meekness !

Here, then, we have the Prayer-Book frankly and fearlessly claiming for the Prayer-Book Man that he is a supernatural being, and dealing with him quite simply as being such. The " mystery " of the Prayer-Book Man's marriage springs directly out of the mystery of his new birth in Holy Baptism.

Let me once more remind you that the Prayer-Book Man never professes to be anything but supernatural. The great mystery of Holy Marriage is all of a piece with the standing mystery of his life in CHRIST.

And having said so much about the mystery of Holy Marriage, and having seen how the mutual duties of husband and wife spring immediately out of that mystery, we shall in the next chapter consider the two other consequences of the mystery of the oneness of man and wife.

CHAPTER XXV

MARRIAGE—II

WE saw in the preceding chapter that Marriage is a great mystery. Its institution in the time of man's innocency rested upon the manner of the creation of Eve, and that in its turn rested upon the manner of the existence of the Church in CHRIST.

The "great mystery" of Marriage consists in this, that a man and his wife "are no more two, but *one flesh*." Out of that mystery spring three immediate consequences:

1. That Marriage cannot be dissolved.

2. That Marriage cannot be within the forbidden degrees.

3. The mutual duties of husband and wife.

We glanced at the third of these consequences in the last chapter. We have now to say something about the two first.

Marriage cannot be dissolved. That means that there is no such thing as divorce, properly so called. Now, to understand this statement we must have a clear idea of what is meant by divorce. Separation—even if it be legal separation—is not divorce. Divorce means the annulling of the marriage bond. The claim of divorce is that it can so annul the marriage bond that it can make it as if it had never existed—

i.e., that it sets the parties free to marry again in each other's lifetime. It is in this sense of the word " divorce " that we say that *there is no such thing*.

There are certain marriages, so called, that were never marriages at all. In such cases there is no question of annulling, for you cannot " annul " what never existed. Such so-called marriages were null and void from the first; consequently, all that is needed in such cases is to recognize their nullity. But such recognition of a fact is not divorce. Given that a marriage has been a marriage at all, nothing can so dissolve it as to make it possible for either party to remarry within the lifetime of the other.

Now, it is here that we put our fingers upon the absolute conflict between Christianity and the English Divorce Act. To understand this, we must be quite clear as to what the State can do, and what it cannot do. The State did not institute Marriage, therefore the State cannot annul it. All that the State can possibly concern itself with is the legal status of its citizens. It is, of course, possible for a State to say that, under certain circumstances, it will not legally disqualify its citizens. In the case in point it is, of course, possible for the State to say that, under certain circumstances, it shall not be illegal for a man to have two wives at once, or for a woman to have two husbands at once (the words " husband " and " wife " being taken in a strictly *legal* sense only). In a word, it is possible for the State to say that, under certain circumstances, it will legalize adultery. But adultery does not cease to be adultery because the State has legalized it. The State did not make adultery any more than it instituted Marriage; consequently it cannot unmake it. Let us be quite

Marriage

(1) Did He permit remarriage? and (2) was the alleged circumstance the circumstance under which divorce is legalized in England?

Now, the answer to these two questions is far too long and detailed for me to enter into here. Those who wish to study the question will find it stated in a comparatively short form in Canon Knox Little's volume on " Holy Matrimony " in the Oxford Library of Practical Theology. All we can do now is to summarize the matter very shortly.

Our LORD speaks with no sort of ambiguity about divorce. He tells us that if a man puts away his wife and marries another, he commits adultery. He tells us that if a man marries a woman who is divorced, he commits adultery. When He had stated the matter in this uncompromising way, His hearers not unnaturally asked, " Why, if that were the case, Moses had allowed divorce?" Our LORD answered that Moses' enactment was a concession to men's want of faith.

" For the hardness of your hearts he gave you this precept." And He goes on to recall them to the original institution of Marriage. " From the beginning it was not so."

JESUS CHRIST, who came " to restore all things," restores to us the original inviolable sanctity of Holy Marriage, and He tells us plainly that the so-called Marriage of divorced persons is adultery. But nowadays people have a weakness for what is called the " innocent party " in a divorce case. The presumed Scriptural ground for the " innocent party " we will consider in a moment. Meanwhile, let us just look at the " innocent party." Presumably it is the " innocent party " who sued for a divorce. But if divorce is forbidden by GOD, how about the " innocence " of suing for it ? Why did not the " innocent party " content himself (or herself) with judicial separation ? Again, if the contract is annulled, it is annulled for the guilty party quite as much as for the innocent. If the contract is annulled, it *is* annulled. You cannot have a contract annulled for one and still binding on the other; whether innocent or guilty, they are either both set free or neither are set free. To speak as if the " innocent party " enjoyed a freedom that the guilty party could not have is entirely to overlook the nature of a contract.

But those who think that remarriage ought to be allowed to the " innocent party " rest upon their own interpretation of another saying of our LORD'S. The text to which they appeal runs as follows: " Whosoever shall put away his wife, except it be for *fornication*, and marry another," etc. From these words it is argued that unfaithfulness to the marriage vow constitutes the one exception made by our LORD to His forbidding of divorce.

Now, if we look at the construction of the sentence, we see that it is at least possible that the words " except it be for fornication " may be taken with the words " put away his wife," in which case, though the " fornication " may be an excuse for putting away, it would not necessarily constitute an excuse for remarriage. But supposing that the words " except it be for fornication " cover the whole sentence and justify remarriage, we are face to face with the question, " What is fornication ?" People have come airily to suppose that of course it means adultery.

It is surely a serious matter to accuse our LORD of reckless looseness of language in a most grave matter.

Marriage

The word correctly translated " fornication " is never applied to sin after marriage, which is always called " adultery." Before you can use this text to justify the remarriage of the " innocent party," you must be prepared to say that when our LORD distinctly said one thing, He distinctly meant another. But supposing that when our LORD said " fornication " He was speaking of fornication, and not of " adultery," how will the case then stand ? He will be speaking of unchastity before marriage, and it is at least conceivable that this would be regarded as making the contract *ab initio* null and void. You will find in the Old Testament that the unchastity of a woman before marriage was punished by death. Now, death does annul the marriage bond. But more than this: presumably the man had entered into the marriage contract on the assumption that the woman had been chaste. If afterwards he found out that this was not the case, the contract was null and void, inasmuch as he had been entrapped into it on false pretences. So that " fornication " does not annul the marriage bond, because the effect of it is that the marriage bond never existed at all ! So that, if we take our LORD as meaning what He most distinctly said, so far from these words constituting an exception to His rule about divorce, they are an additional confirmation of the truth that *there is no such thing as divorce at all*.

But the advocates of the remarriage of the " innocent party " will tell you that the Church has acted in different ways in this respect in various places, and at various times, and that this will justify us in approving of the so-called " marriage " of the " innocent party." Now, this statement as regards the Church requires a good deal of qualification. In the first place, it is not " the Church " as a whole that has acted in various ways, but certain portions of the Church; and in the second place, it was, so far as I know, not a question of whether the Church in any given locality, or at any given time, *approved* of the remarriage of the " innocent party," but whether an " innocent party " who had remarried should or should not be visited with the penalty of excommunication.

Broadly speaking, the laxer view prevailed in the East, while the stricter view obtained in the West. And it is not difficult to see why this should have been so; for when the seat of Empire was moved from Rome to Constantinople, it was the Eastern Church that more especially felt the paralyzing influence of the State, which, of course, would be exercised on the side of laxity, and this would naturally constitute a temptation to Churchmen to go as far as they could in the direction of laxity. It is easy to see, therefore, on what a flimsy ground the whole case for the remarriage of the " innocent party " really rests.

1. It presupposes that when our LORD said one thing, He meant another.

2. It erects the weakness of Churchmen under the pressure of State control into a maxim of the Church at large.

But we are dealing with the Prayer-Book Man; and whatever concessions may have been made to the " innocent party " in Eastern Christendom, the Prayer-Book speaks with no ambiguous voice at all. The Prayer-Book commits itself (and thereby commits us) to the statement that Almighty GOD, in knitting together a man and his wife, has taught us that it should *never* be lawful to put asunder those whom He, by matrimony, had made one.

Marriage

Mark the words: " Never be lawful." There is no hint of a single exception—no room for the " innocent party " for the Prayer-Book Man !

Again, in the form of betrothal, the man and the woman are made to take each other " for better, for worse," till death, not divorce, do them part. And in the solemn joining of hands, the Prayer-Book bids the Priest to say: " Those whom GOD hath joined together let no man put asunder."

So much, shortly, as to divorce. Let us now see how, out of the " great mystery " of Holy Marriage, springs the immediate consequence of the impossibility of marriage within the forbidden degrees of kindred and affinity.

The " great mystery," let me say once more, is that a man and his wife are " one flesh." The consequence of this fact is that a man's wife's relations stand to him in the same degree as his relations by blood; that is, to put it in Prayer-Book language, " kindred " and " affinity " are put on the same level. If you look at the table of forbidden degrees, which you find in the Prayer-Book, you will see at a glance that it is on this principle that it has been drawn up. To violate the table of forbidden degrees in one instance only is to violate the whole principle on which it is based. If, for instance, a man may marry his deceased wife's sister, there is no reason why he should not marry any of his wife's relations.

Let me say once more that, of course, we do not expect the world to recognize the principle that underlies the table of forbidden degrees. Of course not, for the world has not the faculty for the discernment of mysteries; they are, and must always be, " spiritually discerned." Consequently the world cannot see why a man should not marry his sister-in-law, while at the same time it thinks it can see why it may be convenient that he should do so. And so we have the lamentable and ludicrous spectacle of solemn arguments in the House of Commons which have nothing whatever to do with the matter in hand. For, of course, all this pompous twaddle is only possible for those who do not see that Holy Marriage is a Divine Mystery. And we would remind ourselves again that the State cannot make a thing right or wrong. It may legalize what is right, or it may legalize what is wrong; but the fact of legalizing or not legalizing leaves the right and wrong exactly where it was before. As in the Divorce Act the State has legalized adultery under certain circumstances, so in the Deceased Wife's Sister Act it has legalized an incestuous connection. Nothing that the State can do can make a thing right or wrong, *per se*. To the Christian the matter is irrevocably and finally settled by the fact that the " great mystery " of Marriage consists in the mysterious fact that a man and his wife are " no more two, but one flesh."

All arguments as to the desirability of a man marrying his sister-in-law are absolutely futile and beside the point; for the " great mystery," which none of the children of this world know or can know, remains where it always was.

It is more than lamentable—it is simply appalling— to find, as we do, really good people who worship GOD and receive the Sacraments, puzzled as to whether or not it is wrong for a man to marry his deceased wife's sister.

But leaving Christianity for the moment out of the question, the Deceased Wife's Sister Act is, as we

should expect it to be, as ridiculous as it is blasphemous
and impious. For on what conceivable principle can
it be right for a man to marry his wife's sister, when
it is wrong for a woman to marry her husband's
brother ? On what conceivable principle can it be
right for a man to marry his wife's sister, when it is
wrong to marry his wife's aunt, or his wife's daughter ?
There is no principle in the matter at all. The
Deceased Wife's Sister Act is based on a denial of the
" great mystery " of Holy Marriage, and on that
ground it is abhorrent to us as Christians, and all the
arguments from expediency, were they a hundredfold
more cogent than they are, cannot move us one jot.
Let us take an instance which, from the mere point of
view of the world, will show the utter absurdity, as
as well as the abominable wickedness, of the Deceased
Wife's Sister Act.

Two brothers, whom we will call A and B, marry
two sisters, whom we will call C and D.

A and D are both dead. B, taking advantage of
the Deceased Wife's Sister Act, " marries " C. The
" marriage " is legal because C is B's deceased wife's
sister. The " marriage " is illegal, and therefore null
and void, because B is C's deceased husband's brother.
Was anything so childishly absurd ever heard of ?
" Quem Deus vult perdere, prius dementat."

But we have nothing whatever to do with either the
expediency or the absurdity; we know that the whole
thing is wrong from beginning to end, because we know
that the " great mystery " of Holy Marriage is that a
man and his wife (whether the State sees it, or whether
it does not) are " no more two, but one flesh." If
so-called marriage with a deceased wife's sister were a
hundred times legalized, the fact remains that a man

and a woman who avail themselves of this abominable Act are simply living in sin, and as such must be excluded from Sacramental Communion. Once grasp the principle that Holy Marriage is an " excellent mystery," the principle that the Prayer-Book is never tired of proclaiming, and there is no room for doubt or hesitation as to whether divorce is possible, or whether, under any conceivable circumstances, a man may marry his sister-in-law.

CHAPTER XXVI

MARRIAGE—III

W E have, in the two preceding chapters, seen something of the Mystery of Marriage, and the consequences that immediately follow upon the fact of that everlasting mystery. The mystery is that a man and his wife are no more two, but one flesh, The consequences of that mystery are—

1. That Marriage cannot be dissolved. There is no such thing as divorce.

2. That Marriage cannot be within the forbidden degrees; that, *e.g.*, no amount of Acts of Parliament can make it possible for a man to marry his sister-in-law.

3. That the husband is to be to the wife as CHRIST is to the Church, and the wife is to be to the husband as the Church is to CHRIST.

We are now in a position to see how the Prayer-Book deals with Holy Marriage. And first as to the preparation for Marriage. Alas! that so little should be thought about the needful preparation for Marriage. Holy Marriage is essentially the marriage of a Christian man to a Christian woman. The marriage of Christians is, according to our LORD'S teaching, a reverting to Marriage as originally instituted; but it is something even more, and so we are told that members of CHRIST and temples of the Holy Ghost, when they are united in Marriage, do not merely remain each blest by the Spirit as before, but that the grace of the Indwelling Spirit, working through the Divine institution of Marriage, " Makes the Marriage union to be a deeper, more intense, more mysterious interpretation of being than it had been even in Paradise."

How tremendously important, then, is the question of due preparation for Holy Matrimony. This question of due preparation seems to be almost entirely overlooked in too many instances; and is it too much to say that the disastrous failures in married life, of which, alas ! we have so many sad instances, may be traced mainly to the want of due preparation for Holy Matrimony ? Let us, then, consider the subject of preparation for Marriage.

We will divide the subject under two heads:

1. Remote preparation.
2. Immediate preparation.

1. *Remote Preparation for Marriage.*—We will consider this under two heads:

(1) Baptism.
(2) Vocation.

(1) Baptism as a preparation for Holy Marriage. It must be borne in mind that the essence of Marriage lies in the mutual consent of a man and a woman to live together as husband and wife. It is clear that society must recognize this mutual consent, and so we find that this mutual consent, while it is always binding *in foro conscientiæ*, is registered, attested, and legalized by the State, so that it becomes binding in law. There are certain " impediments " which nullify a marriage contract *ab initio*. Given that no such

nullifying impediment exists, the State attests, registers, and legalizes the marriage contract. It is then as binding in law as it is *in foro conscientiæ*. The Office of the Church in relation to Holy Marriage is to sanctify and bless the marriage union. It is plain that occasions may arise in which the State may legalize a marriage that the Church cannot and will not bless. We have, alas! instances of this in our modern English legislation. But what we observe is that neither the State nor the Church marries the man and the woman. The State attests and legalizes the marriage; the Church sanctifies and blesses it; but the essence of the marriage lies in the mutual consent of the parties.

In most countries the offices of the State and of the Church in respect of Marriage are kept quite distinct. There is the civil marriage, by which the State attests and legalizes, which may or may not be followed by the religious marriage, by which the Church sanctifies and blesses. But in England the Church is " by law established." Consequently Church marriages in England are civil marriages as well as religious, and are *ipso facto* recognized by the State. In the case of other religious bodies in England, there must be the separate recognition of the marriage by the State.

This *ipso facto* legalizing of Church marriages in England is merely the outcome of the peculiar position of the Church in England, as being " by law established." Now, we are in a position to rule out certain marriages as not coming under our present consideration—that is to say, we may put out of our consideration marriages that are merely legal, and confine ourselves to the consideration of Holy Marriage.

Our main subject is not Englishmen in general, but the Prayer-Book Man. It will be apparent that Holy Marriage is the marriage of a Christian man to a Christian woman. Marriage is an " Honourable estate instituted of GOD in the time of man's innocency." It may and, alas ! does happen that, through the perversity of fallen man, we have to draw a distinction between " legal " and " holy " marriages; but we never for a moment allow that in the mind of GOD there is any such distinction. If an unholy marriage is legal, that is the fault of the Fall. Marriage, then, as a Divine Institution, is essentially Christian. St. Paul throws a considerable light on this when he is considering the question of heathen marriages in the case where one of the parties has become a Christian. He lays down that if the heathen husband is willing to dwell with the Christian wife, or the heathen wife with the Christian husband, they are to continue to live together. "But," he adds, "if the unbelieving depart, let him depart; a brother or a sister is not under bondage in such case."

Holy Marriage is essentially the marriage of a Christian man to a Christian woman. The State can and will legalize any marriage where there is not an annulling impediment. It may even legalize a marriage that is really no marriage at all. But the Church cannot and will not sanctify and bless a marriage other than Christian. And here we shall easily see how difficulties may arise in England from the fact of our Church marriages being civil as well as religious. But the difficulties as to mixed marriages are minimized by the fact that if a Christian wants to marry a heathen, or heathen wish to marry, they can always have their marriage legalized at the Registry Office.

Marriage

The Registry Office is one thing, the Church is quite another, and we lay it down as a great principle that the Church cannot bless a marriage except it be between Christians. That both parties should have been baptized is, then, the first " remote " preparation for marriage.

(2) *Vocation.*—It is in connection with marriage that the Apostle lays down the great maxim that " Every man has his proper calling of GOD, one after this manner, another after that." In our modern use of the word " vocation " we are apt to confine it to the vocation to the Priesthood, or the vocation to the Religious Life under vows. But Marriage is quite as much the subject of a vocation as the Priesthood or the Religious Life. Every man has his proper gift of GOD, one after this manner, another after that; and surely it is of the first importance that a man or a woman should see and know whether he or she is called of GOD to the married or single life. For some are as distinctly " called " to marriage as others are to celibacy. Speaking of " vocation," one may broadly say that vocation is the direct path marked out by GOD, along which any given individual is to attain to perfection. If a person misses his vocation, or is mistaken as to what is his vocation, that person will have greater difficulty in reaching perfection than he would have had if he had gone along the path marked out for him by GOD. If people find that they have mistaken their vocation, they must not give way to despair; they will have to go a roundabout way, but they must bravely plod on along that roundabout way. But there *is* a straight and direct way for every Christian, and that direct way is the way of vocation. If this be so, it is clear that from the very beginning

men and women should get themselves to work to ascertain what is GOD's Will and purpose for them in their choice of life. They should cultivate a great devotion to the Will of GOD, and pray that they may be led to see and know what that Will is. But this too commonly is just what people neglect to do, and so we find sometimes people who have rushed into marriage when it was not their vocation, and people who have embraced celibate life when their vocation was to marriage. Such people have made their lives needlessly hard and difficult, but, as we have said, they must patiently plod along in their roundabout way. The hardships and difficulties of their life will be like the forty years' wanderings in the wilderness. The Israelites got to Canaan at last, but it took forty years instead of eleven days.

Surely, then, marriage ought not to come upon a man or a woman as a sudden surprise. If people are called to marriage, they ought to know beforehand that they are so called, and be on the lookout for it. Equally, if people are called to the celibate life, they ought to know that they are so called, and be prepared to follow the Call. It is a lamentable spectacle to see men suddenly leap into marriage in their old age. If a man has reached the age of sixty without knowing whether his vocation was for marriage or not, one of two things must have happened: either he has lived the bulk of his life on a wrong tack, or else he has been tempted out of the right tack at the end of it. Do let us start on the journey of life by trying to ascertain and to follow the vocation wherewith GOD has called us.

First, then, every man and woman should pray that they may know GOD's Will for them, and to be enabled to follow it. If people have reason to believe that their vocation is to marriage, then they must bend all the energies of their life to fit themselves for marriage, and the first step in such preparation is purity of heart. " Blessed are the pure in heart, for they shall see GOD."

Impurity of heart or life does more than anything else to darken the understanding and blunt our sense of GOD. Here is a call that is distinct, imperious, and universal; there can be no doubt or question about it ; whether people are called to marriage or to celibacy they are called to purity. Much might be said about the relation of purity to marriage which cannot be said here. But this one thing we do say—viz., that if there is not purity of heart, there is little chance of people knowing what God's Will for them is.

If people are called to marriage, they are certainly called to a life of sacrifice; and here, again, we have a call that is clear, imperious, and universal. The question is not whether a man is called to marriage *or* to sacrifice himself in the celibate life. Certainly not ! All Christians are called to a life of sacrifice; the only question is in which direction that sacrifice is to be worked out and consummated. Think of the duties of husbands to their wives and wives to their husbands, and you will see that marriage is essentially a life of sacrifice. The husband is to love his wife " *as CHRIST did love His Spouse the Church.*" And we know what was the nature of this love of CHRIST for the Church. " He gave Himself for it."

So the love of the husband for the wife is to be a self-sacrificing love. The wife, in her turn, is to be subject to the husband, as the Church is subject to CHRIST. Again a life of self-sacrifice; and this same principle of mutual self-sacrifice is taught in the great precept that the wife has not power of her own body, but the husband; and the husband has not power of his own body, but the wife.

The call to marriage, then, is a call to sacrifice. The sacrifice of the celibate life is in one direction, the sacrifice of married life is another; but both are alike in this: that they are lives of sacrifice lovingly offered in union with the Sacrifice of CHRIST on His Cross.

Do let us emphasize this fact, because in modern English thought and speech it seems as if marriage were looked upon as the opportunity of escaping from sacrifice, whereas the truth is that every Christian is called to follow CHRIST in the bearing of His Cross, and marriage or celibacy are merely marked out as the line along which the life of sacrifice is to be worked out for this man or that. If, then, people have reason to think that their vocation is to marriage, they have to bend the energies of their lives to prepare for marriage by the cultivation of habits of unselfishness and self-surrender; and such persons ought to prepare for, and think out the details of, the management and government of a family and household. How often this is left to come by haphazard as it may, and how lamentable is the result! The great need of society is Christian homes, and it is in and by Christian homes that society is to be reformed. " An Englishman's house is his castle " is our proverb, and a moment's thought will show us what a tremendous vantage-ground this fact gives. We cannot help the evil that goes on outside, but the home is and must be just exactly what the husband and wife choose to make it; but headship and government are hard and weary tasks, and is it not significant that when the Apostle

Marriage

is speaking of the different virtues needed for different states of life, he lays down that the virtue that is needed for those called to rule is not, as we should perhaps expect, justice or mercy, but "diligence"? "He that ruleth let him do it with *diligence*." The responsibility of being heads of families and households again involves sacrifice. Time will not allow us to do more than just mention the essential self-sacrifice of fatherhood and motherhood, that incessant obliteration of self for the good and the well-being of others—that earthly picture of GOD and His creatures. Do let us try and think what it means to be a good father or a good mother, and see what habits of self-discipline must have been formed to achieve such a result.

To sum up these thoughts about vocation:

(1) Every man has his proper calling of GOD. Therefore—

(2) Every man and woman should pray and labour to know what that calling is.

(3) If people have reason to think that they are called to marriage they must devote their lives to fit themselves for it. This they must do—

(4) By persistent purity of heart and life.

(5) By cultivating the habit of self-surrender.

2. We pass to consider the immediate preparation for Holy Marriage. Marriage is, in the wide sense of the word, a "Sacrament of the living"—that is to say, it is not a Sacrament for making bad people good, but a Sacrament for making good people better. Consequently it is assumed that those who come to ask for the blessing of the Church on their marriage are at that moment in a state of grace; in a word, the immediate preparation for marriage is the same as the immediate preparation for Communion. What

359

will not do for the one will not do for the other; nor is this fact left to be conjectured by the Prayer-Book Man, for the newly-married are enjoined by the Church to make their Communion at once. So the Church assumes that they are at the moment in a fit state for Communion—*i.e.*, that they are at that moment in a state of grace. So much for preparation. Let us sum up the conclusions at which we have arrived on this head. Preparation for Marriage is to be : (1) Remote, and (2) immediate.

Remote preparation consists in—

(1) Baptism.
(2) Recognition of vocation.
(3) Habitual training for the following of vocation.

Immediate preparation consists in—

(1) Self-examination.
(2) Contrition.
(3) Confession, if the conscience requires it.

Having said so much on the all-important question of preparation for Marriage, we have but a short space in which to speak of the Marriage Office itself. A very little study of the Marriage Office (which is perhaps the most beautiful of all the Prayer-Book Offices) will show how it carries out the principles that we have laid down.

In the first place, by the publication of banns and the solemn charge to the man and woman, the Church insures that there is no nullifying impediment.

If the parties have perjured themselves, or if they are concealing a nullifying impediment, should such exist, the marriage is, *ipso facto*, null and void. The Church having ascertained that the marriage is one that

Marriage

she can bless, proceeds to hear and witness the solemn betrothal of the parties. First, she questions the man and the woman respectively as to their free intention, eliciting thereby the mutual consent, which alone can constitute marriage. Then the Priest, representing the Church, receiving the woman from the hands of whoever has the authority to give her away, gives her to the man, and the solemn betrothal is dictated to the parties, each in turn taking the other by the right hand during betrothal. Then the ring is given by the one party and received by the other, the hands are solemnly joined, and in defiance of all contrary Acts of Parliament, past, present, and to come, the solemn words are said: " Those whom GOD hath joined together, let no man put asunder."

And all being now completed, the Church pronounces that all *is* complete, and that this man and this woman are, in consequence of the mutual consent, attested before GOD and His Church, and witnessed by the ring and the joining of hands, " man and wife, in the Name of the Father, and of the Son, and of the Holy GHOST." Man and wife, that is to say, according to the Holy Ordinance of GOD Himself.

All that follows in the Marriage Office is subsequent to, and consequent upon, the marriage itself, which has now become a fact—viz.:

1. The solemn blessing on the marriage.
2. Thanksgiving.
3. Prayer for grace and for fruitfulness.
4. The second blessing.
5. Exhortation as to duties.

As regards the said exhortation it will be noticed that it is always to turn upon the fact of the Mystery of Holy Marriage, as signifying and representing the Spiritual Marriage and unity betwixt CHRIST and the Church; and here we must end what has to be said about Holy Marriage. It will be seen that the Prayer-Book Man is not left in any doubt or conjecture as to Holy Marriage. He is fully instructed as to its nature, its institution, and its duties. He will know how to prepare himself for it, and how it is to be accomplished. And we notice how, on the subject of Marriage, as in everything else, the Church appears as light contrasted with darkness, certainty as contrasted with doubt, and order as contrasted with chaos. Step aside in any particular or in any way from the Church in respect of Marriage, and you go back at once to darkness. If the spirit of the world, as represented among us by the Acts of a godless Parliament, undertakes to regulate or interferes with the Divine Ordinance of Marriage, its enactments are certain to be " of the earth, earthy "; they will always be retrograde, and will always tend, as we see them tend, in the direction of laxity and of revolt from the high standard of Christian morality.

Before a question can be raised as to whether a man may have two wives at once, or whether a man may marry his sister-in-law, men must have parted company with the truth of Marriage as a Divine Mystery. And if Christians would, in these evil times, quietly take their stand upon the simple truth of GOD's Ordinance of Holy Matrimony, we should not have the degrading and appalling spectacle that is so common among us, of Christians puzzled and perplexed about things that ought to be to them as plain as the sun in the heavens. That a godless Parliament should make a ridiculous spectacle of its ignorance is nothing

Marriage

to be wondered at; that a Christian should for a moment be perplexed by it is a lamentable and degrading spectacle indeed.

So let English Parliaments say and do what they please; the Church of the living GOD will not turn aside from her tranquil course by one jot for all the Parliaments in the world !

" *Magna est veritas, et prævalebit.*"

CHAPTER XXVII

THE CHURCHING OF WOMEN

WHEN we read quietly through our Prayer-Book, we feel instinctively that we are in an atmosphere that is very different to that of Church life as we know it day by day. It is an atmosphere of tranquil order like that of a well-ordered household, where everything is provided for, and nothing haphazard or left to chance. So in the Prayer-Book we find the Church ready and waiting for her children at every turn of the road of life. Every contingency of life is provided for in a perfectly orderly way. And this is what we should expect, for the Church is the Household of GOD, and in that Divine household all the members of the vast family find themselves considered and provided for.

But this perfection of order is found in the Prayer-Book simply because the Prayer-Book is presenting to the English people the tradition and life of the whole Body. Take the subject of this chapter as an instance. It was not a happy thought on the part of the compilers of the English Prayer-Book that women should give thanks to GOD after childbirth; it is the universal custom of Christendom. Therefore it comes in its natural place in the English Prayer-Book.

But we are compelled to notice here how the fact of

The Churching of Women

the custom of universal Christendom in this respect bears witness to the great truth of the unity of the whole Creation. Men are apt to draw lines between what they call "things religious" and "things secular"; but where is the authority for drawing such lines at all? If GOD is One and His Creation is one, then all created life falls under the head of religion. Let us take the case in point. Childbirth might seem to a superficial observer to be among "things secular." It is a part of the natural order of things. But what about "the great pain and peril of childbirth"? Where does this come from? It is part of the penance for original sin. "I will greatly multiply thy sorrow and thy conception; in sorrow shalt thou bring forth children." So the apparently ordinary and commonplace circumstance of childbirth is rooted in the mystery of sin, and in order to understand such apparently natural (or "secular") commonplaces as childbirth on the one hand, or death on the other, we are thrown back upon the most spiritual of spiritual facts—viz., the fact of original sin. And at once, if for the moment we were able to forget the religiousness of created life at all, we find ourselves in the region of revealed religion, and the "pain and peril of childbirth" has to do with GOD's Revelation.

And inasmuch as "the pain and peril" of childbirth are the outcome of sin, and inasmuch as all men, as a matter of fact, "are conceived and born in sin," therefore the instinct of the Church, under the Old Covenant as under the New, has seen the fitness of something analogous to purification after childbirth, and this universal instinct of regenerate humanity accounts for the Office for the Churching of Women in our English Prayer-Book.

Let us, then, emphasize the great truth of the unity of Creation, and cease to draw our foolish lines between " religious " and " secular." Creation itself is " religious." It is religion that is the " substance " of it. You may think to drive religion out of the door; it will come in again at the window. People may think to get rid of religion out of their lives by discarding Creeds and Sacraments, and rejecting worship, but their children are born into the world, and lo ! here is religion confronting them.

It is, then, the great revealed fact of original sin that accounts for " the pain and peril " of childbirth, and that emphasizes the fitness of the churching of women.

But now we pass to a second thought. The Churching of Women does not in any way stand apart from the rest of the Prayer-Book. It takes its place in the ideal with Baptism, Confirmation, Communion, Confession, and Marriage. And it presupposes this necessary connection in the case of the woman who comes to be churched. It is quietly assumed that she is habitually in a state of grace. It is taken as a matter of course that she has been baptized and confirmed; that she knows how to prepare for Communion, and is in the habit of making her Communion from time to time. Her churching fits in with, and is unintelligent, if not unintelligible, apart from, all the rest. It is an integral part of one solid whole. The ideal is that, after childbirth, she should be churched, and then make her Communion. So much as this, which comprises all the rest, is distinctly stated in the Rubric.

But here, alas ! we are confronted with the great gulf that lies between the ideal and the actual.

The churching of women remains as a custom, and

The Churching of Women

has a strong hold upon the English people as a sentiment. It is not, perhaps, too much to say that in many instances it is almost the only recognition of the Catholic Religion that remains. One cannot but be thankful that it does survive, even in this shadowy and unintelligent manner. It constitutes a " thing that remains " that we can " strengthen " just because it does remain, and herein lies the great value of the existing use of the Office for the Churching of Women. It is touching in these godless days to see how almost universal is the sentiment that a mother should not return to her ordinary occupation until she has been churched, but in the majority of instances it must be feared that it is not more than a sentiment.

But we are thankful that the sentiment is there. In time, please GOD, it may be strengthened into life.

We note, then—

1. That the Churching of women finds its natural place in the Prayer-Book as the expression of the instinct of the Universal Church.

2. That it is an integral part of the whole ideal of Christian life.

3. That therefore it presupposes conformity with the Christian ideal of life all along the line.

And, inasmuch as it remains in actual practice, even when other Christian observances have been discarded, it is of particular value in these days as a rallying-point, and it may very well happen that through faithfulness in the observance of this one part of the Christian life many souls may be brought back to conformity with that whole ideal of which this is an integral part.

CHAPTER XXVIII

THE VISITATION OF THE SICK

WE pass now to consider the Prayer-Book Man in sickness. It is characteristic of true living that the man who lives along right lines is never taken by surprise. To the Christian, life is " simplified "— that is, it is manifestly one solid whole. The wise man says: " In all thy works, remember the end, and thou shalt never do amiss."

" Remember the end." But what is " the end " ? The Christian answers at once: " The end—Everlasting Life." This the Christian knows to be the " end," the cause, the reason, the object, of his existence at all; consequently, to him, life leads quite naturally into death, and death leads quite naturally to resurrection. But take away the knowledge of " the end," and what remains ? Death is too patent a fact to be contradicted or put aside. That the soul is immortal most men believe ; but this life is all that they know anything about, and therefore it is on this life that their philosophy is practically based. " We are born at all hazards, and we shall be hereafter as though we had not been." So dim and shadowy is the bare conception of the immortality of the soul ! And so, as life seems to them the solid fact, and after this life all is dim and shadowy, they not unreasonably bend all

368

their energies to deal with this life. Death is coming to snap it off some day or other; they had better think how to make the most of it while it lasts. The dog who dropped the bone he held to catch at that which he saw reflected in the water was, of course, wrong, because he had not first ascertained which was the real thing. Unless the life to come is at least as solid and real as this life, we had better leave off thinking about it, and deal as we think for the greatest advantage with that span of existence that lies between the cradle and the grave.

All philosophies of life practically resolve themselves into two:

1. The sacrifice of this life to the life to come; or—
2. This sacrifice of the life to come to this life.

But the Prayer-Book Man has no doubt at all about the matter. For him there is no question as to which of these two philosophies of life is to be his. It is not even open to him to weigh the pros and cons of the two views of life; it has all been settled for him long ago. He has been born again; he is " a new creature." The end and purpose of the life into which he has been thus marvellously born is the resurrection of the dead and the life of the world to come. Hence all along the line of his life sickness and death have stood in their orderly proper place as essential parts of the great whole, and so neither sickness nor death in any way take him by surprise. He goes to meet them as he goes to meet any other part of his life.

What we want to see, then, is what the Church has to say to the Prayer-Book Man about his sickness and death. When it is time for him to be confirmed, he is told what to do; when it is time for him to be married, all is straight before him, set out in a business-like way, so that he knows exactly what to do and how to do it. So, too, with his sickness and death. It is all provided for; nothing is left to haphazard. He has not got to cast about when the time comes to know what to do. And so we find, as we should expect to find, that as there is an " Order " for Confirmation and an " Order" for Holy Matrimony, so there is an " Order " for the Visitation of the Sick.

Now, a single glance at the Order for the Visitation of the Sick will show us that it is presupposed that the sick man has sent for the Priest; that he has sent for the Priest for a definite purpose; and that the Priest is to come to him for that specific purpose. It is not that the Priest visiting round the parish has happened to find So-and-so ill in bed, nor is it that the sick man has thought that perhaps the parson may be able to do him some good. Each one knows quite well what he is about. The sick man knows what he wants, and the Priest knows how to give it to him; and so this Visitation of the Sick is an *official* visitation. We rule out of our conception of the Visitation of the Sick mere kindly visits of sympathy, or even the periodical visiting of chronic invalids. The sick man wants something definite, and it is for that definite something that he has sent for the Priest.

Now, the definite " something " that he wants is this : it is essential to him that he should be able to use his sickness as penance; therefore it is essential that he should be in a state of grace. Equally, to say the least of it, is it essential that this should be so in view of possibly approaching death. It is, then, definitely for this—viz., to put the sick man in right Christian relation to sickness and death—that the

The Visitation of the Sick

Priest comes to him. So the Priest's course is quite clearly marked out. He begins with the solemn salutation, for this is not at all an ordinary visit. He then, after an opening prayer, reminds the sick Christian of the beauty and joy of being made like unto CHRIST in suffering; and that there may be no hindrance in the present instance to this likeness to CHRIST, he bids him remember and practically renew the vows of his Baptism; he examines him as to his faith, his repentance, and his charity; he makes sure that he is in charity with his neighbour; and he bids him clear his mind of earthly anxieties by making proper disposition of his worldly goods in case of his death. He then hears his confession, if the sick man's conscience requires it, and gives him Absolution. If the sick man is in immediate danger of death, he solemnly commends his parting soul to GOD.

All this is quite simple, straightforward, and business-like. It fits exactly into its place in the Prayer-Book Man's life; it is all of a piece with everything that has gone before. But now we must turn to look at the actual facts, as, alas! they are in ordinary "Church of England" life of to-day. And when we come to look at things as they actually are at this moment among us English Church-people, we find that the Office of the Visitation of the Sick has become an absolute cipher. Ordinarily speaking, *there is no such thing!* This sounds very appalling, but it is the simple fact. It hardly ever happens that we are called to visit the sick in the Prayer-Book sense of the word. Think what happens in English parochial life of to-day. The parson casually hears through the village gossip that someone is ill. He goes to pay him a friendly visit, but this cannot be, and is not, the Visitation of the Sick. Or a fussy district visitor comes and says: "Mr. So-and-so is ill. Do go and see him." The Parson wonders why he is to "go and see him." Still, in a friendly way he goes. Perhaps he finds that the man did not want to see him at all; perhaps he finds he is glad to have a friendly visit. But in neither case has this sort of thing anything to do with the Visitation of the Sick. The sick man had nothing definite for which he required the Priest. When, therefore, the Priest called, it was not to do that definite something. All that can be hoped for in such visits as that is that they may ultimately, perhaps, pave the way for the Visitation of the Sick. But too often these friendly calls rather hinder than help the Visitation of the Sick. There can be no Visitation of the Sick except at the express desire of the sick man himself. One often wonders what district visitors think we do or can do when they implore us to go and see Mr. So-and-so. They have a sort of vague idea that we shall do something, but I am afraid their ideas on the subject are almost as shadowy as those of the sick man himself, and that is saying a good deal ! But occasionally it happens that the sick man himself wants to see the Priest. This is a good step in the right direction ; but it is obvious that before there can be any Visitation of the Sick, the sick man must not only want to see the Priest, but must also know *why he wants him*.

There often is in a man's mind an idea that it is right to have the Priest to see him when he is sick, and though this may not amount to more than a superstition, it is valuable as far as it goes, and may in time pave the way for the reality. We will not therefore despise this superstitious use of the Priest in sickness, but for the unfortunate Priest himself it is a questionable advantage. Many years ago in the country a farmer was subject to occasional heart attacks. He was not a bad sort of man, as farmers go, but he rarely came to church, and had never received a Communion. The Priest was called up early one morning to go to him. After tramping a mile, he got to the house, to find the man propped up in bed surrounded by the weeping family. He said: " I am not afraid to die." Well, that being all, why had the Priest been sent for ? What can he do in that hurly-burly ? And even if the friends gave him a chance, how can a man in that condition be instructed in the ABC of the Christian religion ? If a man has persuaded himself all his life that he does more right by staying away from Communion than by making his Communion, how are you going to put him straight at such a moment ? If a man has no faith in the power of the Priest to absolve from sin, you cannot at such a moment argue the point as to Absolution. If you have to battle your ground step by step against old ignorance and prejudices, there is no scope for the Visitation of the Sick, as the Church contemplates it. We are not blaming these dear people, nor are we going to attempt to sit in judgment upon them; they are what their circumstances and their upbringing have made them. They are like those people in Nineveh for whom GOD had such tender compassion. " More than six score thousand persons that cannot discern between their right hand and their left hand, and also much cattle." Oh no ! It may be that when the last are first, and the first last, they will be far ahead of some of us who have been better taught. But what we have to observe is that the Visitation of the Sick presupposes desire and knowledge on the part of the sick man, and that where either this desire or this knowledge is lacking there is no place for THE Visitation of the Sick. What a sobering reflection it is that sickness and death, which may come upon any of us at any time, reveals to us the unity of life and of GOD's purpose for us throughout! It is want of the perception of this unity that makes men's lives such a jumble and so chaotic. The Prayer-Book Man reveals to us this essential unity of life and purpose. His Baptism, his Confirmation, his Confessions, his Communions, his marriage, his sickness, and his death, are all obviously of a piece. They are integral parts of one great whole: they have one great end in view: " The end "—" Everlasting Life."

But there is a certain logical unity, too, about the life of the ungodly. If they can live without Worship and Sacrament, why should they not die without them? What will do for life will do for death; what will not do for death clearly will not do for life; for life and death are but integral parts of one great whole. Why should a man want to make his Confession when he is sick if he never wanted to make it when he was well? Of course he will not! What application can Absolution have to approaching death that it does not have to approaching Communion? It has been well pointed out that Communion and death are much alike. In Communion GOD comes to us; in death we go to GOD. The preparation for the one is the same as the preparation for the other!

A word here to the clergy. In what an absurd position does the Visitation of the Sick put a Priest who is not in the habit of hearing Confessions! What becomes of the pompous nonsense that is talked about

The Visitation of the Sick

Confession being a very exceptional thing that is not to be made a habit? By all manner of means let Confession be exceptional, *provided that sin is exceptional;* but the two things must obviously go together, and if a Priest has quietly let people drift into thinking that they are always fit for Communion without Confession, how can he have the face to move a sick man to make his Confession? If he can go to Communion without Confession, he can die without it. It has been a regular part of the Prayer-Book Man's life to make his Confession whenever his conscience requires it; but let us ask those clergy of whose ordinary work the hearing of Confession forms no part, how many deathbed Confessions they ever hear. And, again, if a Priest never goes to Confession himself, and never hears Confessions, how is he suddenly to know what to do if he is called to the bedside of the sick and dying? We can understand the Protestant who fiercely denies the power of the Keys. He is dishonest, of course, as a Priest of the Church of England, but his position is, at any rate, intelligible. But your " moderate " man, who professes to believe in the power of the Keys, but refuses to use it, is a quite unintelligible monstrosity. To him, as to the Protestant, the Office of the Visitation of the Sick must be a dead letter. Is it, then, too much to say that the Office of the Visitation of the Sick is to the Priest and to the sick man alike the test of their grasp of the unity of the Christian life? It comes at any moment as an integral part of a great whole; and it has no meaning at all, except as an integral part of that whole. There is no more reason why a man should die well than why he should live well. People say, " It is a solemn thing to die." Granted. No one will say that it is not, but what we want to impress upon people is that it is just as solemn to be alive to-day as it is to be dead to-morrow; and this surely is the lesson that the Prayer-Book Man teaches us—a lesson that both Priests and people sorely need to lay to heart. It is just as dreadful for people to live out of grace as it is for them to die out of grace. The ignorance on the part of Priests and people, that leads to the shelving of the Office for the Visitation of the Sick, is all of a piece with the ignorance that leads them to discard the Prayer-Book life *all along the line*. The ignorance of the clergy is not to be wondered at when one thinks of their preparation for the Pastoral Office. They are supposed to know the ins and outs of the History of the Canon; they are stuffed with the last fads of the " Higher Criticism "; they have to be *au fait* with the dreary history of the Reformation period; and they are probably warned against much love of the Mother of GOD; but this curriculum hardly equips them for dealing with a simple soul! And until the Clergy can rightly place Absolution in its relation to Communion, they will not be able to make anything of the Office for the Visitation of the Sick. But, even supposing this be done, the ignorance of the sick man remains. What ought to have been the normal habits of a life cannot be supplied in a few days before death; but, still, much may be done in the right direction if only the Priest has made up his mind what it is at which he has got to aim; and a little study of the Office of the Visitation of the Sick will show him the lines along which he is to work even if the Office itself be, for the moment, impossible.

The point, then, that we want to emphasize is the unity of the whole life of the Prayer-Book Man. Let

The Visitation of the Sick

us look at this from the point of view of the Priest. If the Priest is to spend most of his life in making up his mind about what the Prayer-Book sets before him, then the Office of the Visitation of the Sick must be a dead letter to him. One has known people say of the Office for the Visitation of the Sick that that is the part of the Prayer-Book that they do not like. We will not stop now to inquire whether it is quite honest for a man to pledge himself to a book, and then to turn round and say that he does not quite like some integral part of it; but we *will* say that if people " do not like " the Office of the Visitation of the Sick, it is the whole scope of the Prayer-Book Life that they " do not like." You would probably find that Priests who " do not like " the Office of the Visitation of the Sick do not like a good deal besides. Are such people, for instance, quite sure whether Baptism and Communion are generally necessary to salvation? Do they quite see why these Sacraments are thus necessary? Have they practically been in the habit of dealing with them as being thus necessary? Have they realized for themselves, or taught people to realize, the relation in which in the Prayer-Book Absolution stands to Communion? Are they quite clear as to Christian marriage, and the questions that arise out of it?—*e.g.*, divorce, and the table of forbidden degrees? Have they always been in the habit of reciting the Divine Office? We venture to think that if Priests are quite clear about these other matters, they will find no difficulties about the Visitation of the Sick; and, conversely, that Priests who do " not quite like " the Office of the Visitation of the Sick will be found to be quarrelling practically with the Prayer-Book in a great many other matters. If those who have to prepare candidates for Holy Orders would devote a little less time to the History of the Canon and the Reformation period, and would have the courage not to care whether the candidates are or are not "up to date" with the latest fads of Protestant Germany; and if, instead of these things, they would take a little more trouble to set before the candidates the unity of life set out in the Prayer-Book, and the relation of the various parts to the great whole, our Priests would be better equipped than they are for dealing with the souls of men. It may be very delightful to be clever enough to know who did or did not write what, but that interesting knowledge will not in the least help the Priest to perform the Office of the Visitation of the Sick.

And as with the Priest, so with the sick man. If the sick man has lived the Prayer-Book life all along the line—if he has followed the Prayer-Book lines as regards Baptism, Education, Confirmation, Communion, Absolution, and Marriage—then he will know what he wants when he is in sickness and near death. But if he has gone his own way, and refused the instruction that the Prayer-Book gave him at all the stages of his life, then, of course, he will go his own way in sickness.

You cannot isolate the Office of the Visitation of the Sick; it is all of a piece with the rest of the Prayer-Book; and the reason why the Office of the Visitation of the Sick is practically a dead letter is that a great deal of the rest of the Prayer-Book had become a dead letter first.

One word in conclusion about the Unction of the Sick, which has been called the "lost Pleiad" of the Anglican firmament. In its due time, in the providence of GOD, this subject is now coming to the fore. The vagaries of so-called " Christian Science " are showing Churchmen that we ought not to have tried to do without the Unction of the Sick. A leading Bishop has said that if a sick person desires Unction, he ought to have it. There are, thank GOD, Bishops who are ready to consecrate the Holy Oil for the Sick; and Unction is being administered more often than a good many people suppose. As with other parts of our inheritance that we seem to have " lost awhile," so it is with Unction of the Sick. It will not be regained by elaborate treatises or platform speeches. It is a case of *solvitur ambulando*.

Let Priests hold themselves ready to anoint any who may desire it, and Bishops bless the Oils. Let it be understood that the Holy Unction can be had for the asking, and it will not be very long ere we have recovered it.

CHAPTER XXIX

THE PRAYER-BOOK MAN DEAD

WE have now to think of the Prayer-Book Man dead and in his grave. Two things will strike us at once:

1. When we speak of the Prayer-Book Man in his grave, we are speaking of the normal condition of the vast majority of Prayer-Book Men. We are speaking of the Prayer-Book Man as in the main he is at the present moment, so that the study of the Prayer-Book Man in his grave is of supreme practical importance; and yet, is it not so that our thoughts about Prayer-Book Men run almost exclusively on that small fraction that are actually living at this moment? Or if we study the individual Prayer-Book Man, is it not true that we are thinking almost exclusively of that tiny fraction of his life that lies between his cradle and his grave? Is it not the case that when he is dead he ceases to have any practical interest for us? Theoretically, we believe in the immortality of the soul; theoretically, we even believe in the resurrection of the body; but practically, he has become a shadowy entity that has passed out of the region of practical politics.

Why is this? The answer surely is that this is the sign and the outcome of our practical unbelief. We know theoretically that the faithful departed are still living; but practically we deal with them as non-existent, because of the lurking materialism that makes us think that it is only what we can see and handle that can truly be called real. Therefore, the present life of the faithful departed is to us something so shadowy and unreal that for all practical purposes it may be counted as non-existent. And yet, when we come to think of it, how ridiculous and unintelligent, as well as how wrong, is this normal English attitude towards the faithful departed ! What should we think of a foreigner who should try to write about England and the English people, and leave London altogether out of account ? And what shall we think of the judgments and opinions about the Church that are based upon a total disregard of (at the very least) ninety-nine hundredths of Church-people ? Surely there must be something hopelessly wrong about a form of Churchmanship that takes no practical account of the faithful departed !

2. The normal English attitude towards the faithful departed is largely traceable to the weakness (to put it in the mildest way) of the practical belief of Englishmen in that cardinal doctrine of the Christian religion —viz., the resurrection of the body.

Again and again has the Church had to contend against the false spirituality that is the outcome of Manichean thought. Again and again, in one form or the other, has the Church been confronted with that perversity of the thought of fallen man that works along the lines of a dualism of matter and spirit. It is always a virtual denial of the Unity of GOD. In its nakedest and coarsest form it represents matter as the creation of an evil being, while spirit is the creation of

GOD; so that the good god and the evil god stand eternally over against each other. In its somewhat less coarse (though none the less deadly) form we meet it in all those speculations, such as the Gnostic heresies, which spring out of the intellectual difficulty as to how GOD, Who is Pure Spirit, can come in contact with matter—a difficulty which the Gnostic heretics tried to bridge over with their theory of successive " Æons," or emanations, which nevertheless left the intellectual difficulty exactly where it was before. It is not too much to say that what in these days is grimly called " religious " thought is soaked through and through with the Manichean poison. Look along the line of English " religious " thought, and you cannot fail to see the cloven hoof of Manicheism peeping out under the covering of popular Protestantism.

Can we not, *e.g.*, see how, to the average English Protestant, the soul, the affection, the intelligence, are just everything, while the body is practically of no account ? Is it not this that lies at the bottom of the Protestant revolt against the sacramental system of the Church ? They cannot see what the receiving of a Sacrament with our bodies can have to do with our souls. The Sacraments are to them decent ceremonies. They were, to be sure, ordained by CHRIST Himself, and therefore, as positive obedience to a positive command, they must be retained; but the bare idea of a Sacrament being " generally necessary to salvation " is loudly laughed to scorn.

Then, again, as pointing in the same direction, we have the prevalent scorn of fasting, or bodily discipline, as an element of religion; while the same lesson is taught us by the absence of bodily reverence in their religious exercises. Go into a Protestant meeting-house—built in these days amphitheatre fashion, like a music-hall, so that the congregation may settle themselves comfortably in easy seats to listen—and you cannot fail to be driven to the conclusion that these people think that the body has nothing to do with the matter, religion being, in their idea, something that only concerns the soul, the intelligence, and perhaps the affections. And this being their attitude towards the body in life, quite logically they take up the same line towards the body in death. The body is regarded as a sort of case that temporarily holds the soul, or as a sort of cage in which the soul is temporarily imprisoned. When the time has come for the soul to be separated from the body, so much the better for the soul. The case or the cage is no longer needed, and we need not trouble ourselves any more about it. In nothing is the Manichean spirit more truly shown than in the modern English attitude towards the faithful departed, and that in two ways: (1) The supreme contempt of relics, and (2) the practical neglect of the faithful departed.

And now, having glanced at these two wrong lines of thought that are prevalent among modern Englishmen, we will see what the Church has to say to us on both these heads.

1. As to the relative importance of the dead and the living. Sometimes, when it dawns upon us for a moment that the Church Militant here on earth is not quite the whole Church, we will sing in some popular hymn about " the living and the dead "; but St. Paul would have put it the other way about. He tells us that at the coming of our Lord the living shall not " pre-vent " them which are asleep. " The dead in CHRIST," he says, " shall rise first "; " Then we which

are alive and," etc. That looks as if the dead came first in his mind in the order of importance. It looks as if the Church, to him, appears to consist (as in fact, of course, it does) of the faithful departed, with the little, comparatively insignificant, fringe of the living hanging on to the main body. If we accustomed ourselves to think of things as they really are from the common-sense point of view, we should be more inclined to speak of " the dead and the living " than of " the living and the dead." See how the Church keeps this truth practically before us if we would but have ears to hear and a heart to understand. Who is meant when in our liturgical prayers we say " we," " us," or " ours"? Clearly, of course, the whole Christian people, the faithful departed, who form the enormous majority, and those members of the Body of CHRIST who are alive and remain. What do we mean when we pray in the Divine Service that we and the " whole Church " of GOD may receive remission of our sins, and all other benefits of His Passion ? The " *whole* Church "? What does this mean ? People who have substituted " Church of Englandism " for Catholicism use the term the " whole Church " when they only mean the living members of the Anglican Communion. People who are a little more advanced in the intellectual scale are able to see that this is not a satisfactory account of the " whole Church "; but even to them too often the " whole Church " is not more than coextensive with " the whole state of CHRIST's Church Militant here on earth "—*i.e.*, the baptized who happen to be still alive on earth at the moment. But this, though not so grossly ridiculous as the conception of " Church of Englandism," is nevertheless but little less unintelligent. When the Prayer-Book speaks of the

384

whole Church, it *means* the whole Church—viz., the dead and the living. Every Eucharist is, and must be, the offering of the whole Church. The continual remembrance of the Sacrifice of the Death of CHRIST must belong to the dead as much as to the living.

2. As to the belief in the resurrection of the body. The Church knows nothing of a Christianity that is merely to improve the social and moral conditions of earthly life. Her motto is: " If in this life only we have hope in CHRIST, we are of all men most miserable." She stakes her all on the fact of the resurrection of the body. If there is no resurrection, *cadit quæstio*. " Let us eat and drink, for to-morrow we die." The modern idea that the Church is to strip herself of all that is mysterious, and devote herself almost exclusively to " social work," finds no echo in the Bible or in the Prayer-Book. The Prayer-Book Man is carefully taught that the effect of his Baptism is to make him partaker of the Death of CHRIST, so that he may be partaker of His Resurrection. He is to crucify the old man, and utterly abolish the whole body of sin. He is to use such abstinence that the flesh being subdued to the spirit, he may obey the godly motions of the HOLY GHOST, Who is the giver of Life.

The Sacrament of Communion is generally necessary to salvation, because, as was foreshadowed in the Tree of Life, it is the food of Eternal Life. To the Prayer-Book Man life leads naturally up to death, and death to resurrection. Hence the care of the Church for the bodies of the faithful departed. They are to be laid in consecrated ground, in sure and certain hope of the Resurrection of the dead. The Church does not forget, however heretics may forget, that the body is an integral part of the man, and that the salvation of CHRIST has to do with the body as much as with the soul. The trumpet gives no uncertain sound here. The Christian religion stands or falls with the fact of the resurrection of the body, and the resurrection of the body stands or falls, as St. Paul is careful to show us, with the fact of the Resurrection of CHRIST. And now, having glanced at the false and the true ideas of the faithful departed, let us see how these aspects of the case will respectively show themselves in the practical dealing with the Christian dead.

Let us take the false aspect first.

Two things strike us in the modern English idea of funerals:

1. Englishmen are thinking a great deal more about the living than about the dead; they seem to be thinking more of the mourners than of the corpse. The Burial Service is estimated according to the amount of *comfort* that it will bring the mourners. That seems in modern English minds to constitute its chief, if not its sole, value. We have been told lately that we want a more " bright and comforting " Burial Service. One of the silly demands in connection with Prayer-Book Revision was for a more " comfortable " Burial Lesson, and akin to this is the brand-new invention of the " Memorial Service," which has not a shred of authority or precedent in Catholic Christendom. If you are only somebody in society, you will probably now have a " Memorial Service." If you are a big enough somebody, Royalty and the Corps Diplomatique will be represented at your " Memorial Service." The " service " seems to consist of a few tags from the Burial Service, with a " comforting " anthem or two, and one or two " favourite hymns "

of the corpse! Can anything be more supremely ridiculous? The humble poor, thank GOD, have the enviable distinction of having no " Memorial Service." It is an exclusively aristocratic function. Then a little lower down, perhaps, in the gamut of Protestant vulgarity we have the " Funeral Sermon," or the funeral oration, in which the virtues of the deceased are trumpeted forth. It is really hardly a caricature when Bret Harte speaks of the widow, sitting in her pew in the Dissenting Chapel, " enjoying the compliments that were paid to the corpse." Consider all this, and you will see that in the modern English funeral the sympathies are far more with the living than with the dead.

2. The thought of death as a penance for sin (which is the leading thought of Christianity) is to be as far as possible eliminated. Everything about the modern English funeral is to be made as bright and cheerful as possible. Oblivious of the fact that the instinct of Christendom both East and West has pointed to black as the most appropriate colour for the dead, the Church is to be made as white as possible. The coffin must be smothered in white flowers, tied on it or hung about it with endless bits of pack-thread. Sympathetic ladies will go and stick flowers and leaves with hairpins all over the sides of the grave to make the grave look as pretty and " comfortable " as possible. Sickly High Church sentimentality will have the Burial Service interspersed all over with hymns—probably Easter hymns, or hymns about the labourer's task being o'er or things of that sort—no respect being paid to the ludicrous incongruity of all this with the Burial Service of the Church, the solemn sequence of the whole thing being incessantly broken in upon by these abominable

hymns. As like as not the Priest will stick himself into a white stole to match the flowers, etc. What shred or vestige of authority or precedent is there for all this ? None whatever ! The idea seems to be to cover up and obscure GOD's revelation of death as the penance for original sin, and to hide away this truth as much as possible. So we sum up the modern English idea of the funeral in these two ways:

(1) It is for the edification of the mourners, rather than for the benefit of the departed.

(2) We are to obscure and forget as far as possible the solemn truth revealed to us by Almighty GOD— viz., that death is the penance of original sin.

Now, as against these pre-eminently false ideas let us set the practice of the Holy Church.

1. In the mind of the Church it is the dead rather than the living who are to be thought of in the Burial Service. The Church is laying in the grave one of her own children, who, because he is partaker of the death of JESUS CHRIST by his Baptism, will therefore be partaker of His Resurrection. Whatever modern maudlin sentimentality may say or think, the Burial Service is for the children of GOD only. The Burial Service is not to be used for those who are manifestly outside of the Kingdom of Heaven, either because they have never been born into it by the Sacrament of Baptism or because they have been formally cast out of it by a sentence of excommunication. The Church knows perfectly well what she is about in the Burial of the Dead. She is laying in her consecrated place the bodies of her children who are to be partakers of the Resurrection. It is of the dead that she is thinking rather than of the living.

2. The leading thought of the Church is that death

is PENANCE; and penance, be it remembered, means the temporal punishment of sin *that has already been forgiven.* " Death passes upon all, for that all have sinned." They have sinned by being born in sin, even if they have not committed actual sin; and penance witnesses to the great fact that GOD is Perfect Justice as well as Perfect Love. Nay, that He would not be Perfect Love if He were not Perfect Justice. Penance is the keynote of Christian Burial. The colour is not white, but black. If the Church sings a hymn over her dead, it is the solemn sequence, " *Dies Iræ.*" Let Protestants talk, if they will, about people having certainly " gone to Heaven," or, as they blasphemously put it, having " ascended "; the Church knows that this is not so. Of our Lord Himself it is said: " Now that He ascended, what is it, but that He also descended first into the lower part of the earth?" Is it not enough to make one shudder to hear that this or that Dissenting preacher " ascended " on such a day at such a time? If for a moment this could conceivably be so, the only inference would be that these persons are certainly not following in the steps of our LORD! The Church knows that her child who is dead has entered upon his blessed penance, because his sins have been forgiven for the sake of the Name of JESUS CHRIST. We sum up, then, the practical aspect of the Burial of the Dead in the Catholic Church:

(1) It concerns the dead more than the living; the corpse more than the mourners.

(2) It regards death as what GOD declared it to be —viz., the penance of sin.

So, in our dealings with the faithful departed, we are to be guided, not by sentiment, but by attention to the solid facts of the case. The " end " for every child of GOD is " everlasting life," and everlasting life is the perfect vision and the perfect knowledge of GOD. But, as St. John is careful to remind us, we can only " see " GOD because we are like Him. The Beatific Vision of GOD in Heaven presupposes a character that will have made sin morally impossible. Otherwise, we have no guarantee that the life in Heaven will be an abiding one. The " end," therefore, of every child of GOD is that he has come to be perfectly like GOD. This is the solid fact that is revealed to us.

But while it is certain that those who die in a state of grace are undoubtedly saved, there is nothing in the actual fact of death that of itself will transform character. Character is the result of habit, and the character of being like GOD must be formed by habit. Hence the supreme importance of the penance of the grave. If we eliminate the penance of the grave, and allow ourselves to think that a child of GOD " ascended " at the moment of his (or her) death, we are face to face with the appalling thought of a soul entered upon the Beatific Vision without the necessary qualification of being perfectly like GOD !

The Prayer-Book Man, then, at his death is entering upon that gracious and blessed state of penance by which he is to become finally perfect and fit for Heaven, and it is for this reason that the Church follows him with her unceasing prayers. Every Eucharist is, as we have seen, pleaded for the dead as well as for the living, and the ceaseless cry of the Church for her children who have entered upon their blessed penance is: " Grant them, O Lord, eternal rest, and let light perpetual shine upon them."

If people do not pray for their dead they are not in sympathy with the Prayer-Book, for, as we have seen, in the Prayer-Book the dead are continually remembered in public worship. But, leaving this fact for the moment on one side, we note two somewhat opposite errors that keep people from joining with the Church in her prayers for the dead. One is the error that underlies that awful word " ascended "—viz., the terrible idea that our dead go straight to Heaven; the other, and opposite, error underlies the common use of the word " poor," as applied to the dead, as when we constantly hear people speak of a dead friend as " poor " So-and-so. Why " poor "? One cannot but think that the man is thought deserving of pity because he can no longer be engrossed in the affairs of this life. One can hardly call a man " poor " if we realize that he has taken an immense step in advance of us towards his final perfection ! But " poor So-and-so " seems to have dropped out of things altogether !

Do let us, then, discard mere sentimentality, whether in thought or in practice, and take our stand with the Church in fearlessly facing facts as regards the faithful departed; then, and then only, we shall understand the Prayer-Book Man in his death.

CHAPTER XXX

CONCLUSION

THE life of the Prayer-Book Man is one solid consistent whole. The Prayer-Book Man is born again in the Sacrament of Baptism. He is born into that life which grows steadily on till it reaches its full development in the resurrection of the dead. Education, Confirmation, Absolution, Communion, the Last Sacraments, and Burial, all fit into their natural and proper place in the development of the new life that was born in Baptism. From his Baptism to his resurrection the Prayer - Book Man moves steadily onwards. Such is the magnificent conception that the Prayer-Book sets before us, such is the splendid ideal. But, alas ! the Protestant Philistines have invaded the Holy Land, and where all should be order, peace, and plenty, all is chaos, confusion, and starvation. Think of the ghastly absurdity of our being called to the bedside of the dying, and having there and then to argue the point whether a man is, or is not, bound by his Covenant; whether Absolution does, or does not, convey the forgiveness of sins; whether Communion is, or is not, necessary to salvation ! How absolutely terrible this all is ! How absolutely terrible at such a moment to find the fair plant of the spiritual life all choked and overgrown with the poisonous fungus growth of

" views," " opinions," or " schools of thought "!
From the beginning to the end the life of the Prayer-
Book Man is one solid intelligible whole. Tamper
with it at any point, and the Nemesis will certainly
fall. Sow the wind by wrong education, by yielding
to Protestant fictions as regards Confirmation or Communion, by banishing Sacramental Confession out of
your system, or by placing Acts of Parliament in the
place of GOD's marriage laws—sow the wind, and you
will reap the whirlwind of the death of the unbeliever !

It is the great truth of the solid unity of the Christian life that has to be emphasized at the present
moment, and the purpose of this book has been to
attempt to dissipate the clouds of error both in faith
and practice that have so terribly obscured for English
Christians this great truth.

Englishmen are apt to detach this or that portion of
the Christian life from its context, and to look at it
and to deal with it as if it stood alone. We see this
notably at this moment in the case of Holy Marriage,
but the same tendency is observable all along the line.
As against this disintegrating force we insist that the
Christian life must be looked at and dealt with as one
solid whole. Let men take it or let them leave it,
but do not let them think that they can take a part
of it and leave the rest; do not let them think that
they can criticize it at one point and still retain their
respect for it as a whole.

If, then, we put in the forefront the great fact of
the solid unity of the Christian life as a whole, we
shall steadily refuse to allow it to be tampered with at
any point. We shall cease to criticize the Prayer-Book,
and begin loyally and obediently to frame our daily
life according to the ideal that it sets before us; and,

Prayer-Book Ideals

as we do this, we shall realize in everyday life the great truth that the path of the just is as a shining light that shineth more and more unto the perfect day. Life will lead quite naturally to death, and death to resurrection, and the end of that apparently small beginning in our Baptism will be found to be nothing short of the perfect vision and perfect knowledge that constitutes Everlasting Life.

THE END

Elliot Stock, 7, *Paternoster Row, E.C.*